DRESSED TO KILL:
DEATH AND MEANING IN ZAYAS'S *DESENGAÑOS*

ELIZABETH RHODES

Dressed to Kill

Death and Meaning in Zayas's *Desengaños*

UNIVERSITY OF TORONTO PRESS
Toronto Buffalo London

© University of Toronto Press 2011
Toronto Buffalo London
www.utppublishing.com
Printed in Canada

ISBN 978-1-4426-4350-5 (cloth)

University of Toronto Romance Series

Printed on acid-free, 100% post-consumer recycled paper with
vegetable-based inks.

Library and Archives Canada Cataloguing in Publication

Rhodes, Elizabeth, 1955–

Dressed to kill : death and meaning in Zaya's Desengaños / Elizabeth
Rhodes.

Includes bibliographical references and index.
ISBN 978-1-4426-4350-5

1. Zayas y Sotomayor, María de, 1590–1650. Parte segunda del sarao y
entretenimientos honestos. English.   2. Death in literature.   3. Meaning
(Philosophy) in literature.   4. Women in literature.   I. Title.

PQ6498.Z5P372 2011   863'.3   C2011-904979-1

Published with the generous support of the Trustees of Boston College.

This book has been published with the help of a subvention from the
Program for Cultural Cooperation between Spain's Ministry of Culture
and United States universities.

University of Toronto Press acknowledges the financial assistance to its
publishing program of the Canada Council for the Arts and the Ontario
Arts Council.

 Canada Council Conseil des Arts
for the Arts du Canada

 ONTARIO ARTS COUNCIL
CONSEIL DES ARTS DE L'ONTARIO

University of Toronto Press acknowledges the financial support of the
Government of Canada through the Canada Book Fund for its publishing
activities.

for Sarah and Alexandre
who saw me through it

Contents

Illustrations

Acknowledgments

Thanks are small things to offer the people who helped me through the years this book was under way. I offer deepest gratitude to my children, Sarah and Alexandre, who sustained me through the project and everything that came with it, and to my parents, Betty and Graham Brimm, who did the same.

Special thanks to Margie Combs for courage, to Kathy Dorrien for flying the jib and walking the lake path, to Laurie Shepard for intellectual cheerleading, and to Meg Greer for laughter and perspective at crucial moments. I thank Alison Weber, Judith Wilt, Matilda Bruckner, Laura Bass, and Dian Fox for their important, thoughtful feedback on the manuscript. Jim Amelang, María Tausiet, and Antonio Bernat Vistarini provided indispensible bibliographic leads. In the final phase of the manuscript preparation, John Mullen provided more than words can find their way around.

For her energy and sparkling intelligence, I'm grateful to my research assistant, Stacy Brown (Boston College, '08). Leticia Mercado (PhD candidate, Boston College) brought a sharp eye and keen mind to the final draft.

Many scholars and librarians have helped me with the nettle of early Spanish editions of the saints' lives. I particularly wish to thank Mark Dimunation, Chief of the Rare Book Collection at the Library of Congress, for access to the ?1472–5? [*Flos sanctorum*] n.p. before the Library digitized the volume. Barry Taylor, of the British Museum Library, provided invaluable information about the ?1497? *Leyenda de los santos*, and Jan Maarten de Booij at the Koninklijke Bibliotheek in the Netherlands gave me access to the *Leyenda* of Sevilla, 1532.

Robert O'Neil of the Burns Library at Boston College was very helpful with pertinent Jesuitania. Shari Grove, bibliographer in O'Neill Library at Boston College, went above and beyond the call of duty in assisting me, and I thank her. The interlibrary loan staff at Boston College was unfailingly supportive and resourceful.

Research for this book and time to write it was made possible by the generous support of the Fulbright Hayes Program, the National Endowment for the Humanities, Harvard Divinity School, Boston College, and the Renaissance Society of America.

Abbreviations

Aut.	*Diccionario de autoridades* [1723]
d	*desengaño*, 'tale of disillusion,' from Zayas's 1647 *Desengaños amorosos*
DRAE	*Diccionario de la Real Academia Española*
OED	*Oxford English Dictionary*

DRESSED TO KILL

Figure Introduction 1 *Woman Writing a Letter*, Gerard ter Borch, c. 1665. Mauritshius, The Hague, The Netherlands. Kavaler / Art Resource, NY

Introduction:
Setting the Interpretative Baseline

It is time for Zayas ... to be dealt with as an artist.

Susan Griswold

In 1647, María de Zayas published a collection of ten stories in Zaragoza with a rather insipid title, the *Parte segunda del sarao y entretenimiento
honesto* (*Second Part of the Soirée and Decorous Entertainment*). Its original
readers were probably not deceived by this lacklustre marketing, for a
spate of similar titles had followed the 1625–34 ban on novella publication, designed to protect public morality.[1] On the surface, the *Parte
segunda* promised what the public had come to expect from such books,
which were all the rage on the literary scene of mid-seventeenth-cen-
tury Spain: prose fiction tales about love and marriage, sprinkled with
poetry, tales themselves fictionalized as true stories.

The novellas of Zayas's *Parte segunda* are told by noblewomen to an
elite gathering at the Madrid home of Lisis, the charming, smart protagonist of the book's frame tale. Lisis was a familiar character to fans
of Zayas's 1637 *Novelas amorosas y ejemplares* (*Exemplary Tales of Love*),
in which she also figures as the hostess of a holiday soirée at which ten
tales are told. Enthusiasts of Zayas's prose waited ten long years to see
how Lisis's life would be resolved, and double that time separates the
dates on the two books' *aprobaciones*, or approvals for printing. The first
edition of the *Novelas*, published in Zaragoza in 1637, contains a permit
by the Vicar General of Madrid dated 1626, which suggests that twenty
years separate the moment when Zayas presented her *Parte primera* to
the censors and when they saw the *Parte segunda*. It is also likely that

the printer assigned her first book its title, for the author herself refers to it as the *Primera parte* (*First Part*), which she complemented with the *Parte segunda* of 1647.[2] Although all of the novellas in the first collection treat the standard themes of love and marriage, they are varied in tone and objective. Two are comical, three recount frustrated desire, and five end happily in marriage, sometimes against all odds. Most remarkably, the virtuous prayer of the tenth tale's hero resurrects his dead beloved, and they wed.

In both collections of tales, the intention to marry is also Lisis's primary signifying feature, and her chosen partner is Don Juan. He, however, prefers her cousin, Lisarda, and at the end of the 1637 book, Lisis graciously accepts the proposal of Don Diego, a nobleman of merit and stature whom she does not love. Readers of the *Parte segunda* were surely anxious to see Lisis emerge victorious in her struggle to get what she wants and deserves, either by winning Don Juan's affection after all, or overcoming that desire and finding another partner. They would have assumed she would be married or at least engaged again by the second book's conclusion, for that was how such fiction ended when the protagonist was a virtuous member of the nobility. They would be disappointed.

Although the title and structure of the *Parte segunda* were standard fare, and although the fictional objective of finding a spouse was absolutely traditional, what readers encountered in Zayas's second book was far from typical. Lisis remains unwed to the book's bitter end. In stark contrast to the *Novelas amorosas*, none of the tales in the 1647 collection ends happily, and instead each one leads to the violent defeat of virtue. Even though attaining or maintaining a marriage is the declared objective of all the stories' unwed female protagonists, only one manages to marry and survive it: Lisarda, the exception who proves the rule by wedding a foreigner after rejecting Don Juan, an obvious comeuppance for his having spurned Lisis. For their part, the stories' virtuous wives are sought out and abused by a decadent society determined to do away with them, their bodies mutilated and their lives ended literally in death, or figuratively as they enter the convent after insurmountable tribulation in the world.

The dark shadows in the book's interior affect and intensify the unhappy frame tale across the course of the book. When the *Parte segunda* opens, Lisis has recovered from the long illness brought on by Don Juan's rejection, but her attraction to him endures. Nonetheless, she carries on with her plan to marry Don Diego and organizes her second soirée as a celebration of their nuptials, which she says will take place at the conclusion of the final evening's festivities. Three nights and ten horrible tales later, however, Lisis refuses to marry Diego and instead enters a convent as a secular resident. This ending intensifies the failure of marriage in the ten tales, suggesting that the book's central motif is the characters' inability to wed happily or hold their marriages together. In an age when marriage, and the regeneration it symbolizes, was the anticipated finale of urban courtly literature, the *Seguda parte* leads persistently to its failure.

Because Lisis deserves a better ending than she gets, the frame tale frustrates the reader, who closes the book with a lingering unease. Zayas buttresses that frustration with ten tales that likewise recount events that are profoundly unjust, thereby accomplishing the disillusion that she defines as the primary objective of her book. Disillusion, which saturates the culture of the author's generation, was an obsession unique to the Spanish baroque (Robbins 77). Appropriately, then, as the frame tale opens and the storytellers prepare for the soirée, Lisis instructs them to tell only *desengaños*, tales of rude awakening, the better to undeceive virtuous noblewomen regarding the wiles of deceitful men and convince noblemen to treat noblewomen better (118). For this reason, each inlaid story is called a *desengaño*, and since Amezúa's 1950 edition, the volume itself has been referred to as Zayas's *Desengaños*. Disillusion, which is to say the end of innocence and the surrender to artifice, is at the heart of the book, most overtly in the deceit embedded in the diegesis, for the majority of characters practise deception in every story.

Less obvious but more disconcerting is the fact that Zayas and Lisis deceive both their real and fictional publics about the purpose of the soirée itself throughout the entire book. The frame tale opens where its plot in the *Novelas ejemplares* had ended, with Lisis's intention to marry Diego. In the introductory pages, the narrator casually mentions that during the throes of the long illness that preceded her engagement party, Lisis makes a decision ('nuevos propósitos') that she reveals to no one (116).[3] The reader anxiously waits for this secret to be divulged, and the fictional public, unaware of it at all, believes the party everyone is attending will lead to a nuptial celebration. Indeed, the narrator praises Lisis's obedience to her mother's desire that she set her wedding date, saying the young woman responds with 'the answer one would expect of her obedient ways' (la respuesta que se podía esperar de su obediente proceder, 117–18). Not until the book's very end does anyone learn the hostess's secret, that Lisis – not so obedient after all – had decided not to wed Diego before the soirée began. This renders the entire event a teleological ruse designed to deceive, the better to reveal and explain the truth, which falls upon the reader like a chilling fog at the soirée's conclusion: the happy ending is not coming.

Lisis's smokescreen engagement forces disillusion on both her public and that of Zayas. In this way, readers subtly learn what the characters learn more violently, which is not to believe what appears to be happening and instead practise a hermeneutics of suspicion to decipher the truth in a sea of deception. Having learned this lesson, they can reevaluate the tales, thinking their way out of the multitude of conceptual and moral difficulties with which Zayas besets her public inside them. This entails wading through stories murky with equivocation and ethical dilemmas to discern how what happens could have been avoided, a particularly difficult task given that what should have happened is all but absent from the stories. In this negative articulation, the author incorporates the deceptive nature of appearances, a fundamental baroque theme, into the essence of her book and into the praxis of reading it. What appears to be happening is not, and what does not appear to be happening is really what matters. Only in retrospect, thinking the entire thing over, does this become apparent.[4]

For readers today, however, mere thinking does not suffice to disentangle the *Desengaños*, for the muddle of challenges the author presents to her reader does not clear upon closer inspection through a postmodern lens. The narrators, all female, vigorously insist on the need for noblewomen to defend their best interests by not falling prey to the corrupt world that seems determined to eat them alive. They advise each other to take particular care with men, whom some of the narrators describe as inherently deceitful (while others insist that only some men are bad, and those are no worse than some women). A few take the extremist position of rallying noblewomen to bear arms and kill whoever dishonours them. Some vigorously defend the equality of the female soul with that of the male, as well as women's inherent intelligence, which is repeatedly described as unrealized due to lack of education. The book appears to mount a strident defence of noblewomen and prescribe their intellectual and physical strength, as well as their energetic protection of their dignity and reputation. This is only, however, what is said.

What happens seems not only at odds with this defence but appears to undermine it. Not one of the noblewomen characters actually performs any of the recommended strategies, and the only self-defence they practise is retreating from the world that overwhelms them. None possesses or seeks education beyond the ornamental, female variety (needlework, music, poetry), and none strives to do anything except get or stay married. Although they decry noblemen's dishonesty and inconstancy, marriage to these very men remains the desire of every noblewoman character in the tales. If we count God as a male character, since the Catholic nun explicitly weds a male divinity, marriage is the single objective of virtually every female protagonist in the book. Throughout the *Desengaños*, the major features that endow the upper-class female characters with meaning are in fact what we would now call decidedly patriarchal: their sole objective being to marry or remain so, their lives are limited to participation in the dominant sexual and social economy in which women derive their significance from their relationships with men.

The interpretative problems do not end there. One wonders what to do with the fact that many of the ignoble characters and their accomplices are female, and most belong to the nobility. Particularly alarming, certainly today, is the author's gusto for killing virtuous women, first setting them up to die in a patterned style, often after protracted suffering, and then having them done away with in grisly spectacles of dismemberment, bleeding, poisoning, starvation, and beheading. For the characters whose death is social, meaning they enter the convent because they are unable or unwilling to marry, their ending is problematic indeed.

It is difficult to reconcile the author's presumed defence of women with the fact that when her perfect wives realize that their husbands have murderous intentions against them, they remain devoted to those husbands and go down without a word. Similarly disconcerting is Zayas's penchant for focusing her narrative lens on the mutilated bodies of the literally dead wives, only to transform those bodies into paragons of loveliness after the women expire, more beautiful in death than in life. Her tendency to attach sacrificial features to these characters, using words such as 'lamb' and 'martyr,' is discomforting, as is her decision to stylize them as female saints from Catholic hagiography. These idealized, violently failed lives that culminate in violently idealized corpses cast a pall over the author's declared intention to teach women to safeguard themselves and their best interests.

Zayas clearly designed her second book this way on purpose, because the *Novelas amorosas* contain an abundance of female characters of precisely the type exalted by the narrators of the *Desengaños*, who escape the clutches of their imperfect world. The protagonists of two tales, Aminta and Hipólita, kill the men who dishonour them and go on to marry happily, Laura leaves her cheating, abusive husband, and Estela (dressed as a man) is an extremely successful Viceroy of Valencia.[5] These contrasts suggest that the author designed the female protagonists of the *Desengaños* to fail, dressing them in specific features the better to kill them and thereby deliver the sharpest disillusion to her public.

How the apparently discrepant facets of the text reconcile with each other is a vexing problem. Readers today have generally decided that there can be no reconciliation, nor should there be one, finding irresolvable paradox and a plethora of data impossible to arbitrate in Zayas's stories. Recently, critics have allied this indeterminacy with our own postmodern ontological crisis and consider Zayas's second book to be part and parcel of her first. Symptomatic of this tendency, Ruíz-Gálvez Preigo presents the novellas as riddled with indeterminacy, ambiguity, and ambivalence (xxi). Feminist interpretation of Zayas's works intensified the notion that they are contradictory in their paradox. Griswold, writing in 1980, separates Zayas from both the attitudes and arguments in her fiction and the characters who express them, and attributes the varied perspectives represented in Zayas's works to perspectivism itself (107). More recent determinations are more extreme: 'Paradox is at the root of Zayas's work' (Brownlee, Preface xiii); 'Zayas' texts readily lend themselves to multiple and paradoxical readings' (Pecoraro 39); N. Davis refers to 'the disturbing, apparent ideological contradictions in her work' ('Re-framing' 331); Lagreca finds 'perplexing baroque contradictions embedded within and among Zayas's plots' (566); Mujica says the tales are filled with paradoxes reflective of social tensions of Zayas's day (129). It seems, then, that with her fiction and the *Desengaños* in particular, Zayas drops a dark, knotty ball into her reader's lap and walks away.

I suggest that we respond to the author's challenge by picking up and disentangling that ball, proposing two fundamental changes in how we read this important book. The first is to recognize the profound difference in creative registers between Zayas's two collections of tales. Between the time Zayas wrote the *Novelas amorosas* and published the *Desengaños* at least ten and possibly as many as twenty years passed. Distinguishing the two books from each other opens a space for Zayas to develop as an artist and acknowledges that Spain's intensifying difficulties, particularly the Catalan and Portuguese rebellions of 1640, negatively affected the author, whose patriotic bent is manifest. Analysing the *Desengaños* as a predominantly independent text, rather than in relationship to or in conjunction with the *Novelas ejemplares*, also accommodates the contrasts in tone, content, and objective between the two.

Already in 1975, Kahiluoto Rudat observed that Lisis's frustrated affection for Don Juan sets the tone for all twenty tales. Clearly the two volumes fit together, sharing structural organization, the themes of love and marriage, and some frame tale characters. But Zayas radically altered her literary course with the *Desengaños*, and precisely because the two books share structural and diegetic features, the differences between them acquire high relief. One difference overshadows everything they have in common: whereas not one virtuous noblewoman dies in the stories told in Zayas's first book, *all* such protagonists die or fail spectacularly in those of her second, in plots that tease out and expose extreme cases of human weakness and depravity. Thus, while scholars such as Amezúa and Levisi find nothing new in the *Desengaños* (Amezúa, Prólogo vii; Levisi 447), I believe that what distinguishes the author's second book from her first is precisely where Zayas's important literary innovations lie, in how she tropes marriage and the dying or dead female body to render social crisis, splaying the distance between the fictional female subject and what she means.

I suggest further that reading Zayas on her own terms reveals a fundamental order in her second book, a baroque order, extremely violent, highly encoded, and rendered negatively, but ultimately and rigidly consistent. Seeking order for its own sake would be a mistaken critical enterprise. But the *Desengaños*, I argue, are deeply conditioned by seventeenth-century poetics and ideological standards that challenge us to do exactly that. If we engage the interpretative codes and skills that Zayas's first readers had at their disposition to disentangle the *Desengaños*, and if we familiarize ourselves with the book's intertexts which they knew well, that order becomes apparent and Zayas is free to do more with the competing discourses of baroque Spain than describe them.

Chapter 1 adduces three sets of evidence to justify this approach on historical grounds: 1) the censors' praise of the *Desengaños* pointing to the book's conformity with, rather than resistance to, seventeenth-century standards; 2) premodern readers' and writers' support of literature's moral imperative; and 3) baroque poetics exalting difficulty, celebrating the reconciliation of paradox, and defining the act of struggling with a text's meaning as an exercise of moral improvement. Grounded in this conceptual triangle, I examine three central issues of Zayas's text with a seventeenth-century lens, through which the function and meaning of her female protagonists come into focus. Chapter 2 assesses how class interests condition the text, examines what the text (not only the narrators) says about marriage, honour, and violence, and excavates the book's goals from the ruins created by the tales to examine how Zayas's terrible stories meet her fiction's goals using two plots and a fixed cast of characters. From there it is possible to reconcile Zayas's book with itself by revealing how her failed fiancée and wife characters realize the book's objectives, including its declared defence of women (chapter 3). That analysis, in turn, reveals how Zayas uses the convent ending to signify a threatening loss that parallels and augments the literal deaths of the virtuous wives (chapter 4).

The resulting re-evaluation of marriage and women in the *Desengaños* sheds light on when and how the book was influential and opens two avenues for continued thought. The first is what her book calls us to reconsider about women and the Spanish honour code, and the second is what Zayas made possible for later European writers (Conclusion). In this analytic context, Zayas's heady and dangerous poetics comes into view, a representative scheme that stages a beautiful female corpse at the heart of a woman's defence of her sex and her class. The enduring resonance that the trope of the dead woman had in subsequent literary and visual art makes the exercise compelling and important. Trained in how to find and ascertain meaning in the *Desengaños*, the reader sees Zayas's abused, dead, and disappeared noblewomen in light of the darkness she created like no other author before or since.

Critical Premises

What to call the stories in the *Desengaños* is a troublesome question, for two reasons. The fact that titles deeply condition a reader's entry into a text is widely recognized,[6] and in the 1647 edition of the book, the only edition Zayas is known to have supervised, only the first story had one, 'El esclavo de su amante' ('Her Lover's Slave'), while the others bore the page header 'Desengaños de las damas' ('Disillusions of the Ladies'). Eighty-seven years later, an editor added titles to the other nine *desen-*

gaños for the 1734 Barcelona edition of Zayas's complete stories, and those are the names by which the tales are known today. They often privilege the experience of a male character. For example, *desengaño* 6 was baptized 'Amar sólo por vencer' ('To Love Only to Conquer'), positing the vicious Esteban as the protagonist at the expense of his victim Laurela, who dies as a consequence of his lies. Zayas herself makes it clear throughout her book that she wants to centre the experience of her nobly born female characters, as does her title for *desengaño* 1. This problem is compounded by the fact that the frequency with which I refer to lists of tales makes a shorthand method to reference them indispensible. Aware that it might inconvenience readers accustomed to the attributed titles of the stories, I refer to each one using its number and include a reference list of numbers, tales, and characters below that can be removed and used as a bookmark and reference.

In what follows, I support the assertion that Lisis is Zayas's alter-ego and voice of authority, made by Stackhouse, Clamurro, Guillén, El Saffar ('Ana/Lisis'), Merrim, and Greer (*María*). To their evidence, I would add the strategic function of what the book's narrator calls the 'moralizing' (*moralizar*) in the book, referring to the fictional discussions in which at least two characters state an opinion about the story just told. These exchanges allow Zayas to cite Lisis and reveal what is, in the end, the opinion that matters. As Greer says, 'Zayas does not use the frame as a format for true discussion of philosophical difference' (*María* 329–30). Lisis always gets the last word, and no one ever contests her point of view.

I endorse Alicia Yllera's corrective reordering of the *desengaños* in her 1983 edition and cite that edition. Respecting seventeenth-century usage, I refer to the divinity as masculine. Because the Spanish *desengaños* is a plural word, I use a plural verb when referring to the volume. Except for quotations of *Don Quijote*, all translations are mine. I refer the reader desiring more of Zayas's works in English to the Greer and Rhodes translation of selected tales and Boyer's able translation of them all. I have modernized the Spanish of unedited texts according to standard scholarly criteria. In reference to the different registers of imitation in literature, which range from the idealized to the parodic, I employ Northrop Frye's scheme of high and low mimetic (*Anatomy*).

The violent, complex narrative fugues in the *Desengaños* are extremely compelling and make it difficult to see what is going on at the aesthetic levels of the text. Thus, rather than emphasize the differences between the ten stories' narrators, I refer to the narrator whenever possible so as not to distract from the fact that all of those personae belong to Zayas. Readers interested in the nature and functions of those fugal voices will find studies of them in Griswold, Greer (*María*; 'Who's Telling'), and Kaminsky, and analysis of the discursive position of Zayas's authorial voice in N. Davis. Similarly, those interested in postmodern theoretical approaches to Zayas can consult the monographs about her works by Vollendorf (*Reclaiming*) and Greer, and Brownlee's 'Postmodernism.' What follows seeks to bring today's readers to Zayas rather than vice-versa, an approach that stems from my belief that in such stretching we exercise understanding and tolerance of difference. Although I do not pretend to be any less influenced by my life and times than anyone else, I consciously privilege the primary text in its own context to the extent possible.

My analysis of the *Desengaños* stands on the shoulders of previous scholars, particularly feminists, whose attention to María de Zayas has positioned her in the foreground of canonical literature, making possible a project such as this one. Feminism focuses on components of literary works that previous scholarly lenses clouded over or blacked out completely. Having those components clearly in sight now, we can (and, I believe, must) amplify our analytic range to understand and appreciate how Zayas represents a society in crisis by manipulating the figure of the idealized woman to her own artistic ends.

Like many readers of Zayas, I find her fiction difficult, often distasteful, and equally compelling. Having spent years searching for and sorting out the seventeenth-century aesthetic, legal, historical, literary, and religious referents of the *Desengaños*, and having long struggled with the book's meaning, I came to realize something I did not expect. The very enterprise of doing that, of wrestling with the difficulties that the book poses, is in fact part and parcel of the author's aesthetic itself. Resolving those conflicts reveals her extraordinary capacity to capture the complexities of her age in ways that speak not only to women, but to her world at large and through it, to ours.

Second Part of the Soirée and Decorous Entertainment (Tales of Disillusion)

frame tale: **Lisis**, betrothed to **Diego**, loves **Juan** but Juan loves **Lisarda**, Lisis's cousin.

d1: **Isabel** is courted by **Felipe**, but is raped and abandoned by her lover **Manuel**, who plans to wed **Zaide**. Felipe kills Manuel, Zaide kills herself. Isabel becomes a nun.

d2: **Octavia** is dishonoured by her lover **Carlos**, who weds **Camila**. Camila is raped by Octavia's brother **Juan** and then poisoned by Carlos. Octavia becomes a nun.

d3: **Roseleta** is courted by **Juan**, best friend of her husband **Pedro**, but resists him. The **Virgin Mary** saves Juan's life when Pedro seeks to kill him, and then he enters a convent. Pedro bleeds Roseleta to death after Angeliana convinces him that Juan and Roseleta were lovers.

d4: **Martín** listens to Jaime's story: **Jaime** defames **Lucrecia**, and then marries and starves to death his wife **Elena**, believing his **black slave**'s lie that Elena was unfaithful. Jaime goes mad. Martín marries.

d5: **Inés** is violated by **Diego** under the effects of a **Moor's** magic candle, for which her husband, brother, and sister-in-law cement her into their house's chimney, from which a neighbour rescues her. Her family members are executed and Inés becomes a nun.

d6: Laurela is dishonoured and abandoned by **Esteban**, who pretends to be her maid. Her father kills her, arranging for a wall to fall down on her.

d7: Blanca, married to the **Flemish Prince** who has a male lover **Arnesto**, is bled to death by the **Prince's father**, who also kills his own daughter **Marieta**.

d8: a) **Mencía** is stabbed to death by her brother **Alonso** when he discovers her secret marriage to **Enrique**; b) Alonso, in alliance with **Marco Antonio**, beheads his unwealthy wife **Ana** to recover his father's favour and fortune. He and Marco Antonio are executed.

d9: Queen Beatriz is desired by **Federico**, brother of her husband **King Ladislao**, who believes Federico's lies about his wife and exiles her. In exile she is betrayed two times by Federico, in league with a mysterious **Doctor**, but is saved by the **Virgin Mary**, who vanquishes the Doctor. Beatriz becomes a nun, and Ladislao enters a convent.

d10: Gaspar, frightened out of an immoral relationship by a dead body he unearths, is then frightened out of a relationship with **Florentina** after he rescues her from stab wounds and she tells him her story: Florentina has a long affair with Dionís, husband of her half-sister Magdalena. Hoping to wed Dionís, Florentina acquiesces to a plot to wrongly accuse Magdalena of infidelity to Dionís, for which Dionís kills his wife. Realizing his error, Dionís stabs everyone in his house and then himself, and only Florentina survives. She enters a convent. Gaspar weds.

frame tale: **Lisis** enters the convent as a resident, **Juan** dies in a fit, **Lisarda** weds a foreigner.

Figure 1.1 *Kitchen Scene (Allegory of Lost Virtue)*, Antonio de Pereda. Douglas-Pennant Collection, Penrhyn Castle, North Wales. With the generous permission of the National Trust

1 The *Desengaños* at a Distance

under the guise of licit entertainment, may virtue be
illuminated in the precious light of disillusion

(a sombra de lícito divertimiento [la virtud] se halle
alumbrada de la preciosa luz del desengaño)

Calderón de la Barca[1]

Readers of the *Desengaños* find themselves seeking meaning in a jumble of things, reminiscent of Antonio de Pereda's couple searching for virtue in the painting on the left. As anyone knows who has hunted for something in similar conditions, it is helpful to step back and assess one's position. This is a particularly difficult enterprise when under duress, and the *Desengaños* are designed to pressure the reader. However, like Pereda's subjects, Zayas's original readers would find what they sought, not only by calm re-vision, but also by looking at themselves: the key to virtue hangs on a ribbon tied around the woman's waist, exactly where it should be.[2]

If one steps away from Zayas's book with an eye on the patterns in which everything accumulates, it becomes evident that the way in which marriages are unrealized or destroyed is surprisingly straightforward, even though the plots are complex: first one, then several nobly born characters act ignobly, which opens the door to misbehaviour for others in the community who collude with nobility to overwhelm the virtuous. The virtuous are always characters seeking to marry or live a married life.

Because the dominant themes of the novella tradition as Zayas inherited it were love and marriage, the centrality of matrimony in her book is no surprise.[3] What is surprising is that she creates the narrative fireworks of the *Desengaños* using only two plots, both standard in prose fiction and theatre of her day: the courtship tale whose protagonists are unwed, and the tale of honour whose protagonists are married. Analysing the poetics of each, Wardropper points to how the courtship plot can end happily because it treats irresponsible behaviour toward a marriage contract *per verba de futuro*, or a promise to wed. The honour plot, in contrast, represents imprudent acts that violate an extant social contract and a sacrament, a marriage. Whereas in the former, irresponsibility can be treated lightly because the characters are not bound by a life-long public commitment, in the latter, irresponsibility usually costs someone's life ('El problema').

In defiance of these norms, Zayas does not once use the courtship plot's inclination to end happily, and instead consistently refuses to reconcile unmarried lovers to each other. Rather than contrasting stories of courtship and those of honour, the *Desengaños* use both to evidence how the nobility's misbehaviour inevitably produces disaster, in spite of her readers' expectation that at least some of them will end well. The tales of the unwed noblewomen Isabel, Octavia, Lucrecia, Laurela, and Florentina, which form all or parts of *desengaños* 1, 2, 4, 6, and 10 respectively, end in calamity. Less formally remarkable but no less alarming is the fact that the wives fare no better. In fact, every *desengaño* combines elements that make a bad state of affairs worse, and thus the situation with which each story ends is always inferior to the one with which it began, producing a terrible display of what happens when people do what they should not.

The key to reading the book is in the author's set of objectives, which are unfurled in chapter 2. Here we lay the necessary groundwork to capture those objectives in light of the social and artistic conditions that gave them meaning, since what is 'right' and 'wrong' for a noblewoman and nobleman of seventeenth-century Spain, and why the *Desengaños* signify through the lens of the nobility in the first place, is heavily conditioned by historical context. Any reader's success in defining the book's play between what should happen and what does happen is likewise conditioned by how alert that reader is to interpretative skills exalted by baroque artists, for without those skills, the reader sees only the jumble mentioned above. This chapter, then, takes us out of the *Desengaños* to imagine the text in a seventeenth-century context. From that vantage point, the objectives that Zayas establishes for her book are visible, and how the dying and dead noblewoman suits those objectives becomes understandable.

Morality and Class

In spite of the immorality and violence with which the *Desengaños* overflow, its first readers, church and state censors, did not find anything troubling in Zayas's book, although they did find troubling things in those of others. Approving the first edition, Doctor Juan Francisco Ginovés celebrates the volume as 'full of models to reform behaviour … models with which to flee the risks into which some inattentive women hurl themselves' (lleno de ejemplos para reformar costumbres … ejemplos con que huir los riesgos a que algunas [mujeres] desatentas se precipitan).[4] Fray Pío Vives's approval, part of the preliminary materials of the 1649 edition, is dated 23 Sept. 1648 and similarly declares, 'I find nothing in it contrary to our Holy Faith or good behaviour, and indeed see in it a refuge in which female weakness beset by importunate flattery can be protected, and a mirror of that which man most needs for the proper direction of his actions' (No hallo en él cosa contra nuestra Santa Fe, y buenas costumbres, antes en él veo un asilo donde puede acogerse la femenil flaqueza más acosada de importunidades lisonjeras, y un espejo de lo que más necesita el hombre para la buena dirección de sus acciones, np).

These endorsements suggest that Zayas's original readers understood her book as properly instructive and responsive to moralists' critique of novellas as 'violent awakeners to all vice and perpetual instructors in how to attempt and carry it out.'[5] The censors did not fixate on the death and abuse of women in the book that so calls forth our attention today; they appear rather to have seen those features as part of a coherent picture that provided the 'fruit and general benefit' expected of all publications in seventeenth-century Spain.[6] Our task, then, is to recover the assumptions of such a reading to normalize the book within the standards to which they held it. What did Zayas use her violently dead and disappeared women to say to her readers that would provide them with 'models to reform their behaviour' and how does that usage square with her defence of women?

The answer to that question is largely secured in the moral imperative of seventeenth-century literature, explicit in the censors' reports but often overlooked in literary analysis.[7] As Ullrich Langer has indicated, early modern Europeans had a more centred and fixed understanding of moral categories than readers today and belonged to 'earlier Western societies in which moral language was available, enjoyed a certain social consensus, and provided powerful ways of understanding and evaluating individual behavior' (312). According to Langer, the novella was in fact the genre with which European authors most intensively rehearsed their communities' moral axioms. This moral imperative was particularly strong and enduring in Spain, not only because the country was the bastion of the Counter-Reformation, but for reasons inherent to the nation itself. Spanish baroque authors, writing in defence of an imperial state and church in crisis, justified their writing by its potential to improve the status of things or provoke the public to reflect upon betterment. Morality (a system of beliefs that define right and wrong) and ethics (morals in praxis and the systematizing of the same) are at the core of the *Desengaños*, and Zayas has long been described as a moralistic author.[8]

Disentangling the class-conditioned morality that energizes Zayas's book, which is to say how it defines right and wrong for the nobility, allows readers today to understand it intellectually, even though the ideology it articulates is at some distance from current standards.[9] For example, her text's endorsement of the lower classes' inherent inferiority and ontological insignificance grates against twenty-first century liberal ideals about class and identity. The narrator declares that servants are 'domestic animals and enemies,' creatures whom the nobility cannot live with or live without.[10] Zayas uses servants as specular characters who occupy no self and should remain obediently subservient to their superiors, justified by Aristotelian hierarchies of social order that naturalized slavery and servitude. Marco Antonio de Camos articulates this vision in his influential treatise *Microcosmia* of 1595: 'Aristotle says that power and servitude exist naturally and there can be no perfect house or republic in which there is no lord who commands, and servants or vassals who obey' (Aristóteles dice que señorío y servidumbre es por naturaleza y que no puede ser casa o república perfecta que no haya señor que mande, y criados o vasallos que obedezcan, 158).[11]

Zayas's unambiguous legitimization of seventeenth-century class hierarchy conditions her text, such that whenever it portrays a servant's power over a member of the nobility, that power signifies the nobility's failure to maintain proper control over that servant and the serving class's inherent unreliability which justifies that control. When a former servant betrays the noble wife Inés by setting her up to be dishonoured (d1), when the nobleman Jaime believes a lying slave rather than his wife (d4), when Florentina heeds the bad advice of a servant and allows her half-sister to be betrayed and murdered (d10), Zayas is using the empowerment of the lower class over the nobility to signify the deadly consequences of the nobility's moral weakness, of failure to abide by the divinely mandated system of order. Entering the text from within this understanding, it becomes clear that whenever a noblewoman falls under the influence of a member of the lower class, directly or through someone else, she is going to be dishonoured or die, or both, and responsibility for her loss is deflected from the nobility, but not in fact reduced, by the mediating presence of that character.[12]

However, even the reader perfectly cognizant of Zayas's class-conditioned morality is in for a rough ride. Clarifying the ideological principles that the book sustains does not make it easy to distinguish right from wrong in the fiction, because her compounding of wrong acts almost to the exclusion of what is right produces a moral morass in which multiple contingencies – all bad – intertwine with and intensify each other. Furthermore, she problematizes, nuances, and temporizes wrong and right for the nobly born characters, such that being a member of the nobility does not translate into permanent goodness or badness and a nobly born character's wrongdoing rarely translates into being a bad person.

The sixth *desengaño*, for example, tells of a young girl, Laurela, whose virtue is besieged by a lying ne'er do well, Esteban, who poses as a female servant, gains access to Laurela inside Laurela's house, and pretends to be her ideal companion. After Esteban identifies himself as a nobleman, Laurela foolishly (says the narrator, 326) falls in love with him. All of this happens under the nose of Laurela's high-born father, whose honour requires that he defend his property, including his daughter, better than he does. Zayas aggravates these already numerous problems by making Laurela's father a weak married man who seeks a sexual relationship with Esteban, believing him to be the woman he pretends to be. To make matters worse, Esteban withholds his true identity as a commoner and a married man until the moment when he abandons Laurela in public after taking her virginity and stealing her money. At that, her aunt, uncle, and father turn against her and kill her.

Every member of this sad group is guilty of something, and the reader is left with the unhappy job of sorting it all out to determine what message to take from the story. The most obvious guilty character is Esteban, but to blame him alone for Laurela's death ignores the nobly born characters' misdeeds and the fact that when he abandons her, he is sure her father will forgive her ('in the end you are his daughter, and he will realize how little blame you have, since you were deceived' [al fin eres su hija, y considerará la poca culpa que tienes, pues has sido engañada, 325]). The fact that Laurela's body is the only female protagonist's corpse to which Zayas does not attach signifiers of sanctity intensifies the interpretative dilemma, as does the story's failure to censure her murderous father. This suggests that, following the text's own logic, he may have had the right to kill his daughter. To correctly assign guilt and innocence, the reader of the *Desengaños* must juggle multiple questions and assess the text's evidence in relationship to the reading instructions Zayas nested in her book, in order to arrive at the text's own conclusions. The author's original readers – the literate class – would have been highly skilled at doing that.

Reading Baroque

John Beverly indicates that seventeenth-century texts 'tend to justify themselves not by an appeal to the beautiful but rather to the difficult' (9), and indeed, in his 1648 guide to baroque poetics, *Agudeza y arte de ingenio* (*The Sharp Wit and Art of the Mind*), author Baltasar Gracián specifies the appeal of the difficult as superior to any other, saying, 'The more difficult the truth is, the more pleasing, and knowledge that costs effort is most esteemed' (La verdad, cuanto más dificultosa, es más agradable, y el conocimiento que cuesta, es más estimado, 1:99).[13] Prescribing difficulty specifically for the novella, author Cristóbal Suárez de Figueroa insists, 'Novellas, understood with proper rigour, are most clever compositions, whose example obliges to imitation or learning by means of observing the pain of others. The novella should be neither simple or naked, rather crafty and adorned with judgments, source material, and everything else that prudent philosophy can offer' (Las novelas, tomadas con el rigor que se debe, es [*sic*] una composición ingeniosísima, cuyo ejemplo obliga a imitación o escarmiento. No ha de ser simple ni desnuda, sino mañosa y vestida de sentencias, documentos y todo lo demás que puede ministrar la prudente filosofía, *El pasajero* [1617] 72). This difficulty, which requires effort on the part of the reader to produce meaning, makes a text what we now call readerly, a feature Eavan O'Brien attributes to Zayas's *Novelas amorosas* that is even more applicable to the *Desengaños*.[14]

Seventeenth-century authors' conscious engagement of the reader's intellect in their writing and their attempts to awaken their public to 'prudent philosophy' was a response to extensive critiques of printed literature of entertainment, critiques that date from the humanists and intensified through the seventeenth century. According to those seeking to protect the good of the republic, reading fiction excited the emotions and the will without the intellect, leaving readers helpless before the power of their indiscriminate passions and unable to distinguish what was real from what was not. Don Quijote's craziness is Cervantes' brilliant assessment of this problem.[15]

To justify fiction as beneficial as well as entertaining, authors sought to appropriate what Barry Ife calls 'the rapture of reading,' the tendency of readers to engage emotionally with a text, for the cause of moral good. They accomplished this by representing illusion as illusion, creating literary art that never lets the reader lose sight of the text as a text, so the enthralling effects of the untrue were countervailed by the intellect's constant surveillance. Favoured techniques, all well known, included self-conscious narrative voices, plurality of perspectives, fiction inside fiction, and the metatextual characteristic of baroque art, in which artistic works are reviewed inside the works of art themselves. Zayas marshals all of these in the *Desengaños*, most obviously in the Boccaccian frame tale in which characters attending the soirée talk about the stories, harnessing the readers' rapture by fictionalizing responses to the stories inside the book. The need to interpret rather than simply consume the text, then, is explicit in the literary poetics of Zayas's day, and the appropriately educated reader will seek non-literal meaning in stories that in some cases function perfectly well on the literal level. Harnessing rapture, however, was not the only benefit that baroque poetics ascribed to the reading of a difficult text.

Cognitive science has revealed that the human brain seeks order, is wired to make sense of data, and is pleasantly excited when beset with the need to do that.[16] This would have been no news, however, to baroque artists, who intuited that a challenge to the mind piques in the reader what they called the exercise of *ingenio*, the sum of one's imaginative and intellectual abilities. *Ingenio* is most brightly ignited by the means of *agudeza*, which is perspicacity and liveliness of wit, meaning the capacity of understanding. Zayas's contemporaries, such as Spain's baroque poet Luis de Góngora (1561–1627), understood the untangling of a difficult text as an act of moral improvement, and Gracián called *agudeza* the 'nourishment of the soul' (Es la agudeza pasto del alma, *Agudeza* 49).[17] The taxing text, which necessarily signifies through artifice, is also the one that delivers the greatest gratification and moral benefit at once. Zayas's prose, which qualifies as taxing, not only invites but demands the intervention of the reader's intellect, with its syntactic and diegetic difficulty, the complexity of its meaning, and the author's consistent recourse to the representation of what is wrong to somehow convey what is right.

Within this poetics of intensity, Spanish baroque readers and writers greatly esteemed an author's ability to press a variety of meanings into very close and conflicted proximity to each other, which Gracián renders by using the verb *exprimir*, 'to squeeze or twist' (*DRAE*) to describe the intensity of that proximity.[18] The resulting opposition had to be resolved in an exercise that tested the reader's interpretative skill, and the *Desengaños* are rife with such conflicting signifiers, implanted at both the syntactic and diegetic levels. When the narrator states that the *chill* of Don Juan's *lukewarm* behaviour toward Lisis was her highest *fever*, she expertly captures the hostess's conflicted emotional state with three referents of temperature, using two extremes that pass through a middle ('el *frío* de sus *tibiezas* [era] la mayor *calentura* de la dama,' 116; emphasis added). Overall, the book's primary opposition poses hyperbolically bad things that happen to hyperbolically good people.

The most difficult tests of wit in the book occur at the diegetic level, via what happens and how. For example, in *desengaño* 4, an unnamed, ugly, black slave passes through a doorway into the dining room, adorned in costly apparel and sparkling jewels, illuminated by candelabra carried by white servants, to occupy the wife's place at the table next to the white, nobly born husband Jaime (see fig. 1.2). At precisely the same moment, the rightful wife Elena, a beautiful, deathly pale, white noblewoman, is released from her cage in the nearby wall, dressed in rags and emaciated, and crawls into the darkness under the table where she eats scraps left for dogs and drinks from a skull. In this brilliant and startling chiaroscuro moment, Zayas besets her reader with several interpretative dilemmas.

If light and white are good and darkness is not (respecting the terms of Zayas's racism), then both the black slave and the white noblewoman are in the wrong place under the wrong conditions (elevated, illuminated material splendour and darkened, degraded deprivation, respec-

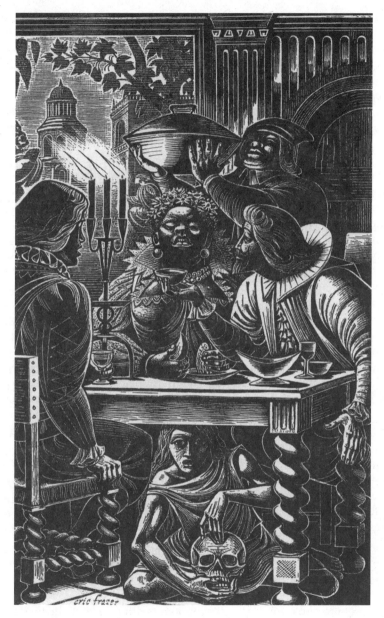

Figure 1.2 Illustration of *desengaño* 4 by Eric Fraser (1902–83), from the 1963
Sturrock translation

tively). The black woman's ugliness is right, in that it is true to early modern racist stereotypes. Her highly visible proximity to the white husband in the position of wife is wrong because it suggests an inappropriate relationship of race and class. The white woman's emaciated pallor, which seventeenth-century Spanish cosmetic aesthetics defined as beautiful, is also right, for whereas baroque ideals of female beauty in France and Italy celebrated robustness, those of Spain emphasized paleness and thinness, a standard that women strove to attain by regularly having themselves bled (Ortega López 253).

The skull in Elena's hands and her tattered attire are attributes from the lives of penitential saints such as Mary Magdalen, and affiliate Elena with repentance.[19] Apparently, the young wife has made a big mistake for which she is paying, something that readers must disentangle as the plot progresses. The highly visual image that introduces the slave and the wife presents conflicting signifiers in high compression, in which white, light, and penance should signify goodness and success but do not manage to do so. The dissonant components of the picture can only be harmonized in light of Zayas's objectives and how the story ends, but this brief display suffices to demonstrate the author's agility in manipulating meaning and the need to read cautiously to countervail the powerful magnetism of the book's high drama.

Contextualizing the *Desengaños* in baroque poetics prepares the reader for contingencies that complicate each other and multiplicities that might appear to contradict each other, but which in the final analysis can and must be resolved. Thus, not only might the book strive to meet multiple objectives, but a single tale may meet several of those objectives rather than just one. Moreover, what one group of readers takes from the book (noblemen, for example) might differ from what the author embedded in it for another group (noblewomen, for another). In this context, the successful reader will determine how the apparently contradictory components of the text, such as encouraging women to defend themselves and celebrating dead women, can be reconciled using internal standards. In a book in which metaphorical meaning displaces the literal, a female character may not mean a flesh and blood female, for example, and the author may condition her to signify differently at specific points in the text. The reader's task is to seek out patterns of signification that provide the clues for how to correctly interpret the book, for a naive or literal meaning violates the text's aesthetic standard.

María de Zayas, Classism, and Social Morality

As she hones her readers' moral capacity by piquing their intellect and challenging their ability to manage multiplicity at several levels of the text, Zayas offers little that challenges hegemonic ideology of seventeenth-century Spain. Using the conservative values of the royalist, Catholic nobility as a baseline, she points instead to how the elite has strayed from its class ideals. By affiliating with her society's dominant group, she enhanced the appeal of her book's otherwise strident message, particularly given its severe critique of the male nobility's foul behaviour. All evidence suggests that this affiliation was authentic to Zayas, and the supreme signifying power of class in the *Desengaños* comes as no surprise, given what we know about the author.

Available historical information about María de Zayas, still scant, allies her with the nobility whose best interests the *Desengaños* represent as under siege by the nobility itself. It is generally agreed that she was born in 1590, and that her father was a Knight of the Order of Santiago, a military order of highest prestige. As a young woman, she likely travelled to Italy, probably Naples, when her father may have had a post. There is evidence that she later participated in, but did not belong to, literary salons in Madrid and Barcelona, and that as an adult she was relatively well connected and well known among the Spanish literati as a poet, novella writer, and perhaps playwright. *La traición en la amistad* (*Betrayal in Friendship*), her only known dramatic work, is extant in an undated manuscript. Although evidence has been found that her friend Ana Caro wrote for money, no such information has surfaced for Zayas, which suggests that she was financially well off.[20] There is no data as yet indicating that Zayas exercised any other profession than noblewoman, nor is it known whether she was married or had children. Serrano y Sanz, whose 1903 catalogue of information about Spanish women writers contains most of what is known about Zayas, cites two death certificates as possibly hers, one of 1661 and another of 1669, but observes that because the name María de Zayas was common, it is impossible to know if either one belongs to the woman who wrote the *Desengaños* (583–7).[21]

Sylvania calls Zayas 'aristocratic to her fingertips, well educated and surrounded with friends of similar station and similar tastes' (4), and Yllera describes her as proud of belonging to the nobility and accepting of the established order (Introducción 21). Some qualifications, however, are pertinent. Had Zayas been of the highest aristocracy, genealogical information about her illustrious family would have survived, and to date none has come to light. She probably belonged to what Romero-Díaz calls the 'middle nobility,' whose members not only wrote but also represented themselves in the seventeenth-century novella (*Nueva* 35).

This would put Zayas in good company, for the majority of authors in sixteenth- and seventeenth-century Spain were from this group, whereas only 2.9 per cent came from the uppermost class (Estruch Tobella 338). Almost the highest elite, the middle nobility identified with the highest elite, to whose status they aspired and whose interests they protected as their own. The uncontested importance of class has a direct impact on the *Desengaños*, most obviously in Zayas's lexicon, for when she writes 'woman' (*mujer*) she means 'noblewoman.' When she refers to a female of another class, she uses a different noun, such as '*vecina*' (neighbour woman), '*esclava*' (female slave), or '*criada*' (female servant). The *Desengaños* are not a defence of women; they are a defence of noblewomen.

Because the signifying class of the seventeenth-century Spanish novella is the nobility, the fictional meaning is invested in their interests, and in Zayas's book, a female character has more meaning and power by virtue of her high birth than by virtue of being female. Logically, then, the author empowers noblewomen by stressing their uncontestable right to respect as nobility rather than their problematic, conditioned rights as women, who lived under prescribed subservience to upper-class men. In other words, class trumps gender in the *Desengaños*. Thus it is not only acceptable but admirable for a noblewoman to cross-dress as the Viceroy of Valencia, as Estela does in the *Novelas amorosas*, because although the change in clothing violates her gender, it does not violate her class, but rather affirms that class's inherent talent for ruling.

In contrast, in *desengaño* 1 when Isabel dresses herself down, wearing the clothes and brand of a female slave and a Moorish one at that, she double hexes herself because doing so demeans her class and assures that Manuel will never marry her. He rejects her for this very reason, asking what on earth she is doing dressed as she is ('¿Qué disfraz es éste, doña Isabel?'), accusing her of vile actions ('semejantes bajezas') and assuring her that if he ever intended to marry her, he no longer does, specifically because she has destroyed her own reputation: 'for the bad name you have acquired with me and with anyone who finds out what you have done' (por el mal nombre que has granjeado conmigo y con cuantos lo supieran, 156).[22]

By virtue of her race, religion, and class, Zayas formed a part of what Maravall calls the 'seigniorial network,' participating in 'a drama of the estates, the gesticulating submission of the individual to the confines of the social order' (*Culture* 35). That social order was extremely rigid in comparison with Western societies today. In seventeenth-century Spain, social mobility was suspect among the upper classes, a situation often cited in reference to difficulties faced by the non-noble classes as their members attempted to buy their way into the nobility. Outsiders to the inbred aristocracy and royalty were not welcome in the elite, and in the face of early modern challenges to aristocratic systems of wealth based on bloodline, land, and reputation (versus the modern wealth of money and political talent), the Spanish upper classes responded by closing ranks, not opening them.[23]

Less considered is how notions of social hierarchy constrained as well as privileged the highborn, which is what Zayas fictionalizes. Nobly born characters in the *Desengaños* cannot escape the identity and obligations that come with their birth; one cannot rise to authentic nobility, but neither can one fall out of it, and noblesse oblige is the book's implicit motto.[24] The gridlock of birthright and responsibility surfaces in how Zayas treats the members of her fictional aristocracy who offend God and each other with alarming intensity. Any unrepentant Catholic sinner is headed to hell, and a sinful individual will deservedly die unconfessed, as does Isabel's dishonest lover Manuel, killed by his virtuous rival in *desengaño* 1. However, Zayas also fictionalizes another option for the nobly born sinners, by far the preferred one: repentance, not only for the sake of their souls but for the sake of the reader for whom they model correct, noble behaviour, even (or especially) after having betrayed their class ideals.

In the *Desengaños*, the way for nobly born sinners to regain their eternal souls is by contrition and exit from the world, entering the convent and thereby fading the stain with which they besmirched their class and disobliged God. Therefore Juan, who regrets his assaults on his best friend's wife (d3), and Florentina, who realizes she committed a grievous error by stealing her half-sister's husband (d10), do precisely that, although they have no religious vocation. Lower class characters committing a similarly egregious offence and regretting it, such as Esteban who violates Laurela (d6) and the black slave who betrays the noble wife Elena (d4), have no chance to die well and are relatively unremarkable (if no less destructive) within the book's class ideology, because their misbehaviour merely affirms the nobility's stereotype of non-noble individuals as naturally dangerous and weak.

Zayas does not interrogate social hierarchy, as did Cervantes and dramatist Pedro Calderón with characters such as a daughter of wealthy farmers who out-performs the nobles' nobility (Dorotea of *Don Quijote*), or the humbly born Isabel of Calderón's *El alcalde de Zalamea*, for whose honour her farmer father risks everything. The question in the *Desengaños* is not whether a person not born to the nobility can be noble or act nobly. The question is what happens when a person born to the nobility fails to behave nobly by not abiding by the codes of behaviour that define the upper classes, such as moral integrity conditioned by violent loyalty to class and clan, dominion over others of class, race, and religion, and self-sacrificing defence of the honour of one's family, class, and nation. The imperatives of class deeply compromise the good noblewomen's ability to function independently of noblemen. While all readers fall into the quicksand of the *Desengaños'* complexity, only those who remain constantly aware of those imperatives will re-emerge.

Reading through Zayas's classist lens also clarifies the distinction between blame and responsibility, key to the book's moral paradigm. Blame, 'imputation of demerit on account of a fault or blemish' (*OED*), implicitly entails two positions, one blaming and one blamed. Responsibility, in contrast, means one person's ability and obligation to respond to a situation ('answerable, accountable,' *OED*) and is something an individual accepts or rejects. Blame cannot solve a problem, whereas responsibility can. In the moral framework of the *Desengaños*, characters who are not aristocrats are guilty of sowing serious disorder and for doing so deserve blame. The nobility, as their social superiors, are responsible for the behaviour of their servants, in the way that parents are responsible for their children and kings responsible for their subjects.[25]

In this understanding, the female slave who tells Elena's husband that Elena is having an affair with a young page is guilty of lying, and she thereby confirms the nobility's low expectations of how such individuals behave. Responsibility for her behaviour, however, lies with Elena's husband, who should have known better than to give unconditional credence to a servant. When he kills the slave on her deathbed after she confesses the truth, her death does nothing to correct the situation because the real problem lies with him. The slave serves Zayas's purpose of testing the husband's disposition toward his wife, a test he fails completely. Thus Jaime gets what he deserves, which is permanent insanity, a narrative equivalent of death in this context and, during Zayas's lifetime, 'synonymous with thoughtlessness and intemperance and ... a source of moral decline' (Tausier 288).[26] Likewise in *desengaño* 5, Don Diego's single-handed attempts to access the virtuous and married Inés fail, and her marriage continues intact. It is when Diego affiliates himself with a former servant of Inés's and then a Moorish necromancer that the young wife's downfall is assured. Although the servant and the Moor are to blame for what happens, Diego is responsible for it, and he is executed.

The genius of Zayas's moral paradigm in the *Desengaños*, however, is how it reveals that irresponsible behaviour on the part of nobles does harm to their victims and society at large that even cleansing acts of justice, such as the execution of the guilty, can never heal. The classism of the book clarifies that, because female as well as male nobly born characters are responsible for their own feelings and behaviour, they are not responsible for the misdeeds of other members of their class, who are responsible for their own behaviour. Zayas works this moral paradigm through her three major character types in the *Desengaños*: members of the nobility who behave irresponsibly, those who do nothing wrong, and those who behave somewhat irresponsibly and are also hurt by the errors of others. Those who do wrong themselves and are also wronged by others are partially guilty or imperfect victims, including Isabel, Octavia, Laurela, and Florentina, unwed noblewomen whose misbehaviour generates at least some of their difficulties (d1, d2, d6, d10). The second type, complete innocents, are the perfect victim characters, the married female protagonists of the honour tales who are wrongly blamed and punished for the misdeeds of others, in spite of the fact that they are not responsible for them. These characters' final removal from the world in which they desired to live culminates in divine confirmation of their worth, as they are either paired with the perfect husband – Christ – in the convent (Inés, d5; Beatriz, d9), or assimilated into the superior realm of heaven via markers of sanctity that God deposits on their corpses: Camila (d2), Roseleta (d3), Elena (d4), Inés (d5), Blanca (d7), Mencía and Ana (d8), Beatriz (d9), and Magdalena (d10).

Irresponsible actions by the degenerate nobility against both the perfect and imperfect victims produces a deficit in the textual economics of responsibility that is acutely intense in actions against the wife characters: Jaime punishes his wife to death for a defaming lie about her told by a slave, Inés is cemented into a chimney for having been the object of a thoughtless nobleman's desire, Ana is decapitated because her husband married her against the wishes of his father, and so on (d4, d6, d8). Using her three character types, Zayas represents how the imbalance created by such unjust behaviour generates a debt to society that can never be repaid, even when the responsible party is punished, because the misbehaviour does irrevocable damage to individuals who have done no wrong.

The more innocent, suffering, and perfect the victim characters are, then, the more able the narrative to deliver the most intense sense of loss. The most intense sense of loss, in turn, moves readers to avoid the injustice in the first place. Victimization is a crucial component in the poetics of the *Desengaños*. It is a narrative strategy that Zayas enlists in the service of her larger textual agenda, and the lingering injustice produced by the suffering and loss of the victim characters weighs heavily on the reader finishing the book.

Dying Catholic

The *Desengaños*, written from within the hermetic seal of noble hegemony, do not interrogate traditional Castilian politics of religion, honour, or violence, and it is precisely because those politics form the ideological walls of her fictional structures that the author can focus on the problems that interest her, which are the consequences of ignoble behaviour on the part of the nobility born to those standards. Obviously, the seventeenth-century class-conscious nobility of Spain was aggressively Catholic. However, in a country sewn together with territories wrested from the Moors, from which the Jews had likewise been expelled since 1492 and where Protestants were never welcome, Catholicism was a political and cultural as well as a religious force. Although Zayas's book is not religious per se, Catholic identity provides the invisible warp and woof of the narrative tapestry, and this seamless, casual Catholicism is manifest in cultural as well as theological mandates. Zayas's original public read her book with a level of religious literacy difficult to imagine today, a literacy that conditioned their reading in two important ways: how its members interpreted the death of a character, and how they assigned meaning to the book's hagiographic intertexts.

Early modern Catholics' familiarity with the end of earthly life and corpses made the dead body a locus of rich meaning for the living, a potential of signification that intensified with the baroque obsession with dying and death. The figure of death, as Martínez Gil aptly puts it, was not an abstraction for them but rather a familiar, intimate character that was part of society, not above it (331), and for an author to take recourse in the 'Christian marvellous' was recommended by early modern literary theorists since Torquato Tasso (Welles, 'María' 304). This familiarity heightened readers' sensitivity to Catholic doctrine on death, according to which the portal to life eternal, and one's fate therein, irrevocably gaped open with one's final breath.

The art of dying well became complex in the seventeenth century, bolstered by a series of books about it. Seventeenth-century death culture defined an exemplary demise as one in which the moribund individual made a will and a full confession, then passed quietly and beautifully away, since pain and illness were deeply associated with sin. By the time the *Desengaños* appeared in 1647, a good Catholic death was not only a life's culminating event, but also a performance for those who watched it happen. Zayas stages such a spectacle with Camila, poisoned by her husband because she had been raped, in which the virtuous woman dispenses wisdom from her deathbed and receives the sacrament before passing on to life eternal (d2).[27]

The fate of one's soul was of paramount importance, and Zayas's first readers would have automatically made a calculation of that fate using textual evidence that readers today only gloss over. Taking the opportunity and time before death to make appropriate amends for sin was the only way for a sinner's soul to get to heaven, and when faced with this reality, nobly born sinners such as Juan (d3) and Florentina (d10) do the right thing by retiring to the convent to do so, or confessing all sin and publicly repenting their misdeeds in hopes for divine mercy, as does Alonso, who eloquently regrets the sororicide and uxoricide he committed before he is beheaded (d8).

How a character died was the standard by which that character was judged, and Zayas's readers would have noticed that almost all of the nobly born characters die innocent or repentant. The two exceptions, Isabel's dishonest lover Manuel and Florentina's married and suicidal lover Dionís, serve as cautionary models to noblemen with a potency it is difficult for readers today to fathom, for their souls were going to hell forever.[28] Reading the victims in light of death standards reveals that one of the reasons Zayas marks the dead bodies of her perfect victim characters with holy signifiers, such as preternaturally flowing blood or a radiant corpse, is to assure her readers that in spite of their bodies' disfigurement and in spite of the sudden, unexpected deaths for which most of them had no time to prepare, God has recognized their authentic identity and received their souls into heaven. The explicit, repeated contradiction between the completely innocent characters' mutilation and abuse and their almost celestial virtue would have alarmed Zayas's first readers as much as it does readers today. Their familiarity with displaced and non-literal meaning, however, would have alerted them to the possibility that the horrors splayed over the bodies of those characters might not be their own, but rather someone else's, a possibility to which we will return in chapter 3.

The saturation of seventeenth-century Spanish culture with Catholicism also provided Zayas's original readers with textual models they brought to the table of their reading. These are models to which readers today have little if any access, due to the way in which the literary canon has been constructed to privilege secular texts over religious ones, in spite of data proving that early modern readers' preferences were exactly the opposite.[29] The first readers of the *Desengaños* were as well versed in the details of romance hagiography as they were in romance chivalry, living as they did during what Sánchez Lora calls 'the era of the saints' (366), when Spanish hagiographers were establishing textual models of the saints' lives for all of Europe.[30] Cayuela cites evidence that by the end of the seventeenth century, hagiography had won over readers at large (*Paratexte* 451), an argument buttressed by Carrasco's statistics proving that hagiography largely monopolized the business of Spanish printing in the sixteenth and seventeenth centuries (363) and Buser's evidence that seventeenth-century Catholics were avid readers of martyr accounts for reasons of religious politics.[31]

Catholicism's exalted cult of the saints in post-Tridentine doctrine contrasted with Protestant iconoclasm, making a political as well as religious statement that nationalist authors such as Zayas took advantage of. That cult intensified the notion of embodied holiness that is central to Christianity, and was particularly well suited to the superficial signifying scheme that Zayas uses in the *Desengaños*. It is a scheme that encodes the material world, including the human body, to bring meaning to the text in accordance with baroque artists' use of the creature as 'the mirror within whose frame alone the moral world was revealed to the baroque' (Benjamin 91). Zayas's first public would have registered the presence of hagiography in the *Desengaños* with an ease and precision all but inaccessible to readers today, a cultural deficit easily remedied by a review of the *vitae* from which Zayas borrows, which is part of chapter 3.

As we approach the text more generally now, alertness to its assumption of hagiographic literacy normalizes some of its peculiar features, such as the irruption of the supernatural into the narrative and the book's heavy push toward death. With her persistent adaptive integration of hagiographic components into the novella, Zayas is accomplishing something new, for her book's objective is not religious, and without violating the theological principles of her faith, she manipulates Catholic codes of meaning to celebrate an earthly, not heavenly, ontology.

In a religious text of the Christian faith, for a saint to die after multiple torments signifies the triumph of God, who welcomes the holy individual into death, which hagiographic poetics in turn specify as far superior to life on earth. In the *Desengaños*, Zayas uses hagiographic forms – the mutilated body of a good person – but curtails hagiographic transcendence, such that innocent human beings die unprotected by the armour of God's will. Put differently, in the urban novella dying badly is a bad thing in every way. However, dying well is not a bad thing, particularly if a character dies amid signifiers of saintliness. But in a narrative such as the *Desengaños*, a narrative that does not strive to celebrate a religious, transcendental ontology, for the character who wants to live and does not deserve to die, death under any circumstances is by no means a good thing. The fact that Zayas consistently allies the symbolic or literal death of a good character with a failure to realize or maintain a marriage affirms the earthly orientation of her text. Although each of the *desengaños* and the frame tale move toward death in the world or death to it, the reader is ever aware that this downward spiral is due to the nobility's dysfunction, not God's will.

Zayas uses the frustration of marriage as well to cut off the ascent of her fiction, by having all of the book's virtuous characters strive to enter or sustain the married state. Although marriage is the impossible dream to which every story in the book aspires, it is an ideological hot spot for readers today, whose postmodern experience of it ill prepares them for Zayas's pre-modern standards.

Marriage in Literature and Life

Marriage is not a pretty picture in the *Desengaños*. Seven out of the nine virtuous wives meet violent ends, six at the hands of their husbands, and the two wives who do not die barely survive their husbands' and families' assaults, one due to the miraculous intervention of the Virgin Mary. One of the unwed female protagonists dies in the aftermath of a false promise of marriage (Laurela, d6) and two others abandon the world in dishonour, each consequent to a man's failure to marry her as promised (Isabel, d1; Octavia, d2). Some of the narrators decry men as inherently unfaithful, which bodes ill for any woman planning to marry one. Regardless, none of the noblewomen characters abandon their aspirations to wed or their fidelity to their husbands. True to the thematic tradition of the novella, those aspirations are their primary signifying feature.

One reason for the predominance of matrimony in the *Desengaños* was strictly literary and symbolic. A standard finishing touch on a plot, fictional marriage in early modern literature symbolized 'the restoration of the good order of society,' a divinely instituted ritual scripted to signify the order and harmony of the entire universe.[32] Artistic praxis demanded that Zayas treat marriage in one way or another, and rather than resist this norm, she manipulated it to her own ends by celebrating it and using its failure to signify the crisis of the nobility and the nation. The female protagonists define marriage as their one and only goal, as when Florentina describes 'tomar estado,' or getting married, as 'the desire of all noblewomen of Magdalena's age and mine' (el deseo de todas las mujeres de sus [Magdalena] años y de los míos, 487), and Isabel says she responded to Manuel realizing that she had to marry someone ('era fuerza tener dueño,' 131). Such direct expressions of the female characters' desire to wed reinforce not only the standard humanist arguments in favour of marriage, analysed by Morant Deusa, but also the plots, which strive toward marriage or the endurance of an extant matrimony without realizing either one.

The book's representation of marriage as deadly for women is often read as Zayas's critique of the institution itself.[33] That interpretation, however, does not square with the highborn female characters' determination to wed and stay married no matter what, a contradiction that demands a readerly act of *agudeza*, or wit. Reviewing period-specific information about matrimony, followed by a scrutiny of how the text uses it, allows the reader to resolve the paradox without assuming that noblewomen want to die, which the book's pro-woman rhetoric disallows.

To challenge the institution of marriage and the heterosexual, reproductive union it legitimizes would have constituted a challenge to a Catholic sacrament, highly unlikely in a Catholic author of the seventeenth century. Furthermore, investigations into the realities of married life by scholars such as Connor, Orlin, and Dopico Black support the supremacy of marriage among the opportunities for Spanish women of the seventeenth-century: 'The married state in early modern Spain was the most commonly desired one for most women because it was the legal structure offering the greatest potential for economic, social, cultural, and political security' (Connor 36). Coontz's recent study of the history of marriage reveals that, around the globe and through the ages, marriage was (and continues to be) 'the most important marker of adulthood and respectability as well as the main source of social security' (7).[34] It bears mention that, as Behrend-Martínez says, the same held for males: 'only marriage elevated a man to full status in early modern society' (1077).

Zayas lived in a society in which 95 per cent of urban oligarchs married, and married each other. Hernández cites statistics to support his conclusion that marriage was a social imperative among the Madrid elite, driven by the need to perpetuate lineage and protect an entire social class as well as a way of life, and was the key to the upper class's 'politics of reproduction' (151–98). The high material and political stakes of noble marriage likely made it difficult for noblewomen to reject; Coolidge's documentation of the pressure exerted on the noblewoman Magdalena de Bobadilla to marry, for reasons of estate, is telling (Magdalena lived from 1546 to 1580 [141–3]). Pressure to wed was also exerted by the Counter-Reformation Catholic Church, whose representatives bolstered the power of sacramental marriage by emphasizing, not denying, its worldly, contractual value (Gil 180).

Demographics during Zayas's lifetime lent special power to the metaphorical weight of matrimony. Spain was then in the full bloom of a population crisis, a crisis understood by Spanish citizens and others to be a primary reason for the erosion of Spanish power around the world. Giovanni Botero's very influential treatise *Della ragione di stato* (*On Reason of State*), published for the first of many times in 1589, refers specifically to the relationship between population and national wealth, specifying that 'if Spain is accounted a barren land this is not due to any deficiency of the soil but to the sparseness of the inhabitants.'[35] Sancho de Moncada, a well-known political commentator seeking precise data to explain the nation's decline, researched and identified a 50 per cent reduction in marriages in the parish where he collected his statistics, and the 1623 report to the Council of Castile on the same problem used tax assessments to conclude that the Castilian population had declined by 30 per cent since the previous collection of records.[36] Whether or not Zayas was aware of the high impact that female emigration from Spain to the New World had on national demographics – at the end of the sixteenth century, 30 per cent of emigrants were women – the fact was that this 'loss of potential population to the Iberian peninsula must have been considerable' (Elliot 11). Writers of Zayas's lifetime were under special pressure to defend Christian matrimony, the only legitimate basis for reproduction, a pressure to which visual artists responded by producing an unprecedented number of idealized representations of the married state (Villaseñor Black 638).

Interpreting marriage in the *Desengaños* entails reading what should be but is not, in the black light of Zayas's negative aesthetic. To read that way, the distinction drawn by lawyer and social theorist Juan Costa in 1584 is helpful: one should not confuse marriage, a divinely ordained state, with married people or those who seek to wed, who bring human imperfections to the altar.[37] Given the symbolic meaning of the institution in literature and the dominance of marriage among the elite, it is logical that the *Desengaños* critique not the institution of marriage itself, but rather the corrupt fashion in which fidelity, devotion, and self-sacrifice are promised and not practised by the ignoble nobility and attacked by the flawed characters of every social class, all failures Zayas passes through her device of marriage. These failures assured the rupture of the very components of the nobility for which the noblewoman was responsible: the guarantee of an enduring, pure bloodline, perpetuation of the social, cultural, and ideological structure, and the concentration of power via matrimonial alliance.[38] The fact that Zayas manages her fiction so that all of the wives of the *desengaños* are virtuous and all of them finish the book either mutilated, dead, or both speaks to human failure, not the failure of what seventeenth-century Catholics understood as the divinely instituted union of men and women.

The *Desengaños*'s persistent fixation on the failure and loss of sanctified human union is an innovative literary construct in which marriage acquires a ghostly presence in the book because the characters consistently break marriage promises and, if a marriage exists, one or both of the spouses die violently. Reading the nobility's failures in marriage as the canvas on which the author critiques her class, it becomes clear that, were the characters behaving in accordance with the standards to which the *Desengaños* aspire, marriage would be the happy ending of every single tale.

The question of matrimony remits to that of reproduction, which in turn poses questions of sexual praxis. The successful marriage in

Zayas's day was not understood as a fulfilling interpersonal relationship, but rather a sexual and economic contract between like members of the republic designed to sustain that republic, in which spousal love was the result of, not the reason for, a union. Catholic ethics before and after the Council of Trent define marriage as sanctified procreation in obedience of divine mandate ('Be fruitful and multiply,' Genesis 1:22), and canon law defined it as human beings' right to safeguard their natural inclination to perpetuate themselves ('natural inclinación a la conservación de la especie,' Ledesma, *Adiciones* 5). Seventeenth-century moral philosophy consistently upholds the notion that it was God's will that people wed and thereby perpetuate order as well.[39] Thus, in her treatise describing virtuous nobility, Countess Luisa de Padilla affirms that the purpose of marriage is to procreate citizens for heaven ('el fin de él ... es procrear ciudadanos para el cielo,' *Nobleza virtuosa* 69). Inside matrimony and out, any means of birth control or abortion violated the commandment not to kill, and any sex act that did not facilitate pregnancy, such as improper positions and excessive ardour, was likewise sinful because it compromised the primary purpose of holy matrimony.[40]

Although the central function of marriage was reproduction, matrimonial taxonomy went well beyond legitimized sex. According to Ledesma, Costa, and other moralists and jurists, divine will was that people marry to provide the hub of human society from which all human intercourse emanated, providing the foundation of households, the city, the republic, and the common good (Costa 310–11). This data indicates that the literary tradition that used marriage to signify the restoration of order reinforced the theological and political metaphor of marriage as a microcosm of correct social organization whose reproductive function guaranteed a stable future. Its failure, then, would signify the opposite, a cataclysmic end to the known social world.

Understood as crucial to the well-being of the country and the people's symbolic relationship to God, matrimony was an institution also manifestly in crisis. By identifying noble decadence as the reason for the failure of marriage, Zayas yoked domestic misbehaviour to political crisis with great success, and in the *Desengaños*, marriage – failed and longed for – is a metonym for the Spanish empire, the safeguard of the nobility's perpetuity with honour and purity of blood. Interpreting Christian matrimony as the metaphor of all that is right and good in the *Desengaños* allows the reader to release its pressurized significance and capture its fullest meaning. In this context, when a marriage fails to take place or falls apart, it signifies much more than two people's inability to get along and poses a challenge to the nation.

Interestingly, Zayas does not attribute marriage's failure to premarital sex. True to the dynamics of seventeenth-century society, the *Desengaños* do not equate such contact with sin, but rather accept it as a prelude to marriage, provided the marriage takes place. In consonance with ecclesiastical and civil law, Zayas and her readers would have categorized what we now call sex in terms that divided sexual intercourse into legitimate and illegitimate acts, depending on participants' relationship to the married state, whether the act was between two people of the same or opposite sex, and, if a woman and man were involved, whether she came to the act a virgin or not, willingly or not.[41] Ecclesiastic and civic standards defined marriage – intended or actual – as the only legitimate context for sexual experience, within which the wife and husband alike had the right to demand intercourse of their spouse. (This is not to say that illegitimate sex, such as prostitution and concubinage, was not socially sanctioned.)

Intercourse between members of the nobility outside of marriage was defined in terms of a man's right or wrong access to someone else's property, to a woman's integrity, and to the honour to which it was soldered. Zayas inflects the early modern interpretation of sex acts with the female voice, drawing her narrative camera close into a noblewoman's experience of violation through attempted or actual access to her body under the wrong circumstances, giving a face to the noblewoman's experience of civic and ecclesiastical marriage statutes gone wrong, in cases of rape and sexual dishonour.

Rape, Reputation, and Honour

The *Desengaños*'s nasty brew of noble failures boils over into rape three times: Manuel violates his fiancée Isabel 'to be sure of her,' which is to say to establish his control over her; Octavia's brother Juan avenges Octavia's dishonour at the hands of Carlos by raping Carlos's wife, Camila; Diego gains repeated sexual access to Alonso's wife Inés while she is unconscious due to the effects of a magic spell (d1 [136], d2, d5). Historical and literary evidence suggests that rape in the early modern world was not interpreted as an aggression against a woman's personal identity as much as an attack against social order, an entire web of relationships.[42] Like most authors of her day, Zayas represents the physical violation of an unwed noblewoman less as unconditional dishonour than as an imperative that the rapist marry the noblewoman he rapes, which is precisely what the law dictated. Jurist Francisco de la Pradilla, as his predecessors, defines the forced deflowering of a woman outside of marriage as *estupro*, punishable under civil and canon law by the rapist's obligation to wed the woman he raped.[43] And indeed, Isabel spends the entire first *desengaño* attempting to get her rapist Don Manuel to take her to the altar (d1). Whereas the young woman reconciles herself to having been raped by Manuel and continues to love him, she never overcomes his failure to marry her.

In literary texts of early modern Spain, the rape of a wife by a man not her husband, or a husband's suspicion of his wife's fidelity, sets off a chain of events that leads to her death, since another man's access to her, or suspicion of the same, theoretically throws into question her husband, father, or brother's ability to control his women and the purity of his bloodline. For him to regain the impression of control, evidence of his failure must disappear, and for a husband to reproduce without stain, the tainted wife, whether guilty or not, must die so he can face his community and remarry. How to interpret this extreme assessment of a threat to a marriage, which surfaces in many Spanish works of theatre and prose fiction during the first half of the seventeenth century, remains a matter of debate. However, historical evidence is beginning to reveal that the purist standards of behaviour and reputation exacted of fictional females were much less exacting for their real counterparts of the noble class. Doña Luisa de la Cerda (d. 1596), of the high nobility, had an illegitimate daughter by Diego Hurtado de Mendoza (equally illustrious) and then went on to marry Arias Pardo, who was wealthier and higher born than both Luisa and Diego (Manero Sorolla).

What María de Zayas would have made of such real behaviour is also up for debate, but in spite of the violence engendered by inappropriate sex acts in the *Desengaños*, she does not represent mutually desired sex before marriage as damning in itself, provided marriage is sincerely intended. The text explicitly distinguishes heterosexual sex (in itself not a problem) from reputation (always a problem when compromised). The *Desengaños* rehearse the relative insignificance of premarital sex with the lusty character Lucrecia (d4). This young, beautiful, and wealthy widow plucks the astounded nobleman Jaime from the street and has him blindfolded, and then brought to her chambers, where she regales him with wealth in exchange for sex and what she thinks is secrecy. Zayas never censures Lucrecia's desire in itself, and has the story's narrator rather offhandedly announce that the young woman plans to marry Jaime as soon as possible (243). The problem is not their sexual relationship. The problem is Jaime's compromise of Lucrecia's reputation when he fails to keep their relationship a secret, to which Lucrecia responds by putting out a contract on his life.[44]

What is damning and spells disaster, whether a couple is having sex or not, is public awareness of that couple's relationship without the sanction of public marriage, which comes as no surprise in a book that uses marriage as the signifier of national prosperity and was written under the shadow of baroque acknowledgment that appearance matters more than reality. In *desengaño* 8, Enrique and Mencía's story specifies that marriage spells virtue, but secret marriage spells trouble (d8). Their dishonour arises not when the two lovers marry against the will of Mencía's avaricious father, but rather when neighbours see them together without knowing they have wed, which ignites the scandal that leads to Mencía's death (377). Similarly, Alonso's marriage to Ana unravels only when the same father discovers his son has married a poor woman (391). A hidden marriage, built on a fault line, will crumble in the *Desengaños*. This suggests that Zayas is extremely interested, not in whether unwed women or men are sexually intimate, but in how the need for secrecy and the unmet promises of marriage create explosive problems for society at large for reasons of dishonour. Readers aware of the text's position in relationship to marriage and sex can raise their expectations for some situations, such as whether a character keeps a promise or not, and lower them for others, such as whether an unwed character is sexually pure or not when marriage is intended and that character's reputation is safe.

Honour, Dead or Alive

Whether and when to raise or lower our expectations with regard to social proprieties of marriage is directly conditioned by how the *Desengaños* represent the famous Spanish honour code, due to the isomorphic relationship in early modern Spain between reputation and honour. The meaning of this honour code, in whose name real nobles did in fact kill each other over apparently ridiculous things such as who went first down a narrow city street or who in a meeting of nobles first removed his hat, is a contested question today.[45]

Honour is central in Spain's famous wife murder plays, written and performed between 1575 and 1675, most intensely between 1621 and 1637 (Stroud 19). These dramas, in which a husband kills his wife for suspicion of or actual marital infidelity, have provoked literary critics to question both the meaning of honour and how historically accurate fictional representations of it are. Historians, for their part, are now challenging the validity of literary texts as sources of data and are seeking information about why, when, and how cases of honour were tried in early modern Spanish criminal courts.[46] Because the *Desengaños* systematically stage the death of an innocent noble wife for reasons of honour, and the tales treating unmarried noblewomen unhinge on problems of reputation, these questions bear directly on how to read the book.

Some critics find that Zayas supports the honour code. According to Levisi, Zayas neither challenges nor reproves the principles on which the social structure of honour is built, and only focuses on its victims (448). Martínez de Portal maintains that none of Zayas's heroines rebel against what she calls 'the fierce code of Calderonian honour' (16), presumably the one that sanctions a husband's right to kill a wife who appears to be or actually is unfaithful to him (whether Calderón sanctions that action or not is another question). Such broad-stroke statements suggest that Zayas supports the very system that is deadly for women in the wife murder plot, an interpretation at odds with the book's ardent defence of noblewomen's subjective status.

Others, in contrast, insist that Zayas loudly protests the honour code. Castillo suggests that the *Desengaños* provide 'an array of incorruptible bodies, to interrogate, even to denounce, the code of honour, which is one of the fundamental pillars of the social system' (94). Williamsen agrees, referring to Zayas's 'heightened critique of the unjust [honour] code' ('Challenging' 147). Vollendorf focuses on *desengaño* 10, Florentina's tale, as a criticism of the hypocrisy and danger to which the honour code submits women ('Te causará' 120). These assessments derive from the apparent contradiction between the honour code's condoning the death of a woman to protect a man's reputation and the vehement defence of women built into the *Desengaños*.

All of this appears to lead to an impasse. However, reading the *Desengaños* in light of seventeenth-century standards regarding the question makes it possible to determine where Zayas positions her book on this important topic.

Without entering into excessive legal intricacies, it bears pointing out that seventeenth-century citizens were obliged to juggle what was called the *fuero interior*, meaning one's conscience as it bore on the fate of one's eternal soul, and the *fuero exterior*, meaning one's reputation in one's social community; as Río Parra indicates, neither was considered 'private' (22).[47] In the early modern period, these codes of behaviour rarely if ever worked in isolation from each other, and when things went well they worked together to produce order. The notion of the absolute monarch, a human, political power invested with God's authority, is an example of the two systems' mutual enforcement.[48] In some cases, however, the definitions of sin (*fuero interior*) and social wrong (*fuero exterior*) were at odds, and that is precisely the point at which Zayas picked up her pen and prioritized them in no uncertain terms.

Civil law, which judges behaviour that is not transcendent, and ecclesiastical law, which judges behaviour that is, conflicted on the question of honour, specifically whether a husband had the right to kill an unfaithful wife. Civil law defended that right, whereas canon law denounced it as a mortal sin. Pradilla's 1639 updating of the Spanish civil law code summarizes previous practice in the Judaeo-Christian tradition, taking for granted that 'adulterer' means 'an adulterous wife,' and concludes that, 'according to a new law of the Kingdom, the penalty for adulterers is that both [the wife and her lover] be handed over to the husband that he may do with them whatever he will, killing them or forgiving them' (mas por derecho nuevo del reino, la pena de los adúlteros es que ambos sean entregados en poder del marido para que de ellos haga lo que quisiere, o matarlos o perdonarlos, 5v).[49]

Standards of the *fuero interior*, however, did not sanction such behaviour, which in a religious context qualified as wrongful killing. In his extremely influential confessor's manual, first printed in Spanish in 1552 and widely published in Latin throughout Europe until 1626, theologian and canonist Martín de Azpilcueta points to the mortal sin explicit in killing one's wife, adding that a man cannot do that even to his own slave ('pues no puede hacer esto aun a su propio esclavo').[50] The liberal social theorist and confessor Francico Escrivà, SJ, whose treatise on class obligations was published in 1613, identifies the conflict between civil and religious codes of behaviour outright: '*God does not want the husband to avenge himself and kill his wife*, though he catch her with the adulterer. *[It is wrong e]ven though human laws do not prohibit it*, condescending to the man's weakness and the weight of indignation that is so strong that it sets his heart aflame, inciting and provoking him to take revenge for that which so grievously offends him' (*No quiere Dios que el marido se vengue y mate a su mujer*, aunque la coja juntamente con el adúltero. *Si bien las leyes humanas no se lo tiene prohibido*, condescendiendo con la flaqueza del hombre y el pesar de indignación tan fuerte que por entonces está abrazando su corazón, incitándole y provocándole a que tome venganza de lo que tan gravemente le ofenden, 103–4, emphasis added).

Awareness of the seventeenth-century citizen's need to negotiate these two standards indicates that, in any of the nine cases in which Zayas's perverse fictional society almost or actually kills a virtuous wife, the author could have insisted on eternal damnation to bring home the wrongness of that event. But she does not. Her failure to insist on religious law, which condemns honour killing under all conditions, is astounding because religious law was the only one that defended the right to life of the very women in whose interests she wrote so fervently.

The fact that Zayas does not condemn honour killing suggests something important that the text bears out: the *Desengaños* endorse the assassination of anyone guilty of dishonouring a member of the upper classes, male or female, in support of the Spanish honour code's most violent tenet and in violation of Catholic ethics that condemned the murder of a human being for reasons of honour. When the virtuous wife Roseleta reveals to her husband that his best friend Juan has been aggressively seeking a sexual relationship with her, she points straight to the solution with no hesitation whatsoever: 'I have met my obligation; now you meet yours' (Yo he cumplido con lo que me toca; ahora cumplid con lo que os conviene a vos, d3 210). Her husband, enraged at the irrefutable evidence in Juan's letters that his wife hands him, plans with her to kill his friend in such a way that no one will ever know of their dishonour, and the reader celebrates this hygienic intention because Juan has done them both a grave wrong. Similarly, when the young and lovely widow Lucrecia begs Jaime not to tell anyone about their trysts and he does, she hires an assassin to kill him for dishonouring her. She has the right to do that since no man, potentially Jaime himself, would wed a woman publicly known to grant sexual favours out of wedlock, and by not respecting Lucrecia's insistence on secrecy, Jaime is ruining her future (d4).

These cases illuminate where Zayas positions her text with regard to honour. Had she taken the religious high road and condemned honour killing in principle, it would have allowed her to protest the killing of the innocent in questions of dishonour. That same protest, however, would have disallowed her text from making the crucial distinction it does: although killing an innocent person in a question of honour was wrong, killing a guilty person was not only right, but commendable and absolutely necessary.

Insisting on proper execution of the honour code, which entailed doing away with those who dishonour, allowed Zayas to equalize noblewomen and noblemen on the question: kill anyone who dishonours you. Nisi, the book's most vehement storyteller, flatly enjoins a noblewoman to do exactly that: 'Because, idiot, if your lover or husband commits an offence against your honour, do you not see that when you do the same you offend yourself and give your husband cause to take your life and your lover to speak ill of you in public? Do not be a weakling, and if you were, kill the one who made you be that way and do not destroy your honour' (Porque bárbara, si tu amante o marido te agravia, ¿no ves que en hacer tú lo mismo te agravias a ti misma, y das motivo para que si es marido te quite la vida, y si es amante diga mal de ti? No seas liviana, y si lo fuiste, mata a quien te hizo serlo, y no mates tu honra, 263). Similarly, after listening to the story of how the innocent Inés is all but killed by her family, the story's narrator postulates that even had the young wife been guilty of adultery, she would have deserved a quick death and not the protracted agony to which she was subjected ('cuando doña Inés, de malicia, hubiera cometido el yerro que le obligó a tal castigo, no merecía más que una muerte breve, como se han dado a otras que han pecado de malicia, y no darle tantas y tan dilatadas como le dieron,' 289).[51]

Directly and indirectly, Zayas sanctions the Spanish honour code that demanded blood of the guilty, and her second book dramatically renders the high cost of confusing the guilty with the innocent when meeting its demands. Positioning the law, honour, and marriage outside her critique allowed her to limit the scope of her critique to the nobility's failure to behave nobly. In a book that construes marriage as the analogue of the Catholic imperial state, such energetic defence of reputation is a political as well as domestic position and, given the author's conservative bent, forms a coherent whole with her text's ideological profile.

It is extremely important to recognize that the penalties for adultery prescribed in civil and ecclesiastical codes of law apply only to guilty parties – adultery must have taken place. Many fictional representations of the problem, in contrast, explore the high drama of the husband who kills his wife because she *appears* to be guilty for any number of reasons, such as misperception, rape, and being accused of infidelity by someone who is lying. These are situations that dishonour the husband and family as much as her actual infidelity, reflective of an age when 'honour and reputation were tangible assets,' and 'Castilian criminal codes attached as much importance to insult as to wounding' (Casey,

'Household' 195, 194). Certainly in many fictional representations of noble dishonour, the woman's guilt or innocence is irrelevant in the face of anyone else's belief in her guilt, and she dies on the altar of perception, which is the essence of baroque honour.

This is the only situation Zayas dramatizes in the *Desengaños*. All of her wife characters are innocent of adultery, and the deadly problem they address is purely forensic: whose word and opinion prevails in such cases, that of the dishonoured, possibly raped woman or that of the accusing, lying, or dishonourable party? Among the four lying parties in the *Desengaños*, three are women and two of them are noble (Angeliana, d3; Florentina, d10). The problem Zayas presents, then, is not only noblemen who fail to control their lust. The problem is the nobility, whose members fail to control themselves and their subordinates.

Standards of Violence

Critical insistence on Zayas's protest of men's violence against women, then, must be tempered with a few textual realities in the case of *Desengaños*, such as the book's explicit endorsement of the honour code, the author's consistent inclusion of noblewomen as agents of wrongdoing, and the generally violent tenor of her book. The problems the author addresses go well beyond male victimization of females, for the book represents violence of many types. This is to be expected, given that, aside from the fact that violence 'was part of the discourse of early modern interpersonal relations' (Ruff 2), it was particularly prevalent in Madrid during the years Zayas was likely working on the *Desengaños*. Tomás y Valiente cites chronicles indicating that the incidence of homicide in Madrid rose annually from 1620 to 1639, making it one of the age's most intense periods of criminal activity (245). As Wardropper indicates in reference to the theatre, authors writing against a background of such normalized violence were hard pressed to find ways to horrify their public ('Horror' 224). Still, literary standards of the day as defined by Zayas's contemporary and theorist López Pinciano demanded perturbing content that was 'prodigious and horrifying' (prodigioso y espantoso), making it imperative to do exactly that (58).

The backdrop of the *Desengaños* is consistently violent. Narrators casually relate harmful outbursts in the relationships between social superior and subordinate, such as a virtuous mistress who beats her servant, a behaviour endorsed at that time (Elena, d4 251–2), and a defective husband who beats his wife, likewise a sanctioned behaviour, provid-

Figure 1.3 Detail, *Via vitae aeternae*, Antoni Sucquet. Engravings by Bolswert, 1620. With the generous permission of the Trustees of Boston College

ed it was not excessive (Blanca, d7 355). [52] True to seventeenth-century standards, law enforcement is violent: Inés's relatives are executed (d5), as are Marco Antonio and Alonso (d8), for example. Guilty characters who appear to escape criminal punishment are promised comeuppance when God settles accounts, and the spectre of hell was violent indeed (see fig. 1.3). Pedro and Angeliana wed after killing Pedro's innocent wife Roseleta, and live in peace, but the narrator leaves them 'not safe from God's punishment, for if he did not deliver it in this life, he will not withhold it from them in the next' (no seguros del castigo de Dios, que si no se les dio en esta vida, no les reservaría de él en la otra, 221). This threat resounded much more loudly in early modern ears than in postmodern ones.

Zayas's poetic justice is also violent: Felipe kills Manuel for having rejected and dishonoured Isabel (d1), the Flemish state is ravaged by the Spaniards avenging Blanca's death (d7), and the murderous husband Dionís impales himself on his sword in despair (d10). The wars

Spain was fighting wage constantly in the narrative background, so much so that going off to war is for men what disappearing into a convent is for women, a narrative *exeunt*. Among these many types of violence, Zayas's text protests only one: punishing an innocent wife for the crime of infidelity.

Zayas's intense scrutiny of specific acts of violence, not violence in itself, is especially potent because by identifying the after-effects of dishonourable behaviour, she portrays like no other writer of her age the irremediable consequences of corrective justice that necessarily misses its mark. The only way to eliminate what she magnificently represents as the devastating effects of noble misbehaviour is to prevent it, for corrective justice by nature reacts to an irrevocable injustice that has already transpired. To maximize the anguish her narrative creates, she arranges for the right person to be punished for a crime in most cases, and the wrong person to be punished for a crime in every case. The *Desengaños* bring home like no other baroque fiction the fact that the violation of social ethics does irreparable damage, a premise that perfectly disables the narrative's ability to resolve anything and creates great unease for the reader.

Nader describes the class of noblewomen to whom Zayas belonged saying, 'Systemic change could not attract them. They were, after all, privileged and worked all their lives to retain and improve their status within the established system' (5). In light of this, it is no surprise that, as Mihaly states, Zayas did not accomplish a sustained critique of seventeenth-century Spanish society's social constructs (720). I add, however, that this was not because she was too weak, unable, or subordinate to do so. Zayas does not critique the institutions of hegemony because her interest, which runs deep and clear through her book, was elsewhere. That interest was in pointing the way out of the moral morass in which she purposefully and artfully mires her characters. How she accomplished that becomes clearer in light of the expectations she set for her book, which we can now examine on the text's own terms.

Figure 2.1 *Between Vice and Virtue*, Paolo Veronese, 1580. Bibliotheque Nationale, Paris / Bridgeman

2 Attending the Soirée

'Oh, would that my understanding
were equal to my desire
to know how to defend women
and please men!'

(¡Oh, quién tuviera
el entendimiento como el deseo
para saber defender a las hembras
y agradar a los varones!)

Lisis, *desengaño* 10 (470)

The *Desengaños* are universally read as a defence of women, and indeed, Lisis summarizes her soirée forensically, concluding, 'I believe the defence of women has been quite well aired '(Bien ventilada me parece que queda … la defensa de las mujeres, 503). However, even refining the author's meaning of 'women' to noblewomen, as I have suggested, still misses Zayas's mark for her book. She points directly to that mark in her narrators' comments across the text and uses the plots of her tales to illuminate it negatively, as if with a black light. It is impossible to determine the meaning of the dying and dead women in Zayas's book without deciphering the multiple objectives she claims to achieve with the text and the tools she crafted to do so, and only precise attention to the text – a somewhat tedious exercise – can bring its fundamental coherence into view under the rubric of those objectives. The reader

who fails to recognize all of them runs the risk of holding the book to standards it was not designed to meet.

The author identifies five goals for the *Desengaños*, distillable to three according to their target audience: 1) to convince noblewomen to respect themselves by protecting their honour and stop deceiving themselves about the ways of the world and the men in it; 2) to convince noblemen to distinguish good noblewomen from bad ones and to respect noblewomen; 3) to move all of the nobly born to behave nobly, specifically abandoning the vices of lust and greed. Whereas the first of these objectives has received an overwhelming amount of critical attention, the second and third are no less important, and all three are crucial to the narrative's integrity.[1] Clearly, the author's most prominent tools in the accomplishment of her narrative agenda are her defeated female protagonists, whose rejected and abused bodies accumulate with each tale like evidence in a case against a serial killer. The question is how meeting those objectives drove Zayas to kill them in the way she did, which can be answered by clarifying what she defines as the purpose of her book.

I. Noblewomen: Respect Yourselves and Abandon Naivety

The *Desengaños* open with Lisis declaring that her pretension in convening the soirée was to defend noblewomen's reputation ('volver por la fama de las mujeres,' 118).[2] Under that rubric, she calls women not only to safeguard what others think about them, but also how they perceive themselves and how well they protect their honour, which produces their reputation. At the end of *desengaño* 9, Estefanía calls women of high birth to responsibility for what happens to them, enjoining her peers, 'Stand up, stand up for yourselves; given that you do not esteem your life, since you put it at risk with every step you take, *esteem your honour* ... for in past ages women were held in greater esteem because they esteemed themselves' (Volved, volved por vosotras mismas; ya que no estimáis la vida, que a cada paso la ponéis en riesgo, *estimad el honor* ... que en las pasadas edades más estimación se hacía de las mujeres porque ellas la tenían de sí mismas, 459; emphasis added).

In this, as in other declarations of this objective, Zayas addresses noblewomen as females with power to use, not as victims of men, chastising them as subjects, not objects, and, as Kaminsky indicates, 'for acquiescing to their own disempowerment' (488). Indeed, the book's

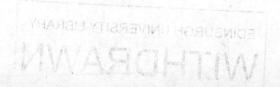

indictment of noblewomen who misbehave is as severe as anything the characters say about men: 'to the woman who is false, inconstant, morally loose and lacking a good reputation one should not give the name of woman, rather that of wild beast' (a la mujer falsa, inconstante, liviana y sin reputación no se le ha de dar nombre de mujer, sino de bestia fiera, 118).

In these appeals, Zayas pairs injunctions to self-discipline and self-respect with regard for honour because in seventeenth-century Spain, individual identity – a modern notion – was inseparable from one's reputation and position in the community. As Maravall clarifies, 'It is not a principle that obliges one to be faithful to oneself, in the sense of realizing with one's actions that internal nucleus of one's own personality ... as *being oneself*. On the contrary, it is the recognition of one's obligation to behave in accordance with the social figure that pertains to each person' (no es un principio que obligue a ser fiel a sí mismo, en el sentido de realizar en sus actos aquel núcleo interno de la propia personalidad ... como un *ser sí mismo*. Es, por el contrario ... el reconocimiento de la obligación de conducirse según el modo que a la figura social de uno le corresponde, *Teatro* 62).

Appropriate to this understanding of community as the font of identity and meaning, the *Desengaños* prescribe the correct functioning of the honour code, which Zayas supports as a set of behaviours designed to protect one's reputation. Her book systematically upholds the correct performance of that code as a noblewoman's best defence against her own weakness and the weaknesses of those around her. Thus, the narrator Nisi introduces *desengaño* 3 stating that 'our intention is not only to entertain, but to advise women to *watch out for their reputation* and be fearful of all the liberties they practise today so that what happened to the women they have heard about and will hear about not happen to them, and also to defend them' (nuestra intención no es de sólo divertir, sino de aconsejar a las mujeres *que miren por su opinión* y teman con tantas libertades como el día hoy profesan, no les suceda lo que a las que han oído y oirán les ha sucedido, y también por defenderlas, 200; emphasis added). Such admonitions define a woman's mindfulness of her honour as her ally in the production of a strong, positive image.

Zayas links the need for noblewomen to respect themselves to her other goal for them, to wake up to the defective nature of human beings around them and accept the political realities of life. One of those realities, which the tales fictionalize several times, delivered a harsh blow to the unmarried woman deceived by a man who promised to marry her, took her virginity, then reneged on his promise. After the Council of Trent, the fundamental principle that validated nuptials was mutual consent (Rodríguez-Arango Díaz 734). Ecclesiastical and civil law of Zayas's day obliged a man who deceived a woman with a promise of marriage to marry her *unless* he could reliably claim that he did not intend to marry her when he said he would. Martín de Azpilcueta Navarro's confessors' manual specifies this clearly: 'The woman deceived in the fashion specified above [promise of marriage] cannot wed another man except when, in a provable manner (judged so by a good and prudent adult male), it is believed that he deceived her, saying that he had no intention to marry her, rather intended to trick her' (La mujer engañada, empero, en la manera susodicha, no se puede casar con otro sino cuando probablemente [a juicio de prudente y buen varón] creyese que es verdad el que la engañó, diciendo que no tuvo intención de casarse con ella, sino de engañarla, 430). Civil law upheld the same statute (Ledesma, *Primera parte* 15), thereby leaving women completely vulnerable to men's disposition to be truthful or not in promises of marriage and putting the prominent literary theme of sexual *engaño*, or deceit, in a new light.[3] It makes Spanish society's insistence on parental supervision of matrimony more understandable, makes equally understandable Zayas's heated critique of noblewomen's gullibility, and justifies her narrators' hot critique of noblemen's practice of deceiving.

Warnings that call noblewomen to interpret the world rather than simply live in it appear in different registers throughout the book, bright yellow signs urging caution. The most obvious appear in editorializing passages that hold female aristocrats partially accountable for what happens to them, as when the narrator opens the second evening of the soirée declaring, 'My tales of disillusion are for men who deceive and women who let themselves be deceived' (Mis desengaños son para los que engañan y para las que se dejan engañar, 258). The narrator Nise cautions that they stay on high alert so as not to fall into the misfortunes that entrap the female characters of the tales, and not 'let themselves be put at risk by deceptions posing as men's love' (dejarse vender de los engaños disfrazados en amor de los hombres, 199).

Francisca, another narrator, offers a similar reality check to noblewomen, but in a lighter tone. Addressing the deceived woman, she exclaims, 'Go on, little idiot, for you deceived yourself, for men should not be believed except when they say "*Domine, non sum dignus*"' (Anda, boba, que tú te engañaste: que a los hombres no se les ha de creer si no es cuando dicen, '*domine, non sum dignus*,' 370). With this Bible verse, part of the ritual of the Anointing of the Sick, formerly called Last Rites, Francisca jokingly recommends that a noblewoman believe a man only on his deathbed. She goes so far as to hold the deceived female responsible for her dishonour, flatly declaring, 'Women provide the cause for which men commit these deceptions, since they believe them' (Y de estos engaños que ellos [hombres] hacen, las mujeres dan la causa, pues lo creen, 370).

The most radical spokeswoman for noblewomen's disillusion is Nise, who concludes a vitriolic diatribe against male disrespect calling her peers to mindfulness of their honour and a radical protective device: 'So, ladies, let us undeceive ourselves; let us defend our reputation; let men die in our memories, since we have a greater obligation to ourselves than to those memories' (Pues, señoras, desengañémonos; volvamos por nuestra opinión; mueran los hombres en nuestras memorias, pues más obligadas que a ellas estamos a nosotras mismas, 222). Zayas immediately nuances this pungent enjoinder, however, when Filis introduces the next tale saying, 'I doubt that women are deceived, for it is one thing to let oneself be deceived and another to be deceived, nor do men likely deserve the blame for everything of which they are accused' (Dudo que ni las mujeres son engañadas, que una cosa es dejarse engañar y otra es engañarse, ni los hombres deben de tener la culpa de todo lo que se les imputa, 227). Although some narrators ventilate extremist views against noblemen's inconstancy and dishonesty, Zayas is careful to offset those radical positions with conciliatory.comments so as not to offend her male public to the point of alienation, for without them, the noble integrity to which her book calls cannot be restored.

Isabel, who tells her own story as a tale of disillusion, is particularly convincing on the point of noblewomen's need to protect themselves, because she herself is evidence of what happens when they do not: she appears at Lisis's house as a raped, rejected woman who has sold herself twice into slavery, recalling her life as 'a tale of disillusion, so that the ladies be advised of the deceits and maneuvers of men, in order that they reclaim their reputation in these times when it is so lost to them' (un desengaño, para que las damas se avisen de los engaños y cautelas de los hombres, para que vuelvan por su fama en tiempo que la tienen tan perdida, 124). Decrying her loss of honour, she reveals how her future began to unravel when she let a servant convince her to read Manuel's first letter to her rather than follow her native impulse to burn it. 'God save us from a letter written at the right time,' she prays in hindsight (Dios nos libre de un papel escrito a tiempo, 134).[4]

In her story, the fullest imperfect victim tale, Isabel repeatedly decries her own behaviour, calling herself the perdition of her bloodline (127), and bemoaning her failure to favour Felipe, her impoverished but truly noble suitor (128). The hapless young woman describes her decision to chase the errant Manuel as the one 'with which I finished ruining myself' (con la que me acabé de perder, 151) and accepts responsibility for her father's sudden death at the news she had run away from home, saying, 'My weak compliance was the cause of all this' (De todo esto fue causa mi facilidad, 152). Repeatedly lamenting her inability to stay the course of defending her own best interests, Isabel implores noble-women selecting a mate to learn from her bad example: 'And oh, weak and ill-advised ladies, how you let yourselves be won over by well-dressed lies, whose gilding endures no longer than appetite!' (Y, ay, mujeres fáciles y mal aconsejadas, y cómo os dejáis vencer de mentiras bien afeitadas, y que no les dura el oro con que van cubiertas más de mientras dura el apetito! 135). In this spirit of despair, not only over Manuel's bad behaviour but her own, she advises: 'Let ladies open the eyes of their understanding and not let themselves be won over by the one from whom they can fear the payback that I got' (Abran las damas los ojos del entendimiento y no se dejen vencer de quien pueden temer el mal pago que a mí se me dio, 136).

Isabel recalls how her doom was assured when she believed Manuel's many false promises to marry her and, her life in ruins, she exclaims, 'Oh weak-minded women! If only you knew, individually and collec-tively, what you set yourselves up for on the day you allow yourselves to surrender to the false caresses of men!' (¡Ay, mujeres fáciles, y si supié-sedes una por una, y todas juntas, a lo que os ponéis el día que os dejáis rendir a las falsas caricias de los hombres! 130). *Fácil*, a word Zayas uses often, literally means 'easy' and is often translated as 'loose,' which has negative sexual connotations. However, in a seventeenth-century text it means the person who changes his or her mind without due reflec-tion, in contrast to the heroic individual whose emblem is thoughtful constancy of word and deed.[5]

Ruing a character's *facilidad* endorses the standard of nobility to which Zayas calls, and the lack of fortitude displayed and lamented by the unwed and undone characters such as Isabel proves how important that standard is, particularly for the single woman seeking to find a suit-able mate. Because of their willing participation in their own undoing, the unmarried female protagonists of the *Desengaños* form the corps of the book's complicit or imperfect victims, who suffer due to their own shortcomings as well as those of others. The unwed noblewomen listening to the cautionary tales of failed courtship can still determine the course of their lives, and Zayas's objectives for the female nobility are designed for them.

In her imperfect victim tales, Zayas imagines young noblewomen who are ruinously naive and/or unworthy of the married state to which they aspire. These characters serve two purposes, one being to pose evidence of how important it is for single women to respect themselves sufficiently to refrain from intimate contact with men until they are publicly married. The other is to illustrate the devastating effects of noblemen's deceptions, and the imperfect victims are ruined by men who promise to wed them but do not. Displaying the effects of dishonour, Zayas invokes the courtship plot and systematically frustrates it for the characters who want and need it most. Isabel, Octavia, and Laurela open their hearts and/or bodies to grossly imperfect men, with disastrous consequences that range from abandonment and claustration (Isabel, Octavia) to abandonment and death (Laurela). Although Florentina's story wrestles with compound problems, it too reveals how she allies herself with an ignoble nobleman and loses everything as a result (d10).

Not martyr characters, the imperfect victims struggle under the burden of responsibility that Zayas casts upon them, as the author relentlessly chastises her unwed female characters for not protecting their best interests and surrendering to men before the time is right. Octavia's abandonment of her resolution to hold Carlos off until marriage ruins her, and Lisarda overtly criticizes the young woman's weakness: 'She already loved Carlos more than was reasonable; for in this one sees how weak women are, that they do not know how to persevere in their good efforts' (Ya amaba a Carlos más que fuera razón; que en esto se ve cuán flacas son las mujeres, que no saben perseverar en el buen intento, 177). The same narrator condemns the noblewoman who cannot control herself: 'Octavia was not without blame, for she let herself be overcome by her love of Carlos' (Octavia no estaba sin culpa, pues se dejó vencer del amor de Carlos, 190).

In her parade of undone single noblewomen, Zayas marches Laurela before her reader, a fifteen-year-old girl ruined when a degenerate rake disguises himself as a female servant, is hired by her unwitting father, and completely compromises her honour. But the author insists even in this case, declaring that Laurela ultimately finds herself, 'where her ungrateful lover took her, or where she took herself for allowing herself to be so easily deceived' (adonde la trujo su ingrato amante, o donde se trujo ella misma, por dejarse tan fácilmente engañar, 326). Parsing Zayas's grammar of blame and responsibility in Laurela's story is difficult because she places the young woman between a rock and a hard place: once Esteban enters her house, there is nothing she can do to save herself. However, although Laurela is victimized by Esteban's extreme dishonesty, her decision to love such a clearly defective man is her own and is what Zayas points to as reprehensible.

The ethical paradigm of the *Desengaños* holds unwed noblewomen responsible for failing to muster the courage of their convictions and failing to deploy the devices that conservative social praxis offers to protect them, such as not taking the advice of servants and never responding directly to a man's desire. Of course it takes two to tango, and every tale condemns the ignoble nobleman who behaves like Manuel. But if both unwed partners in the dance are mis-stepping, which is what the *Desengaños* represent, both of them provoke the fall, which is thus doubly damaging.

Parsing responsibility in a nuanced fashion is crucial to evaluating the book's position on important topics such as love and desire. Isabel, like the other characters who lament a couple's failures in hindsight, does not caution against love or desire per se, but rather against the weakness and artlessness that leads noblewomen to love and desire the wrong man. The wrong man is the ignoble nobleman who displays the faults that the fiction deplores, the very individuals who also must reform to meet the author's goals for them. The discerning reader of Isabel's complicated tale thus realizes that although only Manuel is responsible for raping her and lying to her, she put herself in his path by responding favourably and directly to his advances rather than relying on her parents, particularly her heroic father, to mediate the entire process. Heeding the advice of a servant she later realized had been bribed by Manuel, she seals her sad fate and faces the corrupt world unprotected by the armour of noble social protocol. Her behaviour kills her father, who dies of the shock that she has fled from his care. By positioning Isabel as the first storyteller, Zayas informs her readers from the outset of her objectives for the unwed female nobility, and also alerts them to those objectives' complexity, with which she assails those readers to the book's very end.

The *Desengaños* fictionalize the achievement of the author's goals for the female nobility at the soirée's conclusion, when Lisis and the clutch of noblewomen who follow her depart for the convent, claiming their victory over men and noblemen's victory over themselves by being vanquished by virtuous and noble women ('Hemos de salir vence-dores ... me habéis de dar la victoria, pues tal vencimiento es quedar más vencedores,' 470). Before walking out on her own party, Lisis tex-tualizes herself as the greatest disillusion, since she has learned the pre-scribed lesson and will not remain in the world as it is: 'I myself will be what disillusions you most, for it would be to die of deceit and not live having been warned, were I to let myself be deceived while undeceiv-ing all other women' (Yo misma he de ser el mayor desengaño, porque sería morir del engaño y no vivir del aviso, si desengañando a todas, me dejase yo engañar, 405). Her final act models the self-respect to which all the narrators have called noblewomen throughout the soirée: when the potential for dishonour is greater than your ability to hold it at bay, get up and leave.

In the *Desengaños*, the unwed noblewoman's victory is largely over herself, over her desire to attain something that the fiction represents as unattainable until all members of the nobility conform to the pre-scribed standards. Introducing *desengaño* 6, Matilde equates this vic-tory with self-sacrifice, in the same terms as Lisis, insisting 'the best lot is to conquer oneself rather than being conquered by others. From this was born the Gentiles' practice of killing themselves, because since their souls did not attain eternity, [it must be concluded that] in exchange for not seeing themselves beaten down and defamed by their enemies, they did not esteem life, finding greater honour in dying at their own hands rather than at theirs' (la mayor suerte es vencerse uno así mismo, que no dejarse vencer de otros. De esto nació el matarse los gentiles, porque como no alcanzaban la inmortalidad del alma, en cambio de no verse abatidos y ultrajados de sus enemi-gos, no estimaban la vida, y tenían por honrosa victoria morir a sus mismas manos que no a las de sus enemigos, 293). This defence of kill-ing oneself rather than allowing oneself to be killed allies Lisis's final disappearing act with heroic suicide for the woman who leaves the world in which she wants to live but cannot, because of the dangers in it. In her parting move, the hostess reveals the inexorable connec-tions that bind people together and clarifies that unless all of Zayas's objectives are met, it will do women little good to respect themselves and live in astute awareness of the deceit around them. If they are to remain in the world, the noblemen must also conform to the author's standards for the male nobility.

II. Noblemen: Respect Noblewomen and Distinguish the Innocent Woman from the ·Guilty One

As the epigraph of this chapter makes clear, the *Desengaños* address not only a set of objectives for the male nobility, but the gender-specific problem inherent in how to express them: how to critique noblemen without offending them, given what Edward Friedman aptly calls 'the reality principle of male domination,' specified by Ruff as 'the full weight of religious tradition, civil law, and custom [that] endowed the husband and father with almost total power in the early modern household' ('Afterword' 293, 132). This metatextual awareness is evidence of how Zayas marshals the rapture of reading in baroque style, forcing her readers to stand back from the fiction, aware that it is an act of representation. As we have seen, the interior piece of that experience, the book's diegesis, supports traditional understandings of order in which males rule over females, just as kings rule over subjects and God rules over humanity. Zayas's qualification, explicit in Lisis's refusal to stay in the corrupt world, is that all parties must be worthy of occupying the position they do for that order to sustain itself.

All biographical evidence suggests that Zayas believed in this ideology, and the fact that she dedicated the *Desengaños* to a powerful nobleman, Jaime Fernández de Silva, underscores the book's potential message to the upper-class male public.[6] Whether either of these possibilities is true or not, however, it is clear that representing noblemen's social superiority over noblewomen provided her with valuable evidence in her argument for their improved behaviour, evidence that reaches beyond merely placating the male ego. Honing that argument down to basics reveals its relative simplicity: noblemen are endowed by nature with gifts that oblige them to superior performance of almost everything. Failure to perform in this superior fashion demeans them and the noblewomen over whom they ride roughshod in their irresponsible escapades, and they will be held accountable for such misbehaviour in this life, and if not in this one, then without doubt in the next, where punishment will be severe indeed.

Presenting this argument, Zayas establishes clear differences between the sexes that the equality of their souls cannot erase. The narrators present noblemen as born with the spirit of command and 'male freedom' and the functional upper-class male as 'the sane, well-intentioned man who knows, in the midst of vice itself, how to take recourse in the virtue and nobility to which he is obliged' (el imperio que naturaleza

les otorgó ... libertad de hombres, 228; el hombre cuerdo, bien inten-
cionado, y que sabe en los mismos vicios aprovecharse de la virtud y
nobleza a que está obligado, 117). These qualities tend to overwhelm
the ladies, whom the narrators say nature gifted with weak strength
and tender hearts ('flacas fuerzas y corazones tiernos,' 294), naturally endowed with a retiring femininity ('con recato de mujeres,' 228),
needy of the support and protection of male valour in proportion to
their constitutional weakness ('porque mientras más flaco y débil es el
sujeto de las mujeres, más apoyo y amparo habían de tener en el valor
de los hombres,' 166). Moralists of Zayas's day followed this current,
identifying men's honourable treatment of women with honour itself:
'Love them, honour them, treat them well ... for honourable men do
not dishonour women, much less their own wives' (Amadlas, honra-
dlas, tratadlas bien ... que no es de hombres honrados no honrar a las
mujeres, cuanto más la propia mujer, Escrivà 64).

Zayas's arguments articulate the conservative gender philosophy of
her day, designed to fit like a glove into hierarchies of order. Even liberal moralist authors affirmed the same discriminatory principles of male
dominion and used them to equate power with obligations, as when
Gaspar Astete declares, 'If we consider that man is the head of woman
and the one who has dominion over her, since reason reigns more in
men than in women, since there must be greater fortitude in him than
in woman to resist passion, we can say that the adulterous man commits a greater sin than that adulterous woman' (Si miramos a que el
hombre es la cabeza de la mujer y el que tiene señorío sobre ella, ya que
en el hombre reina más la razón que en la mujer, ya que en él se ha de
hallar más fortaleza para resistir a las pasiones que en la mujer, ya que
el hombre ha de dar ejemplo en todas cosas a la mujer, diremos que más
gravemente peca el hombre cometiendo adulterio que la mujer, 177).

Accessing this logic allows Zayas to leave noblemen holding the
lion's share of responsibility for the disasters that the fiction represents, in which they determine not only their own actions, but also how
noblewomen behave in their wake. Because of men's superior power,
the text's objectives for the male aristocracy are more burdensome and
complex than those for noblewomen. On the one hand, Zayas presents
high-mimetic noblemen as the behavioural model for all men, insisting that by respecting noblewomen, 'the most noble and affectionate
among you will make those who are not like that be so, to imitate you'
(los más nobles y más afectuosos haréis que los que no lo son, por imi-
taros, hagan lo mismo, 335). On the other hand, endorsing their social

superiority allows her to take them to task repeatedly for 'making women bad,' acknowledging the power they have over the female sex and managing to accuse them of misusing it at the same time.

Isabel initiates the complaint against male abuse of power in the first tale: 'The fault is men's, and women follow along behind their opinions, thinking that they do well to do so; for it is certain that there would be no bad women were there no bad men' (ellos [hombres] cometen la culpa, y ellas siguen tras su opinión, pensando que aciertan; lo cierto es que no hubiera malas mujeres si no hubiera malos hombres, 118). Nise throws the blame even harder, protesting, 'Ay! What good women there would be would men just let them be so! But men speak and women listen' (¡Ay, qué de buenas hubiera si los hombres las dejaran! Mas ellos hablan y ellas escuchan, 201). The narrator Laura deplores this problem at length, and then bursts forth with a plea that men leave women to their own misbehaviour rather than make it worse: 'You make them bad, and not only that, but you say they are so. Well since you men are already the instruments by which they become bad, leave them alone, do not dishonour them, for their errors and punishment are heaven's account' (Vosotros las hacéis malas, y no sólo eso, mas decís que lo son. Pues ya que sois los hombres el instrumento de que lo sean, dejadlas, no las deshonréis, que sus delitos y el castigo de ellos cuenta del Cielo están, 333).

The 'bad husband equals bad wife' equation was invoked by male authors of Zayas's day as well, as when Lope de Vega's nobly born, married character Casandra queries, 'because with a good husband, / when did one ever see a bad wife?' (porque con marido bueno, / ¿cuándo se vio mujer mala? vv. 1062–3). Casandra's womanizing, insulting husband proves her point in the negative when his behaviour drives Casandra to an affair with her husband's son. Zayas plays the cards differently to suit her objective to victimize the wife, surrounding her with a cluster of deeply imperfect people who do her in and always including at least one nobleman who knows better than to behave as he does.

While affirming the male nobility's superior power, Zayas drives noblemen to make three changes: distinguish good noblewomen from bad, do not deceive noblewomen, and speak well of women at large. These three goals interrelate with each other and with the text's goals for noblewomen, although the first one has the most immediate and horrifying resonance in the stories' plots. Armed with her narrators' attempts to convince noblemen not to categorize women as a sex before condemning them, Zayas enters the fray of the wife murder text that was especially popular in the theatre during the years she was writing. Her perfect victim tales privilege the wife's experience and intensify her innocence, the better to kill her and thereby meet the text's declared objectives for the male nobility.

The narrators' repeated insistence on the importance of not confusing the innocent noblewoman with the guilty one reveals the juridical nature of the seventeenth-century Spanish novella, studied by Rabell. The explicit goal of Zayas's narrators, to convince noblemen to discern who is guilty and who is innocent before executing anyone, does not condemn the killing of noblewomen, but rather the killing of *innocent* noblewomen. The distinction is crucial because in her plots of wife abuse and murder, Zayas engages an interpretative dilemma, not a moral one; as we have seen, she does not condemn honour killing. She condemns the nobleman's lack of *agudeza*, intellectual engagement, in the determination of culpability, a lack of reasonable behaviour that moves a man to kill the wrong person, who in the *Desengaños* is always a noblewoman.

The man who does away with his wife, sister, or daughter without discerning her guilt or innocence completely erases the female subjectivity that Zayas defends in the *Desengaños*. Because the book buys into principles of male superiority, he also fails to enact justice while having the power and the obligation to do so. The narrator includes this individual among the noblemen whom the *Desengaños* address, dehumanizing him for his underperformance of nobility: 'I speak of those men who, forgetful of their obligations, do other than what is just; such as they will not be men but monsters' (hablo de los que, olvidados de sus obligaciones, hacen diferente de lo que es justo; estos tales no serán hombres, sino monstruos, 118). The practice of condemning women for being women is a subset of the author's larger critique of the male nobility's failure to respect noblewomen and speak well of them. It is a categorical, thoughtless assumption of guilt that provokes noblemen to kill the noblewomen who die in the tales.

When the book opens, the narrator relays the storytellers' delight at having the chance to 'demand satisfaction for so many grievances against men for bearing ill will toward noblewomen and judging them all as one' (satisfacerse de tantos agravios como les hacen en sentir mal de ellas y juzgar a todas por una, 120). Later, as Francisca begins her tale, she specifies that 'our intention … is to prove that there are and have been many good women and that they have suffered and suffer blamelessly in men's cruelty' (nuestra intención … es probar que hay y ha habido muchas [mujeres] buenas y que han padecido y padecen en la crueldad de los hombres, sin culpa, 371). Their determination to convince noblemen to stop damning women as a sex entails moving them to abandon Aristotelian notions about females as inherently defective and guilty, and allow noblewomen to signify who they are, innocent or not.

In ongoing support of the distinction between a guilty woman and an innocent one, Lisis urges noblemen to interpret the world as she urges noblewomen to do the same, but pointing to the need to employ the forensic tool of collecting evidence in a case of dishonour. Even though noblewomen's errant ways have caused men to disesteem them, 'that is no reason, speaking somewhat crudely, to measure them all with the same stick. For it is clear that in a machine as expansive and extensive as that of the world, there will be good women and evil ones, just as there are men of the same types' (No es razón que, hablando en común, las midan a todas con una misma medida. Que lo cierto es que en una máquina tan dilatada y extendida como la del mundo, ha de haber buenas y malas, como asimismo hay hombres de la misma manera, 503). Her conclusion articulates the tempered argument necessary to carry her point. 'I confess that men are partly right, for today there are more vicious and lost women than ever; but they are not right that so many good women are lacking that they do not exceed the number of evil ones' (Yo confieso que en alguna parte tienen [los hombres] razón, que hay hoy más mujeres viciosas y perdidas que ha habido jamás; mas no que falten tan buenas que no excedan el número de las malas, 504). The task of the truly noble man is to distinguish the two, or run the risk of doing away with the innocent, thereby losing a prized resource of the community and damning himself in the process, since killing an innocent person is murder.

Thus, the reason husbands regularly kill their innocent wives in the *Desengaños* is unequivocally related to the message to noblemen inscribed deeply in the book. Since the aesthetics of the *Desengaños* use what is wrong to imply what is right, the innocent must die. Lest the reader come away from her grisly spectacle of dead women with any doubts regarding her position on the matter, Zayas unequivocally articulates her narrators' abhorrence of what her own fiction represents, and no thoughtless husband who destroys his wife goes unpunished or uncensored. When King Ladislao credits his brother's lies about Ladislao's wife Beatriz, the narrator says of him: 'He believed him like a weak man. Great fault in a king, who if he is to carry out justice must lend an ear to the defence if he lends one to the accusation' (Creyó como fácil. Gran falta en un rey, que si ha de guardar justicia, si da un oído a la acusación ha de dar otro a la defensa de ella, 428). Filis, having narrated *desengaño* 4 in which Elena's husband Jaime similarly credits a slave's defamation of his wife, points to how such husbands react thoughtlessly rather than seeking out clarifying information ('[maridos] no aguardan a la segunda información,' 253–4). The result is disastrous: 'Thus we see that there are women who suffer in innocence, for not all of them should be believed guilty, as they are in common opinion' (Se ve asimismo que hay mujeres que padecen inocentes, pues no todas han de ser culpadas, como en la común opinión lo son, 254).

Zayas returns often to the distinction between a killable woman and one who is not, always when meeting her objectives for the male nobility. At the end of *desengaño* 6, Lisis urges caution in judging questions of honour: 'And believe that, although it may seem to you there are many guilty women, there are many more innocent ones, and not all of them who have been violently killed should have been; for if many are punished for good reason, there are many more who gave no cause to be so treated, and if they did, it was because they had been deceived' (Y creed que, aunque os parece que hay muchas culpadas, hay muchas más inculpadas, y que no todas las que han sido muertas violentamente lo debían; que si muchas padecen con causa, hay tantas más que no la han dado, y si la dieron, fue por haber sido engañadas, 334). In the truly noble society envisioned through the author's goals for the *Desengaños*, the guilty die and the innocent do not. It is logical, then, that the fiction drives noblemen toward this ideal by amplifying as much as possible the loss created when they kill an innocent noblewoman.

The other two goals the author establishes for the male nobility are designed to move them away from what the narrators describe as their dishonesty with noblewomen and their overwhelming tendency to speak ill of the female sex, both practices that decrease women's credibility and justify females as objects of attack in the corrupt society. The dishonesty with which noblemen treat noblewomen, which places noblewomen in the unprotected legal position specified above, provokes the harshest complaints of narrators and characters alike, and the narrators repeatedly declare their intention to inspire them to abandon such ignoble behaviour: 'My tales of disillusion are for men who deceive' (Mis desengaños son para los que engañan, 258). Bitter protestations against the deceitful man abound, as when Isabel accuses noblemen of having designs on nothing except female innocence (135).

Nise describes them as experts in deceit (190), while for Lisis they are ancient in the art of deception and as such worse than noblewomen's worst enemies (469, 509). Even the narrator Francisca, who insists that she cannot be persuaded that *all* men *always* look to deceive women, is forced to conclude, 'But that there are many who deceive, who can doubt?' (Mas que hay muchos que engañan, ¿quién lo puede dudar? 368).

Accumulating invectives against defective noblemen, Zayas describes those to whom she addresses her fiction – those in need of reform – as morally weak and therefore womanish, the ultimate insult. Presenting such faulty males as the source of not only personal but national debility, her narrators decry those men's distance from the manly man of Spain's age of conquest, the foundational strategy of what Montesa Peydró calls her 'juxtaposition of a brilliant past with a decadent present' (94). In a long speech at the book's end, the narrator laments that although enemies have penetrated Spain and the king is at war, 'noblemen are at the Prado and on the river, decked out in fineries and womanish clothes' (en el Prado y en el río, llenos de galas y trajes femeniles)[7] or at court, 'wrinkling up your fineries and growing your hair, trampling about in carriages and strolling through meadows' (ajando galas y criando cabellos, hollando coches y paseando prados, 504–5).

Protestations such as these abound in seventeenth-century Spanish texts, in which aristocratic men are held responsible for the nation having fallen off its apex in diatribes accusing them of effeminate foppery and of failure to live up to the ambitious expansionism of their forbears. In her 1637 treatise *Nobleza virtuosa* (*Virtuous Nobility*), composed to advise children born to the nobility, Luisa de Padilla complains, 'The misfortune of our age has gone so far that one sees dancing like women the grandsons of the men who bore the weight of suits of armour upon themselves and weapons in their hands with which they won for those grandchildren everything they now so unworthily possess' (Llega la desdicha de nuestros tiempos a ver bailar como mujeres nietos de los que trajeron casi toda su vida el peso de los arneses sobre sí y las armas en la mano con que les ganaron lo que tan indignamente poseen, 9). Such protests intensify in Baltasar Gracián's *El criticón*, whose first part was published in 1651 with the character Artemia's lament, 'Men are no longer what they were, formed to the age in which they lived and in the old style, which was always the best ... What happened to those good men, to those vestments of innocence, to those good people? Those venerable aged ones, so solid and so true, are no more: yes meant yes and no meant no' (Los hombres no son ya los que solían, hechos al buen tiempo y a lo antiguo, que fue siempre lo mejor ... ¿Qué se hizieron aquellos buenos hombres, con aquellos sayos de inocencia, aquella gente de bien? Ya se han acabado aquellos viejos machuchos tan sólidos y verdaderos: el sí era sí y el no era no, 203). At the same time, preachers railed from the pulpit at the male nobility, denigrated as overly delicate, sensitive, and childish (Aladro 172).[8]

Spanish imperialism made intense demands on noblemen, propelling them around the globe and expecting them to be successful servants of God, the king, women, and the world at once. As El Saffar observes, 'Even more than in other parts of Western Europe, a new vision of what it is to be a man unfolded to meet the demands of an Empire oriented to expansion, change, exploration and conquest' (*Rapture* 66).[9] Capitalizing on the traditional model of the successful nobleman, Zayas attributes masculine effeminacy and cowardice to noblemen's failure to treat noblewomen in the idealistic chivalric fashion that, according to her class's social mythology of the Spanish past, made the Spanish empire possible.[10] In other words, she makes a nobleman's attitude toward women the index of his masculinity and, as such, of his ability to achieve anything positive and masculine. In the gender code of seventeenth-century Spain, positive things defined as masculine included almost everything.

Unconditional respect of women is, therefore, a feature of the *Desengaños*'s ambitions for Zayas's male public, a hyperbolic petition that complements the author's other goals for men. True to form, the fiction represents noblemen's failure to practise that behaviour and the catastrophes that ensue, while the narrators explicitly decry the ignoble practice of speaking ill of women. Asserting that such behaviour declasses the high-born male, Lisis states that, 'the man who speaks badly of women is neither a gentleman, nor noble, nor honourable, though those women be bad, given that as such they should be pardoned on behalf of the good ones' (ni es caballero, ni noble, ni honrado el que dice mal de las mujeres, aunque sean malas, pues las tales se pueden librar en virtud de las buenas, 506). Similarly, the narrator insists that when they defame women, noblemen defame themselves, since they all have a female relative to whom their own reputations are allied (263). According to Lisis, casting such aspersions labels a man as 'discourteous and stupid' (descortés y necio, 404), since a noblewoman's own foolish deeds suffice to defame her (263, 371). Sustaining her emphasis on the defective nobly born male, Zayas makes no plea to noblewomen to speak well of even badly behaving noblemen for the sake of what good men there are, nor does she insult the noblewoman who speaks ill of noblemen.

Invoking public respect for women as a cornerstone of male moral behaviour is by no means unique to Zayas. Such unconditional respect is a hallmark of the hero of Spanish chivalric fiction, whose prototype *Amadis de Gaula* by Garcí Rodríguez de Montalvo was first published in 1508 and initiated a chivalric literary frenzy in Spain. In a telling moment, Amadís assures a damsel he rescues, 'Fear not ... for wherever women are mistreated, since they should be safe, there can be no man worth anything' (No temáis ... que en parte donde las mujeres son maltratadas, que deven andar seguras, no puede aver hombre que nada valga, 286). In a later adventure, he shames a rapist with the reminder that women 'should be very protected by knights' (muy guardadas deven ser de los cavalleros, 447). More than a century later, the ideal endures in works that contrast nobility of birth with nobility of comportment, such as *El alcalde de Zalamea* (*The Mayor of Zalamea*) by Calderón de la Barca, staged in 1636. Therein, the wealthy, beautiful, and humbly born Isabel exhorts the nobly born Don Álvaro to proper behaviour saying, 'For men such as you / must succour women, / if not because of what they are, / because they are women' (Que los hombres como vos, / han de amparar las mujeres, / si no por lo que ellas son, / porque son mujeres, 694–7). In the same play, Isabel's wealthy, arrogant, and honourable father Pedro Crespo includes that very precept in the catalogue of virtues he admonishes his son to follow: 'Do not speak ill of women; / the most humble of them, I tell you, / is worthy of esteem, / for in the end we are born of them' (No hables mal de las mujeres; / la más humilde, te digo, / que es digna de estimación; / porque al fin de ellas nacimos, 1612–15).[11] As Montesa Peydró indicates, Zayas's novelty is not her narrators' stalwart endorsement of chivalric treatment of women; it is the aggression with which she expresses it (109, n. 19).

Zayas is unique, however, for the cause and effect relationship she crafts in the *Desengaños* between the nobleman's regard for women and the recovery of male valour, the cornerstone of the imperial male character. On the surface, these two practices have nothing to do with each other, for presumably a man can be valorous without exalting women. However, the book's narrator insists to her male public, 'Honouring the ladies, they [noblemen] restore their lost reputation' (Honrando y alabando a las damas, restauran la opinión perdida, 264). The final articulation of the message is even more direct: 'Love and honour women,' declares Lisis, 'and you will see how your lost valour revives in you' (Estimad y honrad a las mujeres y veréis cómo resucita en vosotros el valor perdido, 506). This peculiar formula appears in the negative as well, when Lisis attributes noblemen's lack of courage to their low esteem of women and promises: 'Were you to esteem and love women ... you yourselves would offer not only to go to war and fight, but to die, offering your throat to the blade, as in days of yore, and specifically as was done in the day of King Don Fernando the Catholic, when men did not have to be dragged to battle by force or in handcuffs, as is now the case' (Si las estimarais y amárades ... vosotros mismos os ofreciérades, no digo yo a ir a la guerra, y a pelear, sino a la muerte, poniendo la garganta al cuchillo, como en otros tiempos, y en particular en el del rey don Fernando el Católico se hacía, donde no era menester llevar los hombres por fuerza, ni maniatados, como ahora, 504).[12]

Valor, 'valour,' derived from the Latin *valere*, literally means to be well, and by extension the capacity to be worth something of meaning.[13] Zayas's concatenation that makes a nobleman's worthiness conditional on his respect for women harkens to the chivalric ethics she prescribes for the Spanish nobleman and the meaning of the knight's lady therein. Nowhere is the idealized, productive meaning of this relationship more poignantly expressed than in Don Quijote's heated response to his squire's low-brow ideas about women, in which the knight reveals the critical role that Dulcinea plays in his life:

'And don't you understand – you slob, you ditch-digger, you scoundrel – that, without the strength she breathes into my arm, I wouldn't be able to kill a flea? Just tell me, with that lying viper's tongue of yours, who *won* this kingdom, and who cut off this giant's head, and who made you a count – all of which I consider as good as done with, finished, over – except Dulcinea's strength, lent to my arm as the mere instrument of her glorious deeds? She fights through me, and she conquers through me, and I live and breathe in her. I take my life and my very being from her.' (200)

('¿Y no sabéis vos, gañán, faquín, belitre, que si no fuese por el valor que ella infunde en mi brazo, que no le tendría para matar una pulga? Decid, socarrón de lengua viperina, y ¿quién pensáis que ha ganado este reino; y cortado la cabeza a este gigante; y héchoos a vos marqués, que todo esto doy ya por hecho y por cosa pasada en cosa juzgada, si no es el valor de Dulcinea, tomando a mi brazo por instrumento de sus hazañas? Ella pelea en mí y vence en mí, y yo vivo y respiro en ella, y tengo vida y ser.' 352–3)

Although Zayas's text is concerned with less ethereal females, Cervantes' identification of Dulcinea as the engine of Don Quijote's heroics and his meaning reveals how Zayas could solder respectful treatment of women to a man's access to everything worth having and doing. In this context, chivalric behaviour signifies extreme merit and the sovereignty of the Spanish nation over the world as Zayas knew it.

Zayas bases her critique of the Spanish nobleman on the inversion of this model: unlike the knights from Amadís de Gaula to Don Quijote, her nobleman has cast his lady and all ladies into the dirt, thereby losing his most valuable asset, necessary ally, and noble identity itself. In this spirit, Lisis laments, 'Since honouring common women is an obligation, what about those who are not common? Since among the many who vituperate and insult them today, not one is found who defends them, can there be greater misfortune? [What a shame it is that] even gentlemen do this who, when they are singled out as gentlemen, promise to defend women, [and then] let themselves be carried away by vulgarity, without considering how they fail to be who they are and the faith they promised!' (Pues el honrar a las mujeres comunes es deuda, ¿qué será en las que no lo son? Que entre tantos como hoy las vituperan y ultrajan no se halle ninguno que las defienda, ¿puede ser mayor desdicha? ¡Que ni aun los caballeros, que, cuando los señalan por tales, prometen la defensa de las mujeres, se dejen también llevar de la vulgaridad, sin mirar que faltan a lo mismo que son y la fe que prometieron! 333). This formula relies on a hyperbolic idealization of Woman: respect for women engenders male valour, and male valour produces and sustains empire. That formula's inversion, which is what the tales represent, reveals what happens when failure to engage the cause (respect of women) renders the effect impossible (valour). The end of the empire is assured, leaving the chivalric ideal haunting the text like an unquiet ghost.

This nostalgic program for noble behaviour is important because its fictional, chivalric nature denaturalizes and objectifies Woman into a cultural icon that Zayas not only affirms but exalts. Her invocation of male valour as the by-product of esteem for women situates her readers in this retrograde paradigm, alerting them to its presence in the text as part of the desired ideal to which the tales strives, always unsuccessfully. Thus, according to the behavioural prescription of the *Desengaños*, noblemen should privately and publicly esteem noblewomen, and failure to do so will produce the opposite of what chivalric ethics accomplished, not only personal disgrace and failure, but the disgrace and failure of the entire nation. The rejected noblewoman, then, signifies not only her own misstep produced by her failure to respect herself and live astutely. In the *Desengaños*, she can also serve as an analogue of masculine and social failure, personal as well as political.

At her book's end, just as Zayas fictionalizes the realization of her objective to move noblewomen to self-respect and vigilance, so she represents her male public as won over by her book's arguments on their behalf. The gentlemen attending the soirée consent not once but three times that they need to accomplish all of them: distinguish the innocent from the guilty noblewoman, abandon the practice of deceiving noblewomen, and respect and speak well of them all. These lessons are rendered as learned when, in a highly artificial turn of events, Don Juan admits that speaking badly of noblewomen is an abominable vice (289). He later declares on behalf of all the males in attendance at the soirée, 'We admit defeat and confess that there are men who, with their cruelty and tricks, condemn themselves and render women blameless' (Nos damos por vencidos y confesamos que hay hombres que, con sus crueldades y engaños, condenándose a sí, disculpan a las mujeres, 366). Leaving no room for doubt, Zayas has them all acquiesce yet again, affirming that there are good women who suffer in innocence due to men's deceits (398). By repeatedly representing the surrender of her fictional male public to her designs, the author assures her male readers of how possible it is not only to treat noblewomen better, but thereby to achieve great things once more.

III. Nobility: Abandon Lust and Greed

Identifying the text's discrete objectives for female and male aristocrats presented above requires culling the book to locate passages in which Zayas defines them, sifting them out and lining them up in two columns for evaluation. Her objectives for the nobility as a whole, which she does not articulate directly, become visible by passing the entire text through those first two sets of objectives like a sieve. What does not pass through are two prescribed behaviours – both rendered negatively – that reach beyond the gender-specific formulas for improved behaviour and apply to everyone in the nobility. If we scrutinize what remains in the sieve, we see misbehaving characters of both sexes practising two vices with which Zayas metonymically represents lack of self-control: adultery and greed. Both were sins of lasciviousness or lust.

Seventeenth-century lasciviousness is not uncontrolled sexual desire, but rather a larger sin of over-indulgence in weakness and excess. Covarrubias defines it as a moral offence: 'incontinence of the spirit, inclination, and propensity to venereal things, soft and pleasurable, delightful and deceitful in this matter' (incontinencia de ánimo, inclinación y propensión las cosas venéreas, blandas y regaladas, alegres y chocarrescas en esta materia, 702a). As such, it was the perfect vice for Zayas to use in her portrait of a nobility that has lost its hold on its own identity, a group whose misbehaviours catalyze entire chain reactions of misbehaviour.

In seventeenth-century canon law, adultery meant illicit copulation with a married individual and was one of six sexual practices that fell under the category of lasciviousness.[14] Four protagonists seek an adulterous relationship: Juan, compelled to possess his best friend's wife (d3); Diego, who cannot control his appetite for sex with the married Inés (d5); Federico, obsessed with his brother's wife Beatriz (d9); and Florentina, who loses control over her desire for her sister's husband (d10).[15] Although all these characters wreak havoc on the lives of the innocent, neither Juan nor Federico are successful in possessing the object of their desire, in both cases due to the intervention of the Virgin whose symbolic hyper-purity serves as the antidote to their lack of the same. In their transgression, which is limited to adulterous intentions, Zayas manages to encapsulate both the problem (lust) and its solution (self-control). Although Inés repeatedly resists the onslaught of Diego's desire, she succumbs to his alliance with a Moorish necromancer, whose status as Other represents Diego's alienation from the nobility whose values he has abandoned.

Florentina and her married lover Dionís are the book's only fullblown adulterers, and consequently the violence their relationship begets is the greatest of all the tales: twelve people die in its wake. All of the lust-driven characters in the *Desengaños*, however, are unwed members of the nobility who desire a married person. The fact that every one of the marriages under the siege of this illicit desire falls apart confirms Zayas's use of marriage as an index of the stable, symbolic future to which the defective nobility denies itself access with its dissolute behaviour.

Zayas also uses material greed, a variety of lasciviousness in canon law, as a symptom of the nobility's drift from heroic virtue by severely chastising characters who fail to esteem virtue over wealth. Greed was a particularly effective tool for her because the admirable member of the traditional Spanish nobility, certainly in seventeenth-century fiction, does not signify in terms of finance beyond being simply and generically wealthy. Only defective characters desire or esteem money for itself, and the perfect noble individual communicated meaning in terms of more ancient markers of worth such as bloodline, title, and land that produced financial resources. The ideal nobly born person did not work for this income, relying instead on family resources to produce whatever was needed, which in turn provided ample time and resources to practise generosity, a fundamental noble virtue (in part because it signified financial well-being). Zayas suggests the superior merit of virtue over wealth in the heroic character Felipe, Isabel's nobly born suitor whom she initially rejects because of his poverty and too late recognizes to be a superior man (d1).

Refining the contrast between greed and virtue, Zayas unravels *desengaño* 8 on the financial obsessions of the patriarch Don Pedro, an obsession that costs two noblewomen their lives. Greed drives him to prohibit his daughter Mencía from marrying so his son Alonso can inherit his estate undiluted, even though Mencía's beloved, virtuous, and wealthy suitor Enrique asks him for her hand. Enrique, the foil Zayas creates for Pedro and Alonso, is the only character in the book celebrated for his generosity with his material resources (372). Not surprisingly, he is almost killed in his attempts to stay married to Mencía, and Mencía dies at the hands of her brother, who does away with her on behalf of their father.

In the story's second half, Alonso inherits the paternal defect and weds the poverty-stricken, nobly born Ana for love and has a child with her, then beheads her when his father threatens to disinherit him for having married a poor woman. That same vice does him in when he is caught stealing stockings from a store, is identified as his wife's assassin, and garrotted. The poetic justice of the tale's denouement reveals the importance of generosity in the noble heart, for Zayas arranges for justice to be generous to Ana's son: he inherits the entire estate of his avaricious grandfather, the estate for which his mother died. In this implicit exaltation of noble generosity, scripted negatively in the consequences of its lack, the aristocracy is not only obliged to generously distribute resources, but have those excess resources at their disposition to distribute. Felipe, Isabel's impoverished suitor, would really not be an acceptable mate for Isabel, wealthy though she is. Zayas relies too much on traditional formulas of noble goodness, in which wealth is understood as a correlative of merit, for Felipe to do more than point to the importance of virtue in a nobleman.

To summarize, the objectives of the *Desengaños* unfold along the diachronic axis of the text, as what transpires illustrates the consequences of failing to realize them. To convince noblewomen to abandon naivety and practise self-respect, Zayas offers unwed female characters who suffer the extreme effects of ingenuity. These are Isabel, whose positive response to Manuel's attentions and belief that he would marry her lead to her ruin (d1), Octavia, who suffers the same fate because of Carlos (d2), Lucrecia, who wrongly trusts Jaime with her reputation and is dishonoured by him (d4), and Laurela, who believes Esteban's promise to marry her if she runs away with him and dies for having thereby dishonoured her family (d6).

By enlisting her dark poetics, Zayas meets her objective to drive noblemen to respect noblewomen by offering dishonest suitors of noblewomen who promise marriage, take sex, and then renege on their promises, ruining the lives of the women they claimed to love: Manuel (d1), Carlos (d3), and Esteban (d6). To urge noblemen to distinguish the innocent woman from the guilty one, she imagines wife characters who are wrongly discredited by their familiars, revealing the horrifying consequences of not only noblemen's failure to distinguish virtuous women from vicious ones, but also the aristocracy's failure to behave nobly, which puts them in league with the lower classes. These include Camila, (d2), Roseleta (d3), Elena (d4), Blanca (d7), Mencía and Ana (d8), Beatriz (d9), and Magdalena (d10).

Lastly, to draw the nobility back to the practice of noble virtue, Zayas arranges for characters of both sexes to practise lasciviousness in the form of adultery and greed: Juan, Federico, and Florentina are all unmarried lovers who act on their desire for someone else's spouse, leading to death and destruction (d3, d9, d10). Blindness to the merit of virtue over wealth moves Isabel to reject Felipe in favour of the morally bankrupt Manuel, while greed drives Mencía's brother Alonso to kill Mencía and later his innocent wife Ana (d8). These characters operate in the shadow of their own mistakes, in whose darkness their specific purpose must be evaluated. The fact that their errors overlap with and mix with the errors of others makes the discernment of responsibility complicated, but not impossible.

Zayas engages her multiple objectives along the fiction's synchronic axis as well, such that at any given time in a plot, more than one character is doing something wrong. Thus a single story, such as that of Isabel and Manuel in *desengaño* 1, can meet as many as three distinct objectives – 'Noblewomen, respect yourselves'; 'Noblemen, respect noblewomen'; 'Nobility, behave nobly' – illustrating why the book is hard to decipher. From the perspective of Isabel, her experience is a cautionary tale for unmarried women. To a nobleman, the story illustrates the consequence of inconstancy and failure to respect not only Isabel, but the married Angeliana, with whom Manuel has a long affair, and his Moorish betrothed Zaida, who kills herself in the aftermath of his inconstancies: the consequence for Manuel is death. Entering the text as members of the nobility at large reveals the price of ignobility from the highest vantage point, which brings into view the mistakes of Isabel, Manuel, and Angeliana as well as the disasters that ripple out from their misbehaviour: the death of Isabel's father, a high-mimetic nobleman actively and heroically engaged in serving his king; the empowerment of a servant over her mistress (Claudia, whom Isabel lets convince her to break with decorum and respond to Manuel's attentions in the first place); the loss of a beautiful, intelligent, and nubile noblewoman (Isabel); the death of a nobleman who should have known better than to do what he did (Manuel); the death of his Moorish bride-to-be, who kills herself when Manuel is stabbed to death; and the death of the noble but impoverished Felipe, Isabel's constant lover who kills Manuel to avenge her dishonour and himself dies at war.

This brief analysis of *desengaño* 1 illustrates how the tales' consistency comes into focus by applying Zayas's three objectives to parts of appropriate tales and the perspectives they represent, rather than expecting every passage to satisfy just one of them. Similarly, the narrator Filis's insistence that women arm themselves is one of the most cited passages of the book: 'Well then [ladies], let us cast aside our fineries, flowers, and curls and defend ourselves, some with our intelligence and others, with arms!' (¡Ea, dejemos las galas, rosas y rizos, y volvamos por nosotras: unas, con en entendimiento y otras, con las armas! 231). Clearly this display is not meant to teach men to respect women or distinguish the innocent from the guilty, nor does it constitute a general call to good behaviour. With declarations such as Nisis's, Zayas meets her first objective, to inspire noblewomen to self-respect, and neither this exclamation nor any like it can be used to urge a feminist meaning on the entire book without suffocating the author's other two arguments and confounding her agenda to seek the collaboration of noblemen and noblewomen in the production of order. Zayas separates the passages encouraging women to educate and defend themselves from the interior fiction – the ten tales of disillusion – protecting the negative aesthetics of the stories that demand a death sacrifice as the most potent display of noble dysfunction. The book's cries for women to defend and respect themselves are prescriptive, whereas the female characters' failure to do exactly that are descriptive, in the negative style of the tales.

Similarly, the sugar-coated, apologetic statements made to men by some of the narrators and characters serve Zayas's objective to sway noblemen to respect noblewomen and mitigate the insults that most of the narrators deliver to the male sex. Filis, narrating d4, exemplifies this conciliatory practice, pointing to noblewomen's responsibility in not deceiving themselves and adding that 'nor do men probably deserve blame for everything they are accused of' (ni los hombres deben de tener la culpa de todo lo que se les imputa, 227). In such reconciliatory passages, the author sympathizes with her nobly born male characters and public. That sympathy does not violate her support of the female nobility, for were things as they should be, women and men would work together to sustain order. If noblewomen respect themselves but noblemen do not, self-respect would serve women little, and vice versa. The intensely interwoven texture of the *Desengaños* allows problems to compound each another, thereby accurately assessing how trouble begets more trouble when almost everyone is misbehaving.

Most important, Zayas's good wife characters cannot serve her objective of teaching women self-respect without disabling the way in which the author parses her narrative to support multiple objectives simultaneously, to envision an entirely functional society by crafting one that is perfectly dysfunctional. The tales with married protagonists, which end with the wife's expulsion from the world, are designed to convince noblemen to respect noblewomen, distinguish the guilty woman from the innocent one, and lead the nobility to self-control and control over others by exemplifying the disastrous consequences of not living up to those standards. The female reader learns through *escarmiento*, caution inspired by someone else's bad experience, in the stories in which the wife dies. But this benefit is collateral to their primary function, which is to illustrate the consequences of wrongly blaming noblewomen for transgressions they do not commit and the disastrous effects of a serving class empowered by the misbehaving aristocracy.

Although Zayas uses only the courtship and dishonour plots in the *Desengaños*, she combines them in single tales like clauses of a sentence, working different combinations of her three goals throughout. *Desengaños* 2, 3, and 8 are interwoven plots that each recount a double-barrelled disaster. The second tale relates how Carlos dishonours

Camila, and follows with the rape of Carlos's wife, Camila, by Octavia's avenging brother, to conclude with Carlos's murder of his raped wife. The third tells how Roseleta and Pedro overcome Juan's attempts to dishonour Roseleta, only to ignite again when Juan's former lover Angeliana sets Roseleta up to be murdered by her husband so Angeliana can marry him herself. The eighth story begins with the undoing of Mencía and Enrique's secret marriage by her brother Alonso, and continues with Alonso's marriage to Ana, whom he kills so he can inherit from his father. All of these two-part narratives rotate on a defective nobleman (Carlos, Pedro, Alonso) who wreaks double havoc, always in alliance with a secondary character of compromised morals in the story's second half.

In these double-trouble stories, Zayas manages to fictionalize all of her three objectives, always in the negative, representing what happens when not one of them is met. The second tale, for example, could have ended once in disgrace, but engenders a mutant offspring that draws it to end again, in disgrace *and* death. This structural hyperbole spins a web of causes and effects in which wrong behaviour inspires only more wrong: had Octavia not consented to Carlos's illicit desire ('noblewomen, safeguard your own interests'), had Carlos not lied to Octavia ('noblemen, do not deceive women,' 'nobility, abandon lust'), Juan would not have been led to violate Camila, and Carlos would not have blamed her for his mistake and killed her ('men, distinguish guilty women from innocent ones'). The story ends in a tangle of rage, as Carlos sets off after Juan and they both disappear, like Victor Frankenstein chasing the monster he created: 'It was suspected that Carlos had gone off in search of his enemy Don Juan, if by chance he got a fix on where he was, but no one ever heard a single thing about either one of them thereafter' (Sospechóse que Carlos había partido a buscar a su enemigo don Juan, si acaso supo parte segura donde estaba, mas de ninguno de los dos se supo jamás nueva ninguna, 194).

The objectives Zayas establishes for her second book, some for noblewomen, some for noblemen, and some for all the nobility, provide the reader with a guide through the twisted and tormented paths of the *Desengaños*. Everything in the book, down to the minor characters, falls into line behind them. Using nobly born protagonists who should be predisposed to noble behaviour by virtue of their bloodline, she crafts stories that reveal how the nobility's betrayal of its obligations and responsibilities threatens its very existence. Monitory fiction, the *Desengaños* strive to see the disasters they represent overcome through the realization of the objectives the author sets out. The narrator Laura briefly envisions the conditions under which that can happen: 'Honouring the ladies, they [noblemen] restore their lost reputation ... and may the ladies be sensible and modest, for this being done there will be no need for tales of disillusion' (Honrando y alabando a las damas, restauran la opinión perdida ... y lo demás es bajeza, y las damas, sean cuerdas y recogidas, que con esto no habrán menester desengaños, que quien no se engaña no tiene necesidad de desengañarse, 264).

Awareness of what Zayas claimed to accomplish with the *Desengaños* alerts the reader to caution when treading the compound fractures of the plots, to be alert to practices of signification that are not literal, and to evaluate what happens in the fiction in light of conservative social ethics. The hegemonic ideology that energizes the book had no room for major challenges to patriarchal discourses, and the only way to represent women within their constraints was to relinquish their meaning as individuals, surrendering it to something else. Remarkably, Zayas manages to satisfy her book's commitment to its own ideals without sacrificing the virtuous agency to which the same book calls noblewomen. She realizes this accomplishment most potently with her perfect victim characters, the dead and dying wives of the *Desengaños*.

Figure 3.1 *St Lucia*, Antonio Tempesta, *Roman Virgin Martyrs*, c. 1591. With the generous permission of the Warburg Institute

3 Dressed to Kill:
Death and Meaning in the *Desengaños*

The worst is only a place to start.

Terry Eagleton, *Sweet Violence*

The story is always the same.

Step one. She is young, she is virtuous, and she is beautiful or wealthy, or both. She marries her husband by consent, not choice, for like a good noblewoman, she does not desire anything or anyone until she is married, and thereafter she seeks only her husband's happiness and her honour.

A man desires her to an uncontrollable extreme and pursues her. If this man is the one she marries, he marries her in knowing violation of his or her father's will. If she is already married, the pursuing man is not her husband, and he tracks her down in total disregard of her integrity and that of her spouse. This illegitimate desire for her, real or believed to be real by the man who matters, dishonours her and her family. This unworthy man is in collusion with someone else, sometimes a jealous noblewoman or a flawed member of the family, sometimes a lower class, non-white, or non-Catholic person who represents evil: a black female slave, a Moorish necromancer, a commoner who pretends to be noble, the devil disguised as a scholar.

Sometimes she is aware of the corner into which the pursuing man and his accomplices have painted her and knows there is no escape: to seek help is to manifest her dishonour, and to be silent is to be complicit in it. The pursuing man's desire, whether realized or not, ruins her reputation. She does everything she can to extricate her life and her honour from the clutches of wrong, remaining faithful and devoted to her husband. If she knows that a man has behaved dishonourably toward her, she knows she is going to die for it. Aware that there is nothing she can do to save herself, she surrenders to her fate with dignity.

Step two. Believing he has been dishonoured in appearance or in fact (and the two are of equal importance), her husband or powerful male relative turns against her and seeks to destroy not only the pursuing man but her as well. He does not realize she is innocent, or knows she is and does not care, for her violation means more to him than her person. He etches his mutilated honour and the misbehaviour of others onto her body, often aided by female and male colleagues in the wrong. Poisoned, starved, blinded, cemented into a chimney, locked into a hole in the wall, decapitated, or bled to death, that body takes on a horrifying appearance that is radically inconsonant with who she is: a perfectly smart and lovely young noblewoman. It suffers to the brink of death or dies.

Step three. Having been tormented to unbearable lengths, or dead, that body turns its appearance around as if by miracle, communicating redemption. Its whole or its parts glisten with enduring symbols of life, recovering a literal or symbolic beauty greater than the woman's own when she was alive and well. She takes that beauty, a powerful embodiment of who she was and everything she represents, with her when she departs from the world.

So it goes with Zayas's perfect victim characters, seven of whom lose their lives (Camila d2, Roseleta d3, Elena d4, Blanca d7, Ana and Mencía d8, Magdalena d10), two of whom die to the world by ending their lives in a convent after barely surviving their familiars' attacks (Inés d5, Beatriz d9).[1] They are white, Catholic, high-born wives of noblemen and are, to a greater or lesser extent, protagonists of the stories at whose narrative epicentres their bodies lie. There is no doubt that the disappearances and deaths of these characters are the most horrible and startling of the many disasters that ensue in the *Desengaños*.

The hyperbolic innocence of these noblewomen, combined with the hyperbolic torments to which they are subjected, provides the *admiración*, great surprise, crucial to novella poetics, and places the extreme of right (innocent wife) and wrong (what happens to her), into tight, baroque opposition. The fact that Zayas accomplishes all of this using dying and dead bodies is likewise true to baroque culture, whose emblem of preference was the corpse (Benjamin 166). The interpretative problems that the perfect wives present are not of theme or style, but of meaning: what do these women's sufferings and post-mortem loveliness communicate in a book whose primary objective is the reformation of the immoral nobility?

We have established that Zayas uses the *Desengaños* to celebrate human marriage by deploring the nobility's failures to produce and sustain it, that she uses marriage as a metonym of national prosperity, and that she calibrates a nobleman's worth in proportion to his respect for women. Because the narrative uses the negative to imply the positive, it renders the worst possible state of marriage and so the impending doom of the corrupt nobility, as well as calamitous results of noblemen's failure to respect noblewomen or recognize their innocence. To move the aristocracy away from lust and greed, Zayas arranges for the worst possible events to result from the practice of those vices. This puts intense pressure on the perfect wife because she is the character of most value and so the one whose loss best displays the high cost of misbehaviour.

But we have also seen how vehemently the book's narrators enjoin noblewomen to self respect and agency, which puts the author in the dilemma of how to save the very characters she had to torture and kill to satisfy her other objectives. Although the perfect victims serve the goals for the male nobility and the nobility at large, there had to be something about them that would keep the text from endorsing the violent deaths of the innocent. The fact that Zayas managed to accomplish all of this is a tribute to her genius and a test of her readers' wit. Like most tests of wit, this one entails leaving the box in which it is easiest to think. In this case, the box is realism, or reading literally.

Wife Abuse and Murder, History and Fiction

Following Lara's 1932 belief that Zayas is describing seventeenth-century life in Spain with high fidelity (31) and Amezúa's 1951 insistence on Zayas's 'constant and profound' realism ('Doña María' 15), readers today most often assign a literal meaning to Zayas's perfect victim characters, finding that in them the author represents the condition of women in seventeenth-century Spain by means of biographical, if fictional, referents. The accumulation of details with which Zayas describes women's dead bodies gives a 'concrete reality to their tortures' (Levisi 449), and suggests historicity. According to a literal interpretation, which is to say any reading that leaves intact the relationship between a character and what she means, each noble female protagonist signifies her experience in history, and her demise, the end of her life. This approach justifies assessment of the book's violence as 'sadistic, over-stated, and counter-effective,' depicting 'the brutality that accompanies the self-serving notion of men's honor' (Levisi; Kaminsky, 491).[2]

Many read the tales quite literally, finding that the *Desengaños* contain documentary evidence of seventeenth-century violence against women. In 1978 Foa propounded that Zayas set out to represent the true circumstances of women of the age ('propone representar la verdadera situación de la mujer en la época,' 'María' 129). More recently, Boyer describes the *Desengaños* as 'a chilling catalogue of what today we call domestic violence' ('War' 124), Gorfkle finds the book to be 'a shocking testimony of violent acts that men perpetrate against women, including rape, torture, extortion and murder, apparently ubiquitous in the author's social milieu' (11), Williamsen points to Blanca's endurance of her husband's beating as the battered wife syndrome ('Death' 620), and Vollendorf draws a sobering parallel between the patterns of violence against women today and those represented in the *Desengaños* (*Reclaiming* 112; 'Reading').

A literal reading of Zayas's dead wives makes it possible to reconcile the pro-women rhetoric in the book with the virtuous characters' deaths: they are accurate, straightforward testimony of early modern domestic abuse, and Zayas attaches holy signifiers to their dead bodies as a means of protesting their demise, the patriarchy that killed them, and the Catholic church whose signifiers of martyrdom she appends to their bodies (Grieve).[3] This is the prevailing understanding of what the so-called martyr characters of the *Desengaños* mean, and, had Zayas limited her book's objectives to a critique of the patriarchy, this would work. As we have seen, however, her target was much larger and her relationship to the patriarchy nuanced.

On the surface, literal readings appear to be supported by historical evidence that women were in fact endangered and killed for questions of honour. Such evidence includes Vigil's citations from Barrionuevo's tabloid *Avisos* from early modern Madrid (152–3) and Gil's tables of petitions for divorce brought to the diocesan tribunal of Barcelona from 1565 to 1654, in which women plaintiffs who accused their husbands of cruelty and/or physical abuse, death threats, or attempted murder account for 70 per cent of all cases (200). In data cited by Ruff from the diocese of Córdoba and Granada from 1500 to 1800, 73 per cent of the cases that came before the ecclesiastical tribunal were related to male domestic abuse (139), as were the vast majority of divorce petitions studied by Casey in Andalusia from 1600 to 1800 ('Household').

In relationship to literature, and certainly the *Desengaños*, this evidence poses as many questions as it resolves, because Zayas's protagonists are exclusively noble and royal, and no historian has yet produced substantive data about high-class domestic abuse. The cases Vigil cites involve members of the non-noble classes, and though his primary case is a working class couple, Gil does not specify class in his statistics, nor does Ruff. In her interesting study of the litigation of unmet marriage promises in sixteenth-century Navarre, neither does Dyer, and in the data presented by Barahona 'most of the plaintiffs come from society's lower orders' (32), as do those presented by Taylor and Casey ('Household'). Even though this is the period that Kagan describes as Spain's heyday of litigation, these studies suggest that members of the upper class very rarely appear in court cases of dishonour, and instances when they do are limited to those in which lower-class female claimants were brave enough to accuse noblemen of having misused them, or to upper-class litigation for material goods in which litigants took recourse in violent behaviour.

As Pitt-Rivers insists, 'No man of honour, least of all an aristocrat, was prepared to remit to the courts the settlement of his affairs of honour' (30), and Castan prudently indicates that such cases that come to justice are few, and those that do almost always involve a member of the lower class (514). Recent studies of Spanish noblewomen suggest that, although they frequently litigated to protect their economic interests, they did not go to court to protect their social interests such as their honour.[4] Lamentably, then, the few sources of historical data about the honour code – civil and ecclesiastic tribunals – are the least likely sources to reveal how the upper classes resolved such offences, since the stakes of noble marriage with regard to property and bloodline were so high as to make secrecy in cases of dishonour imperative. Nobly born men and women had nothing but more dishonour to gain from taking their dishonour to court.[5]

According to Ruff, the majority of early modern domestic abuse, including rape and wife murder, occurred within social classes, not between them, was far more common in the early modern period than it is now, and was generally 'unchallenged by the social and legal structures of early modern western Europe.' Moreover, he specifies, early modern domestic violence 'flourished behind a wall of silence maintained by all affected by this behaviour' (132). All evidence suggests that the upper class of Zayas's day lived behind a screen of privilege that protected their interests of secrecy to an extent that cuts off access to information about how they treated each other behind closed doors.

The extent to which this is true, and true of the upper classes, makes it likely that the kind of terrible abuse of noblewomen that the *Desengaños* represent did indeed happen. However, given that we will probably never know to what degree, it is impossible to pinpoint exactly how Zayas's second book is true to early modern reality. Parker-Aronson's observation that 'the catalogue of abuses to which Zayas subjects her female characters stretches credulity' (540) is understandable. However, domestic abuse that stretches credulity endures to this day, in events such as those of 23 May 2005, when police rescued an eight-year-old girl who had been raped by a familiar, stuffed into a dumpster in a landfill, covered with concrete slabs and rocks, and left for dead. Appalling upper-class wife murders are ongoing, such as Dr Paul Greineder's 1999 decapitation of his wife in an elite Boston suburb, and since such offences are now less easy to hide than in Zayas's day, they are increasingly documented, acquiring a profile of their own.[6]

The violence against noblewomen in the *Desengaños* faithfully renders the real depravity of some human beings. What stretches credulity are the supernatural components that Zayas weaves into her fictional plots around those acts of violation, and how the text accumulates elements of pathos to the extreme. These unreal features would have increased her text's truth value since in Zayas's day, 'a true representation, one that seeks to expose the world as it actually is,' was non-realist (Robbins 68).

On the complicated question of the text's historicity, three things are clear. First, historical accounts of violence against early modern women similar to episodes in Zayas's second book suggest instances in which reality imitates fiction rather than vice-versa. This would be the case, for example, of the real father who made a wall fall on his daughter to kill her, as happens in *desengaño* 6, since this method of doing away with a dishonoured female appears in several seventeenth-century works of literature.[7] Second, whether or not the acts of violence against the wife characters carried out in Zayas's book are historical, the fact that she followed literary models for much of that violence calls for attention to its pervasiveness as a cultural pattern. Third, the consistency with which those violent acts propel the narrative into the realm of the supernatural is clearly not true to standards of positivist experience and must be addressed.

Montesa Peydró cites Place's research on the tales' literary sources to call readers away from historicist readings of Zayas's fiction (78), and as Boyer wisely suggests, it is important to distinguish between realistic referents and realism in Zayas's fiction ('Introduction' xxvii).[8] As Place ('María') and Sylvania have indicated, some of the stories' models date back to folklore. The most glaring of such sources is the romance vita of St Beatriz of Rome, printed in the second *Flos sanctorum* published in Spanish as the *Leyenda de los santos* (*Legend of the Saints*, 1497), which Zayas embellished to great effect as *desengaño* 9.[9] Violence against an innocent wife is explicit in this text of Catholic hagiography, as is the violence against women in the other hagiographic models embedded in the *Desengaños*, which we will examine shortly.

While the *desengaños* contain historical detail, their content is so clearly influenced by identifiable textual models as to oblige the reader to a non-literal reading of it, such as Vollendorf's passing mention that Zayas uses the violated female body as a sign of cultural decline (*Reclaiming* 58). In short, in her second book, Zayas may be reporting acts of violence that followed long-standing models of what we now call abuse, models that consumers of romance texts of hagiography could find in abundance, represented as sanctioned by God's will therein. These models are more alarming than they would be had Zayas made them up, for they reflect deeply ingrained ideas about women, men, and their bodies. There is no doubt, however, that Zayas stylizes those acts of violence to serve her artistic objectives.

The dead body in the *Desengaños* calls down the divinity, whose signifier that body becomes. It is on this shift of meaning, preceded by another, that I focus here, for the time and place to die in which Zayas positions the perfect wife has an aesthetic function consonant with the clearly declared goals for her book. Reading as a baroque reader makes it possible to locate the clues nested throughout the text suggesting that the female body tells a nuanced and complex story, a story aligned with baroque poetics that displace meaning and unsettle boundaries.

The reader attuned to the difference between responsibility and blame, and to the importance of that difference in questions of ethics and justice in the novella, is alert to the fact that a primary feature of Zayas's perfect victims is how the corrupt society blames them for misdeeds for which they are not responsible, forcing them to pay with their lives for the mistakes of other women and men. Blaming the victim is an act of projection, and the projection of patriarchal interests and dramas onto the bodies of female characters is a long-standing literary practice (Zeitlin), particularly acute in early modern Spanish literature whose theme is honour (McKendrick, 'Honour'). All of Zayas's wife murder stories spin on the axis of honour's effect on marriage, as do Spain's wife murder plays, which illustrate what happens when a female character is not a subject, but rather an object with which men are negotiating their power. Mulvey aptly summarizes this long-standing practice saying, 'Woman then stands in patriarchal culture as signifier for the male other, bound by a symbolic order in which man can live out his phantasies and obsessions through linguistic command by imposing them on the silent image of woman still tied to her place as bearer of meaning, not maker of meaning' (7).

Aware that this displacing tradition objectifies women, readers today are understandably reluctant to implicate female authors in its praxis, particularly a writer who defends the subjective status of women as energetically as does Zayas. The same thinking suggests that it would be remarkable indeed were an author not only able to objectify her female characters without compromising her pro-women agenda, but actually transmit it most effectively by doing so. But contextualizing the *Desengaños* in baroque literary theory reveals her doing exactly that.

The Waltz of Death in the *Desengaños*

Nieves Romero-Díaz points the way out of the opposition explicit in the *Desengaños*'s pro-women statements and the author's relentless subjugation of her virtuous protagonists to systematic abuse, observing the direct relationship between social crisis and the female body, in which Zayas symbolizes 'the fissures, rupture, and dismemberment of traditional order' (las fisuras, ruptura y desmembración del orden tradicional, *Nueva* 138). Refining and specifying this notion of the wife character as a symbol indicates that, after the sacrificial setup of her perfect victims is accomplished, Zayas uses their barely living and dead bodies to mean something they are not, and their passive demise is not speaking their experience, but something else. Tracing the steps of these characters' waltz with death makes it possible to track their subjectivity and its loss.

Step One. The Perfect Victim

The death of the innocent noble wife was the ideal metonym with which to render the future of the entire ruling class, because the married woman's primary function was to reproduce. The virgin might serve as 'a map of the integrity of the state' (Stallybrass 129), but the perfect wife mapped posterity as well as integrity, and designing her perfect victims as wives allowed Zayas to create in them the most high-mimetic, conformist women of which her society could conceive. Their conformism provides her vampirizing narratives with the blood they need to signify the most extreme loss possible, and they bait the imperfect members of the nobility to perform as the narrative needs them to – terribly.

Marriage was the ideal canvas on which to paint the suffering of the innocent noblewoman because, unlike her unmarried counterpart, the nobly born discredited wife was captive to a behavioural code that demanded she submit to the very power that would kill her, and an accusation of sexual infidelity left her unable to stay and unable to go. In *desengaño* 5, Inés's husband announces his intention to move to the outskirts of Seville, where he plans to murder her. The unwitting wife acquiesces: 'To which Doña Inés responded that she had no other pleasure than his' (A lo cual doña Inés dijo que en ello no había más gusto que el suyo, 282). This conundrum produces an airtight victimization, because the wife cannot take steps to defend her best interests without violating the precepts of virtue that bind her irrevocably to her husband, and Zayas needed the wife to be virtuous and helpless in order to be a perfect victim. The horrible circle, like the wife caught in it, is perfect.

The narrative ritual Zayas created with which to kill her perfect victims begins with tests of the wife's worth, creating in her an ironic hero whose heroic nature must be proven for her death to have any impact. In *desengaño* 3, for example, Roseleta's energetic defence of her honour and that of her husband in the face of Juan's desire for her is testimony to female intelligence and integrity. Moreover, it works. Thanks to her vigorous virtue, her husband Pedro accepts the evidence of his best friend's dishonourable intentions and relies on her to take equally energetic steps with him to defend their honour. It is not until Pedro turns against his wife, wrongly believing accusations made by Juan's former lover Angeliana, that Zayas throws Roseleta into victimization and passivity.

Inés is the most tested perfect wife, proving her worth independently because her husband is away on business when Diego begins his assault on her virtue (d5). She discerns that the dishonourable rake believes he has slept with her, when he really slept with a prostitute wearing one of her dresses. Responding by hiding the royal magistrate in her house, she calls Diego in to explain his version of their relationship, discretely revealing her problem to a civil authority. The servant and prostitute are punished (blame), but Diego remains free, chastised but more desiring of Inés than ever (irresponsibility).

Because Inés is so intelligent, virtuous, and determined, the only way Diego can have his way with her is to render her unconscious, which he does under the spell of the Moor's magic candle that puts her in a somnolescent state. Although he is sorry she is clearly out of her senses when she comes to his bed 'because of the damned spell' (con el maldito encanto, 277), he has his way with her regardless. The candle, equivalent to the virtuous wife Camila's faint before she is raped (d2), allows Zayas to render the perfect wife unconscious at the moment of assault, since a woman's consciousness under such circumstances would imply her consent. By the time the candle is lit, Zayas has revealed Inés to be a formidable force of wit and virtue.

Zayas systematically proofs her perfect victims in one way or another. In *desengaños* 2 and 3, a dishonourable man attempts to gain the favours of a virtuous wife; when he fails, he violates her. She pays the price of his behaviour, in parallel plots that incisively illuminate the author's testing strategy. In *desengaño* 2, Carlos's wife Camila responds to Juan's aggressive attentions in accordance with social protocol, ignoring his words, ripping up his letters unread, and finally threatening him cruelly (191). Protecting her husband from the dangerous obligation to call Juan out ('por excusarle el riesgo,' 190), the young wife does not inform her husband of his onslaught, showing how she sets her spouse's wellbeing above her own. Her failure to tell Carlos about Juan's attentions, nonetheless, makes it possible to hold her responsible for not doing so, which some of the frame-tale characters do as they review the story (195). In a clear move to shake her perfect victims free of all responsibility for what others do to them, Zayas sets up a similar situation in the very next tale, in which a dishonourable nobleman pursues a married noblewoman, but has the wife, Roseleta, fully inform her husband of their impending dishonour. Her husband kills her regardless, as did Camila's.

The first phase of the wife narrative consistently posits evidence of her merit, on the one hand, and her innocence, on the other. This patterned resistance and failure reveals that it is not in spite of the virtuous wives' efforts on their own behalf but because of them that Zayas has them die, since their actions in defence of their honour, while unproductive, prove their value and bring meaning to their loss. However, by formulating the paradox of the situation in which the married woman cannot control her dishonour yet does not deserve it, Zayas demands that her readers think their way out of the trap in which she captures them, using means inaccessible to the wife characters ensnared in a no-win situation.

In baroque poetics, paradoxes are celebrated as the ultimate tropes, lauded by Gracián as 'monsters of truth' (mónstruos de la verdad, *Agudeza* 1:225). He describes 'the weightiness of opposition' (las ponderaciones de contrariedad) or 'the reconciliation of opposites' (concordancia de contrarios) as 'the concept that poses the greatest difficulty to clever intelligence' (el concepto que más le cuesta al ingenio, 1:105). According to Gracián, *concordancia de contrarios* is the proximate placement of conflicting signifiers whose meaning poses a paradox but is saved from falling into irreconcilability by an act of able wit, in an exercise as difficult as it is meritorious: 'To unite two contradictory extremes by the power of discourse is an extreme proof of subtlety' (Unir a fuerza de discurso dos contradictorios extremos, extremo arguye de sutileza, 1:105).

Elaborating on the artistic strategy of taxing a reader's brain with a text, Gracián describes narrative instances in which a character is placed in a double bind, an apparently paradoxical situation that a readerly intervention can and should reconcile. His most exalted example is precisely the corner into which Zayas paints her perfect victims, the chaste Susanna's dilemma in the face of the elders who would defile her, a popular topic in baroque art. In Origen's rendition, which Gracián cites, Susanna states, 'If I consent, I die; if I resist, I will not escape you' (*Agudeza* 1:107; fig. 3.2). This is the dilemma in which Zayas places her perfect wives, and they do die.

According to Gracián, morally repugnant dilemmas such as this one are the most praiseworthy of all *concordancias de contrarios*, for they can only be reconciled by the sharpest exercise of wit, and moreover, 'by means of a most praiseworthy disillusion' (con un bien digno desengaño, 1:107). What marks baroque paradox as artful and appropriate, then, is not the static conflict inherent in the opposition of terms, but rather the artist's ability to create a paradox whose bristling conten-

Figure 3.2 *Susanna and the Elders*, Artemisia Gentileschi, 1610. Schloss Weissenstein, Pommersfelden, Germany. Photo Marburg / Art Resource NY

tion produces improvement in the reader. The perfect victims' dilemma in the *Desengaños* is morally repugnant to an extreme that argues in favour of equally extreme gratification for the reader able to decipher the means to resolve it. This is the problem with which Zayas besets her reader after the first step of her perfect victim's waltz with death: what should one take from the experience of the wife who is doomed if she does nothing and will die if she does anything? Holding that dramatic question in painful abeyance, the reader watches as her situation only gets worse, a worsening that increases pressure on the reader to discern how the story's unfolding horrors could have been avoided.

Step Two. Mirror of a Mired World, Reluctant God

In the first step of Zayas's death trap, the virtuous wife signifies who she is, taking actions to protect her reputation or simply being perfect, lovely, and innocent. Her meaning is thus consonant with her inner and/or outer beauty and her actions, and she is neither object nor mirror of anyone or anything else. In the second and third steps, in contrast, her identity is overwhelmed and her body acquires a specular function such that it signifies who is in control of her, first the wrong-minded nobility and their minions. The wrongs done to her, always by more than one person, overwhelm her own meaning as long as she remains in the clutches of those who would make her go away as the easiest and false solution to their problem. Camila's body, poisoned, swells with the pressure of Octavia and Carlos's affair, for which she paid the price when Octavia's brother raped her to avenge his sister's dishonour; Roseleta's body bleeds to death, drained of life by Juan's uncontrolled lust, Angeliana's lies, and Roseleta's wrongly avenging husband; the flesh of Inés rots in the chimney into which her family cements her, as if to make disappear the dishonour done them by Diego's lustful aggression, and so on.

Although the corporeal violence against the virtuous wives is extreme, Zayas does not allow it to register somatically; it does not hurt, which is surprising in a text that privileges the victim's experience.[10] When King Ladislao's henchmen cut Queen Beatriz's eyes out as punishment for her presumed solicitation of the king's brother, the narrator points not to the subjective experience of the heroine but to her appearance to others, underscoring her function as a visual object whose meaning is allegorical: 'They took out her eyes, the most lovely eyes ever seen in that kingdom. She was in the power of men. How rich! To blind and to deceive is the same thing, for it is said that the person deceived is blind in that deceit' (Le sacaron los más bellos ojos que se habían visto en aquel reino. Estaba en poder de hombres. ¡Qué maravilla! Cegar y engañar parece así, en el modo, que es todo uno, pues el que está engañado se dice que está ciego de su engaño, 430–1).

As Greer suggests using the example of Inés, the wife is 'punished for the desire she aroused in others' (María 275–6), in an act of projection often portrayed in the wife murder plot. Intensifying this dissociative analysis reveals that Zayas constructs a cause and effect relationship, not between what the innocent wife does and what happens to her, but rather between what shows on her body and what her guilty tormentors believe of her. Blinding has been a penalty for adultery since biblical times and was frequently represented in baroque literature as such (Stroud 26). As the narrator says, Beatriz is neither blinded by deceit nor symbolically blind herself; she wears Federico's moral blindness and Ladislao's blindness to her innocence. It is their lack of vision that she displays to the reader, and the projected nature of her suffering protects her from the meaning of that suffering.

Failure to represent pain in circumstances when the body is deeply pained is a standard feature of Christian martyr accounts and late medieval art, both acculturated systems of representation dating from times when bodily malaise was associated with guilt and fear. Within this system of belief, only the sinful suffer illness and pain. Highly graphic renderings of the Christian martyrs' torments, which came into vogue in hagiography and the plastic arts at the end of the fifteenth century, portray the martyrs in a blissful state of impervious endurance, reflecting their power to transcend physical reality thanks to the presence of God (see fig. 3.3 and fig. 3.4). The association of pain and illness with sin and guilt continued firm into the baroque period throughout Europe, whose population was beset by inexplicable and relentless waves of plague and other uncontrollable illnesses.[11]

Baroque authors often use pain to signify sin, as in the trickster Don Juan's agonizing screams on the way to hell: 'I am burning up! / Do not burn me / with your fire!' (¡Que me abraso! No me abrases / con tu fuego! Tirso 2836–7). Taking the high-mimetic route, Zayas uses release from somatic experience to affirm the righteousness of her perfect victims. Thus, her virtuous wives sometimes endure excruciating physical suffering, but the text does not allow that they feel it. Camila's body distorts to monstrous proportions, 'her arms and legs seemed to be huge columns and her belly swelled a rod's length from her waist;

Figure 3.3 Woodcut accompanying vita of St Eulalia of Mérida, *Flos sanctorum* (Seville 1532), 254r

only her face was not swollen,' and while bed-ridden, 'she was like an apostle, speaking a thousand good counsels and giving good advice to her female servants' (sus brazos y piernas parecían unas gordísimas columnas, y el vientre se apartaba una gran vara de la cintura; sólo el rostro no tenía hinchado ... estaba como un apóstol, diciendo mil ejemplos y dando buenos consejos a sus criadas, 195.)

There is nothing monstrous about the virtuous Camila, yet according to the seventeenth-century discourse of physical malady, her physical monstrosity signifies guilt. What several guilty characters have done to her, however, is fully monstrous, including the foolishly naive Octavia, Octavia's bother Juan, Camila's husband Carlos, and Carlos's greedy father. The wife's body is the locus where those characters' actions accumulate, fester, and kill. Zayas underscores Camila's moral distance from what is happening to her body (she is not guilty and she is not afraid), by disavowing the pain Camila's body clearly endures, driving a signifying wedge between the woman herself and the meaning of her tumefied limbs and torso. The normal dimensions of her head, distinct

Figure 3.4 Xylograph accompanying vita of St Barbara by Martín de Lilio. *Segunda parte del Flos sanctorum* (Alcalá: 1558), 142r

from the rest of her, reinforce the dislocation of the wife from what is wrongly done to her.[12]

Even when stylizing the dying wife as a martyr less obviously, Zayas hyperbolizes her agonies without hint of the character's physical discomfort. As she reaches the end of her ability to endure her enclosure in the chimney of her house, Inés's lament is not of the pain produced by the rotting of her flesh to the bone, but rather the injustice of her situation: 'How, Lord, do you permit that they usurp your justice, punishing with their cruelty that which you, Lord, will not punish?' (¿Cómo, Señor, permites que te usurpen tu justicia, castigando con su crueldad lo que tú, Señor, no castigarás? 284). Her brief complaint of 'pains and misfortunes' (dolores y desdichas, 285) solders the loss of her physical well-being to her ontological anguish, for she feels completely abandoned by God.

In this fashion, Zayas divorces the signifier of virtue – the wife – from her authentic, subjective identity – honourable woman – and uses her body to mean the moral state of those around her, who are corrupt, metaphorically blind, and lacking integrity, graphically drawing the consequence of ignoble behaviour into view where it can horrify her reader. She thus uses the wife's body to make evident the only thing that is right under those circumstances: the revelation of what is wrong. Neither male characters nor unmarried female characters of the *Desengaños* lose their ability to signify themselves to this extreme, nor do they perish in the ritualized, protracted but painless fashion in which the perfect wives do.

SINNER SAINTS AND WIVES

The reader sensitized to the hagiographic poetics of displaced signification explicit in the perfect victims' sufferings awakens to another set of hagiographic attributes that Zayas attaches to them. These are the icons of the classic female sinner saints, including Mary of Egypt, Mary Magdalen, Theodora, and Thaïs, all women who transgress the sexual norms for women of their society and devote long periods of their lives thereafter to penance. Not coincidentally, the legenda of all these female saints hold them responsible for their sins of the flesh as well as men's inability to resist them. The abbot who seeks to move St Thaïs to abandon her life of exuberant sexuality reminds her, 'You must account to God for not only your soul but for those who sin because of you' (tienes que dar razón a Dios no solamente de tu ánima mas de los que pequen por ti, Voragine 136r).

Most obviously adorned in this fashion is the mute Elena (d4), who bears the penitential icons of Mary of Egypt and Mary Magdalen, reformed sinners whose primary signifying feature in the Catholic tradition was repentance.[13] Indeed, in the early modern hagiography, the Magdalen was credited with initiating the sacrament of reconciliation, or confession, which is institutionalized regret. As Jesuit hagiographer Pedro de Rivadeneira has it, Mary Magdalen is a mirror of repentance ('espejo de penitencia') whose first encounter with Christ is in the Bible, 'so that with this example of bitter grief and penitence, we regulate our own, and, because of what she did to cleanse her sins, we might know what we should do with ours' (para que con este ejemplo de tan amargo llanto y penitencia, regulemos nosotros la nuestra, y por lo que ella hizo para lavar sus pecados, sepamos lo que en los nuestros debemos hacer, 479a).[14] By associating her virtuous wives with these portraits of sorrow, Zayas intensifies their already specular function, using each one to image behaviour appropriate for the person looking at her. Having signified who she is and lost the battle against vice, she continues to fight for virtue by horrifying the spectator with vice's pernicious residue.

This dynamic is especially visible in the figure of Elena, whom Zayas paints though the eyes of the young visitor Martín. He watches in astonishment as Elena crawls out of the wall enclosure in which Jaime keeps her locked, 'so very beautiful, to such a great extreme, that Don Martín decided that this woman exceeded all the beautiful women he had seen, but was so thin and colourless, that she seemed more dead than alive, or gave indications that her death was immanent' (tan hermosísima, con tan grande extremo, que juzgó don Martín ... que ... excedía a todas, mas tan flaca y sin color, que parecía más muerta que viva, o que daba muestras de su cercana muerte, 236). Although born to the highest nobility, the tearful Elena wears nothing but sackcloth with a rope belt, her hair modestly covered with a crude linen cloth.

The drama intensifies: 'In her hands (which looked like flakes of white snow), she held a skull. Don Martín, deeply moved at seeing strings of crystalline pearls drop from her lovely eyes, determined that if the quality of her beauty were so manifest in that clothing, in more exquisite attire she would be a portent of world class. And when she arrived close to the table, she went under it' (Traía en sus hermosas manos [que parecían copos de blanca nieve] una calavera. Juzgó don Martín, harto enternecido de verla destilar de sus hermosos ojos sartas de cristalinas perlas, que si en aquel traje se descubrían tanto los quilates de su belleza, que en otro más precioso fuera asombro del mundo; y como llegó cerca de la mesa, se entró debajo de ella, 237). The fact that Elena never says a word allows Zayas to privilege the visual spectacle she provides, which grafts penitential markers of the female sinner saints onto the idealized female body of the European poetic tradition, in a baroque juxtaposition of opposites (see fig. 3.5).[15] The overlay suggests what is right (Elena's loveliness) horribly blended with something very wrong (the attributes of the prostitute saints). Further evidence indicates that Zayas was working this overlay into a poetics, the better to realize her book's objectives.

The high-born, virtuous Camila, raped by the brother of her husband's former lover, emerges from that violation wearing the same iconography. Dressed in plain, thick wool used for mourning clothes, the young wife sheds endless tears and dares not raise her head (d2 194–5). Similarly, Beatriz spends years in a cave retreat, wearing penitential garb and surrounded by Magdalenic icons: a crucifix, a scourge, a book, and an isolated landscape (d9, see fig. 3.6). Zayas hyperbolizes this iconography for Beatriz, providing her with a very large cross and an entire library, including books of hours and saints' lives (in which Beatriz could presumably read her own story, 454).

The female sinner saints, who did commit transgressions, exemplify what to do *after* having gravely sinned. Soldered to these figures, Elena, Camila, and Beatriz do not mean themselves in these penitential details, for none of these women has done any wrong. Others, however, wrongly accuse them of having done so. What those others have done to them, moreover, cries out for admission, repentance, and reconciliation. By embracing regret and exercising purgation, Zayas's perfect victims become specular, objectified female characters whose final moments in the world are devoted to communicating a corrective message to the very individuals responsible for their demise.

Zayas's most complex hagiographic manipulation is the tale of Inés (d5), the *desengaño* for which scholars have not identified any textual precedent, but in which Zayas's seventeenth-century readers would have heard strong echoes of the legenda of two popular female sinner saints, Theodora of Alexandria and Thäis. Lisis refers to Theodora when she contrasts that saint's disposition to live an entire life in penance for having been unfaithful to her husband, with real women's unwillingness to do the same: 'For one no longer finds a St Theodora of Alexandria at every step, who for just one mistake she made at her husband's expense, did so many years of penance' (Que no se hallan ya

Figure 3.5 *Saint Mary of Egypt*, José de Ribera, 1651. Museo Filangieri, Naples, Italy. Scala / Art Resource, NY

Figure 3.6 *Mary Magdalen in the Desert*, Bartolomé Murillo, 1665–75.
Museenköln, Cologne, Germany

a cada paso Santas Teodoras Alexandrinas, que por solo un yerro que cometió contra su esposo, hizo tantos años de penitencia, 332).

The version of the St Theodora legend from which Zayas borrows appears in the same late fifteenth-century *Leyenda de los santos* from which she culled the other hagiographic components in the *Desengaños*. In this romance legend, the protagonist is a noble, beautiful wife of a wealthy man. The devil, piqued by her saintly behaviour, makes another man fall in love with her, and this man sends her letters and gifts, to no avail. Observing his minion's failure, the devil provides him with an enchantress, who manages to do what the human man could not: she convinces Theodora that God does not see deeds committed at night. Foolishly naive, Theodora sleeps with her lover under the cover of darkness. Subsequently in great distress, she seeks out an abbess, who informs her that God sees everything. In despair over her sin, Theodora dresses as a man, joins a nearby monastery, professes, and quickly acquires renown as a holy man (Voragine [1472] 131v–2r).[16]

Zayas nests the first part of Theodora's vita into *desengaño* 5, which describes the temptation of Inés, leaving all the basic components of the narrative intact: the virtuous wife happily married, desired by another man whose efforts to access her are ineffective until he joins forces with an evil practitioner of magic, after which he succeeds. Unlike her saintly counterpart, however, Inés does not submit to the inopportune desire of Diego and stands firm in her virtue. Where the saint's life inscribes female debility in the face of carnal temptation, Zayas inscribes resistance, and has Inés go down against her will.

As Inés's problems intensify, the author weaves another penitent sinner saint from the romance tradition into her tale. The spectacle of the young wife's body, emerging from the chimney in which her family kept her immured for six years on a diet of bread and water, is laden with hyperbolic epithet. The author completely exposes Inés and everything her abused body represents, describing her blue eyes blinded by extended darkness, her previously golden hair turned white as snow, her scalp aboil with vermin, her bones protruding from her skin, which is pale as death itself. But that is not all; her abundant tears have worn tracks into her skin and her clothes are 'turned to ashes, so that most of her body was visible; her feet and legs bared, for her body's excrement, since she had no place else to go, had not only consumed but eaten her flesh itself down to the muscles with wounds and worms, of which the putrid place was full' (hechos ceniza, que se le veían las más partes de su cuerpo; descalza de pie y pierna, que de los excrementos de su cuerpo, como no tenía dónde echarlos, no sólo se habían consumido, mas la propia carne comida hasta los muslos de llagas y gusanos, de que estaba lleno el hediondo lugar, 287).

Similar to the description of the beautiful and skeletal Elena and resonating with the blinding of Beatriz, this passage contains horribly inverted tropes of life-giving female beauty – golden hair, clear and light eyes, rosy cheeks and luminous complexion – that Zayas wrenches from European love lyric and skins alive. Inés's body is 'hyper-present' (Routt 618) and overwhelming. It is the picture of wrong, radically disassociated from the meaning of Inés herself.

In European folklore, excrement is associated with the diabolic (Scribner), and its corruption of Inés's lovely flesh points straight to the moral corruption in which she has wrongly been mired, on the surface by the Moorish enchanter's unholy spell (blame), but in fact by Diego's uncontrolled lust and her family's failure to distinguish the innocent wife from what has been done to her against her will (irresponsibility). Eaten by parasites, Inés's skin manifests the vicious consumption of her waged by Diego, his low-class accomplices, and Inés's nobly born family. The chimney from which she emerges barely alive inverts the symbolic virtue of the hearth, with its archetypical associations of nourishment, warmth, and comfort, in tandem with Inés's wrongly inverted meaning.

The hagiographic source to which Zayas harkens in this episode is the romance vita of Thaïs, a pagan sinner saint who willingly and knowingly engaged in excesses of the flesh; her legend opens declaring, 'St Thaïs was a public woman' (Santa Thaïs fue mujer pública, Voragine 136r); a 'public woman' was an indecorous one. After her conversion to virtue, Thaïs allows herself to be shut into a tiny cell to do penance for sins she did in fact commit. The source vita describes the purifying actions of Abbot Panucio on behalf on the sinner, as he locks her into a monastic cell and arranges for her to be fed a minimum of bread and water. As he departs, Thaïs asks, 'Father, where do you order me to do that which nature demands and needs be done?' He replies, 'Here in your cell, just as you have deserved' (Padre, ¿dó me mandáis hacer aquello que demanda y ha menester la natura? … Aquí en tu celda, así como tú lo mereciste, Voragine 136r). Thaïs, converted to Christian ethics, cleanses herself of sin for three years, enclosed with her own body's waste that symbolizes her affiliation with the demonic. Thereafter, God informs the abbot that her penance has earned forgiveness, and the redeemed Thaïs, not at all disfigured, 'lived fifteen years in God's service, and thereafter died and went to paradise' (vivió quince años en servicio de Dios, y después murió y fuése al paraíso, Voragine 136v).

The contrast with Inés is clear in Zayas's secularizing transformation of the convent cell into the chimney and her radical alteration of the narrative's meaning. Like St Theodora, St Thaïs wilfully and wrongfully indulges in fleshly pleasure. In contrast, Zayas repeatedly describes Diego's enchanted intercourse with Inés as rape and the consequence of diabolical influence, external to the heroine: 'forzada de algún espíritu diabólico,' she succumbs to 'la fuerza del encanto,' and goes to Diego 'como quien era llevada por el espíritu maligno' (forced/raped by some diabolic spirit; the force/rape of the spells; as one taken by a malignant spirit, 277; 277; 279, emphasis added). Thaïs went joyfully to where Inés is forced to go, not only to bed with a man not her husband, but into isolation with her own excrement for having done so.

According to the theology their vitae represent, Mary of Egypt, Mary Magdalen, Theodora, and Thaïs not only deserve and rightly seek the penitential extremes to which they are subjected, but those extremes make possible their salvation, and thereby the salvation of all other sinners who follow their model. Camila, Elena, Inés, and Beatriz do not perform repentance, they model it for the guilty who behold their stories. In this way the Desengaños effectively invert hagiographic poetics: although dressed like saints, Zayas's dying and dead wives do not call readers to imitation and positive admiration, but rather to effect what change is necessary to avoid their suffering and death.

By systematizing the punishment of the innocent, Zayas produces a potent display of what happens when the innocent woman is conflated with the guilty one; this is part of her second narrative objective. She does not release the wife's subjective state until the man in charge of her misinterprets her, making the mistake even clearer. Vice belonging to others crawls its way over her body as she is done away with, in corporeal metaphors of society's decay and brokenness that reflect the nobility's severed relationship to the ideal: she is poisoned and her body swells, discolours, then dies (Camila, d2), life is slowly drained out of her as she bleeds to death (Roseleta, d3; Blanca, d7), starved of food, air, and light, she slowly expires (Elena, d4), her flesh rots on her bones, enclosed in darkness and embedded in excrement (Inés, d5), her body is stabbed so many times it lies bathed in its own blood (Mencía, d8; Magdalena, d10), her head is severed from her body and both are cast into dark enclosures (Ana, d8); her eyes are put out and she is violently pursued for crimes she did not commit (Beatriz, d9). The overwhelming wrong done to the perfect victim costs her capacity to mean herself, and her apparent passivity in the face of her own demise is a hagiographic signifier that declares her innocence. That passivity is not the consequence of the wife's desire to live or die, but rather the manifestation of how she has already lived.

By the time the reader has passed through the setup and sufferings of each perfect victim, the solution to the paradox that their situations present begins to reveal itself. The intense impossibility of their situations manifests not only the systematic torment of goodness by a people born to much better standards, but the irrevocable nature of the damage such treatment does. Once the good wife is dishonoured, nothing and no one can save her. There are two possible ways out of this dilemma, one traditional and the other, taken by Zayas.

Gracián cites the traditional solution to the dishonoured woman's paradox, which is for her to embrace death as heroic evidence of her virtue. He elaborates this thinking, following Origen: To be a corrupt person is what it really means to die. But to suffer and die at the hand of corruption is not death, 'for in virtue lies immortality' (Si consentís, no moriréis, antes al contrario. ... que en la corrupción de la torpeza está la muerte, y en la pureza la inmortalidad, *Agudeza* 1:107). 'Die,' is the message, 'but do not interpret that death as defeat, for in fact it is victory.'

Zayas, bound to defend the subjective rights of noblewomen, rejects the notion that the death of a good woman for someone else's misbehaviour is a good thing. The only way out of what the tales describe again and again is to avoid the dishonour in the first place, which directs the reader straight to her book's objectives of noble reform. The perfect victims provide explicit proof that if noblewomen respect themselves but noblemen do not, and the nobility as a whole fails to reform, the good wife and everything she represents will disappear.

For Origen's solution to work, the text must invoke a morality according to whose standards life eternal is more important and better than life on earth. Without denying the supremacy of one's eternal fate, Zayas powerfully reinforces the wrongness of innocent women's death by absenting God during their torments and inscribing on their bodies a potent contrast between martyrdom and murder.

THE RELUCTANT GOD

Zayas's first readers would have noticed the difference between the isolation from God in which the perfect victims of the *Desengaños* endure their torments and the unison with God in which authentic saints endure theirs. When the authentic martyr cries out for help, God listens, and most often does not need to be called in the first place. As soon as the Romans strip St Inés naked, God immediately cloaks her body: 'She was immediately covered with hair as if by clothing' (Fue luego cubierta de cabellos como de vestiduras, Voragine 40v). Many romance vitae of female saints stage a serial display of God's presence and power over the body of the woman to which the pagans seek access. After God repeatedly restores St Agueda's body throughout her lengthy torments, which include the cutting off of her breasts, the saint asks to die, an event she envisions in most positive terms: 'Take my soul and make me go to your glory' (Toma la mi ánima y hazme ir a la tu gloria). The response is immediate: 'And saying this, she died and went to paradise' (Y diciendo esto, finóse y fuese para paraíso, Voragine 61v). The cries of Zayas's dying wives, in contrast, go unheard, creating immense anguish for the reader who wonders why God keeps missing his cue.

The case of Inés is paradigmatic, if the most extreme. As her nocturnal and unconscious sexual liaisons with Diego continue, the young wife's distress intensifies, for she remembers their trysts as one would a dream and awakens every morning exhausted. God appears indifferent to her circumstances as her terrible situation fails to improve, 'neither by commending herself, as she did, to God, nor by taking recourse in her confessor, who consoled her as much as possible, and she desired that her husband come as soon as possible, to see if with his presence her sadness could find a remedy' (ni por encomendarse, como lo hacía, a Dios, ni por acudir a menudo a su confesor, que la consolaba, cuanto era posible, y deseaba que viniese su marido, por ver si con él podía remediar su tristeza, 279). Inés's husband does not come home to help her, and when he does he discredits her, and without him or God she is completely undone.

The young wife's pleas to the divinity intensify while she is cemented into the chimney, where she continues imploring for succour, and her prayers go unheeded for six long years. She is 'always crying and begging God to relieve her from such a pitiable martyrdom ... ever lamenting her misfortune and calling upon God to help her' (siempre llorando y pidiendo a Dios la aliviase de tan penoso martirio ... siempre estaba lamentando su desdicha y llamando a Dios que la socorriese, 283–4). The text specifies that Inés's isolation is total. Having removed her from all human contact, her family separates her from symbolic contact with God as well, leaving her 'tyrannized by lack of access to the divine sacraments and hearing Mass' (tiranizada a los divinos sacramentos y a oír misa, 284). God appears deaf to the poor woman's cries, so much so that she desires death, but hangs onto life for the sake of her soul and so as *not* to challenge the wisdom of God: 'What I fear is not death, which I rather desire; losing my soul is my greatest fear' (lo que temo no es la muerte, que antes la deseo; perder el alma es mi mayor temor, 285–6). It is, in fact, not God but God's supposed human agents, the nobility, who have abandoned the virtuous wife to die. In the sacred narrative, God appears promptly to succour his own. In the secular narrative, the dying woman lingers on through prolonged suffering, alone.

As Inés's prayers go unheeded, death begins to stalk her. This allows Zayas to plot the wife's apparent distance from God at its greatest extreme, a distance that serves not as a measure of God's wisdom or power, but of how far the woman in the chimney is from the functional nobility who should be God's agents on earth. After withholding the divinity from Inés throughout the course of her protracted torments, the narrator reveals that, in fact, God was in control of things all along: 'God wished to give her suffering and save her life that she not die in desperation there, and so that such a rabid wolf as her brother, and such a cruel basilisk as her husband, and such a cruel lioness as her sister-in-law, bring about their punishment themselves' (Quiso Dios darla sufrimiento y guardarle la vida, porque no muriese allí desesperada, y para que tan rabioso lobo como su hermano, y tan cruel basilisco como su marido, y tan rigurosa leona como su cuñada, ocasionasen ellos mismos su castigo, 288). Inés pays the price of God's (Zayas's) decision to protract her torments, the better to exact justice of her tormentors.

Zayas's persistent creation of extreme, violent suffering for her perfect victims is not gratuitous, masochistic, or sadistic, nor is it designed to simply scandalize. It inscribes those sufferings in the reader's experience of the text by assaulting the virtuous in intense, compounded ways that mimics the pressure suffered by virtuous women captive to the malicious nobility. Suffering such as theirs has a teleological, moral function in that the greater that suffering, the more punishment deserved by those who wrongly persecute them. Its function is also aesthetic, for those trials provoke the greatest possible anguish in the reader, who must watch in horror as the power of wrong assaults the bodies of the innocent in multiple ways and over protracted periods of time.

Had Zayas allowed heaven to intervene on behalf of her perfect victims any earlier, she would have greatly reduced the power of the horrors produced by the ignoble nobility and thereby reduced the effectiveness of her narrative to reach her objective of societal reform. If God descends, whether through a hero, a twist of plot guided by the divine hand, or any other supernatural means, the portrait of earthly chaos is reduced and the responsibility of humanity is less: if God will solve the problem, then the misguided nobility need not do it. In the interests of intensifying the need for change, Zayas extends and intensifies not only her characters' sufferings, but also their unheard cries for help. Dancing on the edge of modernity's notion that God in fact might not be there at all, Zayas pushes the divinity as far out of her narrative as possible, hanging onto the ontology of Catholic belief by a thin but unbreakable thread. It is because Zayas needs God restrained to the very limits of her suffering characters' mortal existence that she affirms God's will that their suffering go on as long as it does. She could have stopped those sufferings at any moment, had she so chosen.

It is precisely at the nexus of divinity and humanity, where transcendence needs to happen, that Zayas unleashes her secular paradigm from the holy one. Christ and the martyrs, empowered by God, can mediate the sins of the world because they have power and transcendent meaning and, within the sacred context, they signify what is right. Zayas's perfect victims are not empowered to do anything but suffer and then disappear. In a book whose plots strive toward marriage, this disempowerment enhances the book's focus on the human social economy, not the divinity.

Zayas consistently describes the sufferings of her innocent wives as martyrdom and sacrifice. Lisarda says, 'Camila lived like a martyr' (Camila vivía mártir (d2 195); Lisis describes Roseleta's end as 'that martyrdom' (aquel martirio, d3 223); Martín assures Jaime that heaven will give Elena 'reward for her martyrdom' (el premio de su martirio, d4 253); Blanca is 'the innocent lamb ... innocent victim sacrificed by the rigour of such cruel enemies' (la inocente corderilla ... inocente víctima sacrificada en el rigor de tan crueles enemigos, 361).[17] Lisis's revelation of Christian martyr tales as the fabric from which the narrators cut their stories establishes the importance of hagiography in the book (504). However, the *desengaños* make it clear that although that fabric may have been holy, the garment into which Zayas's book sewed those accounts is not.

For the martyr paradigm to function, the group that persecutes the martyr must be Other in relationship to the martyr's beliefs, as the pagans were Other to the Christians. Zayas's dysfunctional nobility is not Other to the women it persecutes; it has merely strayed from the ideals embodied by those women. The *Desengaños* do not bleed for radical change, but for reform – a return to what was. Zayas's victim characters are secular martyrs, bereft of transcendent meaning because they live under the control of the seriously flawed humanity unable to recognize its own values in the women it kills.

Step Three. Gone: The Beautiful Dead

Zayas makes no secret of her overt manipulation of her perfect victim's appearance to serve her artistic ends, correlating physical loveliness and noble virtue with startling metatextuality. The narrator Francisca says that Mencía had to be beautiful, because 'it seems that misfortune evokes greater compassion in the beautiful woman than in the ugly virtuous one' (parece que compadece más la desdicha en la hermosa que en la fea virtuosa, 372), adding immediately thereafter that the combination of nobility, beauty, wealth, and virtue is so astonishing in a woman that it works like a magnet that draws people in ('parece que por lo admirable de ver juntas en una mujer nobleza, hermosura, riqueza y virtud, no sólo admira, mas es imán que se lleva tras sí las voluntades,' 372). Zayas's devil, frustrated by Beatriz's ability to win the hearts of everyone around her, complains to Prince Federico that beauty 'is a spell that moves everyone to mercy' (es un hechizo la hermosura que a todos mueve a piedad, 451).

The power of a beautiful woman was a standard literary tool, visible in texts such as Lorenzo de Ayala's 1603 adaptation of Bandello's novellas in which he describes female beauty as 'the most natural and truest magnet known … it draws souls unto itself' (la más natural y verdadera piedra imán que se sabe … atrae a sí los ánimos, 191). Cervantes puts a class spin on the topic, of which Zayas takes full advantage. Don Quijote declares, 'In good blood beauty gleams and glows more gloriously, more perfectly, than it does in beauty which is humbly born' (Sobre la buena sangre resplandece y campea la hermosura con más grados de perfección que en las hermosas humildemente nacidas, 897).

The *Desengaños* represent what the virtuous wife is worth in the third step of her story, when the divinity swoops down on her dying or dead body and speaks the ultimate truth through her by transforming her mutilated limbs into radiant beauty before whisking her away. Whereas Zayas does not mark the bodies of the imperfect victim with supernatural features, even though one of them dies (Laurela), she consistently dresses those of her perfect victims in exaggerated loveliness. All of the nine perfect victims exit the narrative in this fashion, and no other characters do so.

Inés and Beatriz, the two wives in the *Desengaños* who survive their torments only to disappear from sight, evidence the most radical transformation from abused flesh to corporeal perfection (d5, d9). After having used their bodies to portray what is wrong, Zayas ultimately employs them to reveal what is right by inverting their physical degradation, moving them from the control of vice to that of the ultimate good. That fact that these are the two characters most intimately affiliated with saints enhances their idealization, when in their final transformation Zayas allows her reluctant God to speak through their flesh.

Remarkably, when Inés is finally removed from the chimney of her house, her beauty blossoms like a cactus flowering in warm rain. Cared for by interventionist agents of goodness (her kindly neighbour, civic and religious authorities), she is completely healed except for the blindness that has no cure, and upon being put in the convent, she acquires renown as 'among the most beautiful women there are in the kingdom of Andalusia' (de las más hermosas mujeres que hay en el reino del Andalucía, 288). The transformation could not be more extreme: Zayas has taken Inés's body to the depths of degradation and corruption, walked it to the edge of life, and finally raised it to be a paragon of loveliness, all in tandem with who controls that body. In the process, Inés herself – the feisty, intelligent, and virtuous wife – quietly disappears. Once she is dishonoured, Inés is never released from enclosure nor does she act on her own behalf, but rather passes from two destructive enclosures (Diego's house, then the chimney) to one that is protective (the convent). This affirms that Zayas was not interested in female autonomy per se; she uses the female body as a device to measure and expose the moral environment in which the woman is living. Her scheme allows her to fictionalize one of her book's moral precepts by measuring the worth of the male nobility in terms of how its members treat noblewomen. That treatment contrasts sharply with what those noblewomen deserve, which God articulates with indisputable authority as each perfect victim exits the tale.

The story of Beatriz contains a similar transformation of an even greater degree, for Zayas intensified the sacred signifiers and romance magic of St Beatriz's vita. In a detail she added at the tale's end, when King Ladislao becomes aware of the grievous wrong he did his wife and regrets it, the high-mimetic power of his repentance is manifest on his wife's body when Beatriz's flesh recovers the exact appearance it had at the story's outset, jewels and all, as if none of her many trials had ever transpired. The minute the queen identifies herself to her repentant husband, 'she saw herself, and everyone saw her, with the royal garments that she took from the palace when she was led away to have her eyes put out ... not a single jewel missing from those that the huntsmen took from her; as whole in her beauty as before, without the sun or the air – although she spent eight years in the cave – having aged her beauty a single minute' (se vio, y la vieron todos, con los reales vestidos que sacó de palacio cuando la llevaron a sacar los ojos ... sin faltar ni una joya de las que le quitaron los monteros; tan entera en su hermosura como antes, sin que el sol, ni el aire, aunque estuvo ocho años en la cueva, la hubiese ajado un minuto de su belleza, 465). Like Inés, Beatriz loses her signifying autonomy after her husband rejects her. Thereafter she serves as the instrument through which the devil and the divinity contest their power and in the end, disappears in a blaze of beauty and material splendour with which heaven endorses her virtue and merit.

The cadavers of the wives who completely die make an even more radical turn to beauty in narrative gestures that seem macabre now, but in baroque Spain spoke clearly and simply of the presence of God. After her father-in-law orders his surgeon to begin bleeding his son's wife to death, Blanca faints away, 'so beautifully that it would have moved to pity the one who most abhorred her' (tan hermosamente, que diera lástima a quien más la aborreciera, 363). Beauty radiates through her dying body and into the earthly realm, where it harkens her wrongminded husband to reconsider his ways. The faint and loss of blood give her an extreme pallor, the height of Spanish baroque attractiveness, which Zayas reinforces with her name, which means 'white.'[18]

Blanca's post-mortem loveliness is so great, 'tan linda' is she, so beautifully does she die, that her husband is compelled to try and stop the murder, swearing to his father, 'I give you my word that, as long as I have known Blanca she has not seemed more lovely to me than now. For the sake of this beauty her daring deserves pardon' (Os doy palabra que, cuanto ha que conozco a Blanca no me ha parecido más linda que ahora. Por esta hermosura merece perdón su atrevimiento, 363).[19] Although Zayas represents Blanca as beautiful from the beginning, it is in death that she is *most* beautiful and only then is she able to move her husband away from vice, when heaven is speaking through her. Four years later, the young wife's corpse is returned to Spain, disinterred, and found to be 'as lovely as if she had just died, a sign of the glory the soul enjoys' (tan lindo como si entonces acabara de morir [señal de la gloria que goza el alma], 364). As the nobly born characters' ignobility requires the reinforcement of the lower classes and evil to be effective, so virtue is only empowered when it bears the stamp of heaven.

Zayas gifts all of her virtuous wife characters with the same beauty as they exit the secular social economy, if not with long narrative flourishes then with clipped ones. Of Roseleta, bled to death by her husband, the narrator says, 'They found the lovely lady dead, and since she had been bled, she was the most beautiful thing that human eyes had ever seen' (hallaron la hermosa dama muerta, que como se había desangrado, estaba la más bella cosa que los ojos humanos habían visto, d3 221). Gaspar finds Magdalena's cadaver where it lies in her bloody bed, 'with so much beauty that it seemed a marble statue sprinkled with the rosy hue of dawn' (con tanta hermosura, que parecía una estatua de marfil salpicada de rosicler, d20 482). Elena's death position is iconic, her arms and fingers cruciform and 'her face, although thin and wan, so lovely that she looked like an angel' (el rostro, aunque flaco y macilento, tan hermoso, que parecía un ángel, 252).

Although Mencía's death is recounted quickly, her undead corpse lingers in life. When her secret husband Enrique comes to steal her away from her avaricious family, he meets with a supernatural spectacle. The minute his hand touches her door, it loudly swings open, revealing a closed room inexplicably filled with light. Seeking its source, he finds 'the beautiful lady stretched out on the *estrado* in disarray, bathed in blood, which although she had been dead since noon, flowed then from the wounds as if they had just been delivered, and next to her a lake of the bloody humour' (la hermosa dama tendida en el estrado, mal compuesta, bañada en sangre, que con estar muerta desde mediodía, corría entonces de las heridas, como si se las acabaran de dar, y junto a ella un lago del sangriento humor, 382).[20]

Mencía's luminous cadaver warns Enrique to flee the wrath of her brother, and her speaking corpse recalls the miraculously resuscitated body of the thief who saves Juan's life in *desengaño* 3,[21] as it anticipates the cadaver whose moans call Gaspar away from the danger into which his association with an immoral woman has put his soul in *desengaño* 10. By trespassing the threshold that rightly separates life and death, these undead corpses point to the behavioural boundary wrongly crossed by the living and are cautionary voices from heaven. Mencía's body continues undead a year later, when Enrique moves her cadaver into a tomb. He then finds her 'so beautiful that it seemed that death had no jurisdiction over her beauty' (tan hermosa, que parecía no haber tenido jurisdicción la muerte en su hermosura, 385).

Ana's death, in the same tale as Mencía's, is particularly gruesome and reminiscent of a Christian martyr's last moment. The young wife, unaware of her husband's plan to murder her to get back into the good graces of his greedy father, innocently follows him into a private garden (d8). Alonso steps behind her and cuts off her head, after which he and his companion Marco Antonio stuff her body down a well, then bury her head in a seaside cave (see fig. 3.7). God's justice catches up with Alonso, says the narrator, and when he is caught stealing stockings from a store, his other crimes come to light. On the scaffold about to be executed for having killed his sister and his wife, the terrified man has Ana's severed head dug up and brought to him. It is found to be 'as fresh and lovely as if it had not been buried in the earth for six months' (tan fresca y hermosa como si no hubiera seis meses que estaba debajo de tierra, 397).

In the fictional world of the *Desengaños*, bereft of heroes, heaven speaks to human beings through the dead. The metamorphosis from abused body to paragon of beauty is clearly a justiciary moment when God intervenes to pronounce a divine verdict of innocence in the case of each perfect victim. Moreover, the exalted loveliness in which Zayas encases the corpses of her perfect victims publicizes what the corrupt society on earth has lost, which is virtue, traditionally and strongly affiliated with beauty.[22]

MEANING AND DEATH

Zayas goes the tradition one more, however, by endowing her appealing corpses with a double charge, one of virtue, and one of appealing female flesh, whose augmented attractiveness she displays exactly at the moment when God removes them. Her text calculates the loss of the wife's enduring desirability in human society's earthly terms, allowing heaven to make off with all the perfect women in the book, who are most lovely when they are gone. This poetics allows Zayas to perform, nine times, a literary comeuppance and settling of accounts, as if saying to the grossly imperfect nobility, 'Behold the price of your behaviour.'

This second, earthy meaning is explicit in how Zayas swerves her borrowings from hagiography away from the sacred narrative at the very last moment, for although the final beauty of Zayas's dying and dead women is supernatural, it does not follow the pattern of hagiography. Martyr saints in early modern hagiographies may die in blazes of

Figure 3.7 Illustration of *desengaño* 6 by Eric Fraser, from the 1963 Sturrock translation

light and pools of flowing blood, but they are not stunningly beautiful in death. The hyperbolic appeal of Zayas's dead wives is her personal touch, a symbol of the wives' virtue that the unworthy world rejects and the author's proclamation of exactly what the corrupt world has lost. Thus, in the *Desengaños* the point is not that the most beautiful woman is a dead woman. The point is that God marks the body of the woman wrongly tormented and/or killed as worthy by bestowing on her flesh what her world most esteems, which is physical loveliness.

The beauty of Zayas's female cadavers rightly alarms readers today, who see it chained to the debilitating if not pornographic twisting of women into objects. However, as Jehenson and Welles observe, 'the intense anxiety the denigration elicits is not associated with sexual orgasm but with pathos and sympathetic identification' (187). Having already witnessed how Zayas employs the female body to register the moral dysfunction of individuals around her, it is easier to observe her objectifying that same body again, but at the idealizing end of the mimetic spectrum, using post-mortem loveliness as poetic justice. The perfect victim becomes most beautiful precisely when no one will ever again enjoy her for, whether dead or in the convent, she is gone. The punishment is thus perfectly suited to the crime, for what is lost is what is desired: tantalizing physical appeal that disappears, taking virtue with it from a world that has lost its purchase on correct behaviour.

Cultural historians define the function of beauty since early modern times as a commodity that makes a woman visible (Nahoum-Grappe 86), and in her close-ups of her dying and dead perfect victims, Zayas needs them to be more visible than ever. Moreover, as Nahoum-Grappe states, 'Beauty was also an unreliable but effective tool for social action, especially when women were prevented from using other tools (whether legal, cultural, economic, or political)' (95). Because Zayas ties the hands of her female characters in order to make them the most highly prized women imaginable to the dominant group, beauty is their most valuable resource, and the author invokes it to the greatest extreme at the moment when they disappear. The final statement made by their beauty, however symbolic of virtue it may be, is configured in the language of the earthly social economy. Their physical appeal speaks not of God's gain but rather of humanity's loss, cutting off the transcendent meaning of the hagiographic texts that she so ably utilizes in their stories.

Grieve suggests that Zayas's use of the female martyr's life is subversive: 'According to Zayas, women should reject the secular martyrdom sanctioned by society's view of civilized behavior – marriage – and seek refuge in the communities of women afforded by the convents' (104). Pons, in contrast, finds that because hagiography is a rhetorical system whose purpose is to consolidate belief, it was more productive for Zayas to use it 'straight' rather than subversively (595). Further consideration suggests that, although the material and diegetic signifiers that Zayas grafts onto the bodies of her innocent noble wives are in fact hagiographic, the meaning of those signifiers when produced by the corrupt human community, instead of God, works in contrast to but not against their meaning in an authentically sacred text.

The dead wives of the *Desengaños* embody deeply lamentable incidents of ideological carelessness, of failure to abide by the divinely ordered strictures of truly noble behaviour. It is through the meaningless sacrifice of admirable yet disempowered women that Zayas brings home the consequences of that carelessness, masterfully wielding hagiography to do so. Authentic martyrs are not only ideologically Other to those persecuting them, but their lives and deaths are orchestrated and celebrated by a divinity whose kingdom promises the reward deserved by those willing and able to defy the wrong order in which they live. The believing reader of hagiography understands the death of the martyr as affirmation and justification of the reader's own faith. As such, that death is right. The saint triumphs in defying those who seek to control her, only to finally die at their hands and thereby affirm her God's superiority to all earthly paradigms. She enters the conflict with a desire to die firmly and rightly in place.

Returning once more to the fifteenth-century *Leyenda de los santos* from which Zayas extracted the hagiographic components of the *Desengaños*, we find authentically sacred martyr stories. For example, the young saint Eulalia secretly abandons her parents' house and travels to Barcelona, where she enters the throne room of Diocletian. Aflame with conviction and ready to perish for it, she begins to provoke him. Diocletian responds to her insults, demanding, 'And who are you who speak to the judge so insanely and presumptuously?' She retorts, 'I am Eulalia, slave and servant of my Lord Jesus Christ' (¿Y quién eres tú que tan loca y presuntuosamente al juez hablas?; Yo soy Eulalia, sierva y servidora de mi Señor Jesu Cristo, Voragine 63v).

The furious Roman orders her tortured, and after that she is burned alive. Throughout, Eulalia sings, 'Almighty God, behold me here and help me. And Lord of my soul, receive it' (Dios todopoderoso, heme aquí y ayúdame. Y Señor de mi ánima, tú la recibe). The flames engulf not her, but her persecutors, before her soul ascends to heaven in the form of a white dove (Voragine 63v). A real martyr such as Eulalia is a conscious and willing participant in this entire display, and her execution exudes meaning in the religious ontology served by the plot, which necessarily propels the story's meaning beyond the limitations of human life. In the context of the martyr tale, death is the best thing that can happen to the servant of God, and both God and the martyr ardently desire that death, which promises to supersede the defective human world and unite the martyr with the divinity itself.

Though Zayas affiliates her noble female wives with martyrs, there is something deeply troubling about them. Unlike martyrs, the wife characters are unwilling participants in the spectacle of their own sacrifice, for at the moment when the determination is made, not one of them wants to die. Any reading that respects the author's defence of female subjectivity must acknowledge and accommodate this. Inés's cries for release from her enclosure are telling, for the narrator describes her as 'ever weeping and begging God to relieve her from such a distressing martyrdom ... she was ever lamenting her misfortune and crying out to God to help her' (siempre llorando y pidiendo a Dios la aliviase de tan penoso martirio ... siempre estaba lamentando su desdicha y llamando a Dios que la socorriese, 283–4). She is on the verge of suicide, an act it is virtually impossible for an authentic martyr to commit. The dying woman declares, 'Many times I imagine making a rope with my own hands to finish myself off, but I immediately realize it is the devil, and I beg help from God to free myself from him' (Muchas veces me da imaginación de con mis propias manos hacer cuerda a mi garganta para acabarme; mas luego considero que es el demonio, y pido ayuda a Dios para librarme de él, 285–6).

Zayas abandons her virtuous spouses such as Inés to flail about in human shortcomings to the point of death, and as we have seen, withholds the divinity from them. The author uses God to bring home the difference between right and wrong on the body of the dying or dead wife, consistently making the reader wait out her suffering, and then – as late as possible – release her or her body from it. After surviving six months in her horribly swollen and disfigured body, Camila is ready to expire, not because she seeks union with God or because her death signifies a triumph over an enemy, but because she literally cannot take any more. God himself comes to get her: 'When she was alone in her bed, she heard a voice saying, "Camila, your time is now arrived." She gave thanks to God because he wanted to remove her from a life of such affliction; she received his sacraments and died the evening of the following day, to live eternally' (Estando sola en su cama, oyó una voz que decía, 'Camila, ya es llegada tu hora.' Dio gracias a Dios porque la quería sacar de tan penosa vida; recibió sus sacramentos, y otro día en la noche murió, para vivir eternamente, d2 195).[23] Waiting until Camila's endurance is exhausted, Zayas's divinity rescues her, reaffirming her identity as a highly prized and wrongly maligned wife.

Zayas designs the lingering beauty of her innocent wives to punish the living rather than exalt the glory of God. Appropriately, she restricts the desire of her fictional female characters to the most conservative parameters, in that the noble wives in the *Desengaños* are not only defined by their wish to safeguard their marriages, but their husbands' dissatisfactions of any sort, real or potential, are the only source of these perfect spouses' troubles. Perfectly submissive to the social order that Zayas represents as marriage and speaking the wrong actions of her husband and his allies, she dies meaning not her self but their error.

Designing her wives as paradigms of virtue whose interests go no farther than to please their husbands allowed Zayas to deliver the greatest impact with their elimination, and they portray something quite different from self-sacrificing Christian behaviour. Completely and remarkably bereft of any features that resist conservative notions about 'good' women, these *perfectas casadas* (perfect wives) are obedient, committed to the conservation of family honour, and abide by social strictures regarding female comportment. Inés, assaulted by Diego, loved only her husband (267); Ana is noble, chaste, retiring, and lovely (387); Elena protests to her husband of eight years that life apart from him is not life at all (248). Serving up to the dominant group precisely what conservative social ethics prescribed as the ideal wife, Zayas consistently displays how that same group tortures and eliminates the very individual it claims to desire and, as she proves, desperately needs.

However, the certain logic of hagiography, according to which earthly standards are successfully inverted by a divinity at work beyond those standards, is notably missing from the *Desengaños*. As the perfect wives suffer, Zayas's God watches in horror, not delight, 'offended and weary of enduring such enormous crimes' (ofendido y cansado de aguardar tan enormes delitos, 396). In the *Desengaños*, Zayas withholds divine intervention on behalf of the sacrificial victim until after the moment of death and beyond, precisely because the sacrifice is *not* welcome to the Catholic God; the systematic elimination of women whose sole desire is to preserve their marriages does not strive toward order, but rather away from it. The *Desengaños* thereby register wrongness precisely where rightness is required for transcendence to occur.

There is no triumph for Zayas's dead women who, unlike their model martyrs, live in a world that has no reason but its own hypocrisy for abandoning God's will. Devoid of heroic characters and an activist divinity, the *Desengaños* display the consequences of aristocratic failure to perform heroism using human beings whose imperfections the author projects onto the most innocent among them, emptying holiness itself of its rightful meaning and distancing God from creation. That distance produces the despair for which the tales are rightly famous.

A seventeenth-century Spanish Catholic would have been unable to celebrate and sanctify the victim of abuse in a book whose salient point is that such abuse is not only wrong, it is avoidable. Whereas the authentic martyr joyfully dies to witness something great, powerful, and holy, Zayas's martyrs die in witness to human failure, not in accordance with divine will but in spite of it, for nothing *except* the display of their own disappearance and the stunning darkness they leave behind. The damage inherent to their demise is precisely where Zayas uses hagiography to make her point. Although the perfect victims' heroic endurance of suffering accrues points in their individual accounts of salvation, the text makes it clear that they have been killed in an act of wrong, and their haunting corpses signal with deadly precision not the rewards of virtue but the terrible consequences of straying from it.

Although Zayas produces the sacrifice of the innocent, although she borrows hagiography's method of contrasting right behaviour (the martyr's) with wrong behaviour (the killing of the martyr), and although she celebrates the abused and/or dead flesh of the sacrificed woman, she is careful to distinguish between martyrdom and murder. Premeditated murder qualifies as sacrifice only when the gain realized by a sacrificed person's death transcends the loss of the person's life (McCracken 57). One of the greatest tributes to Zayas's literary genius is how she uses the sacrificial setup to point to its meaninglessness when wrongly enacted, signalling the dangerous loss that such wrong enactment produces. The wife characters are killed to placate the ire of the dominant group, inflamed by its own corruption. The sacred signifiers in which the author enshrouds their bodies are designed to differentiate between meaningful ritualized death orchestrated by God and the meaningless taking of human life by defective and irresponsible individuals in defiance of God's law.

Zayas's pro-women discourse reconciles with the suffering of her perfect victim characters over this distinction. In the frame tale, at a remove from her perfect victims, she argues that noblewomen should enhance their power and education. Those goals, however, can only be realized in tandem with the book's other stated objectives, which she illuminates negatively with her narrative black light, inside the tales. When noblewomen respect themselves, when noblemen respect women, and when the nobly born embrace true nobility, order will return, and with order, God himself. In accordance with her negative aesthetics and projected meaning, the perfect victims of the *Desengaños* speak not to women who should be active agents of their own lives, but to the female and male members of the nobility who have relinquished their own values and their own future in prosperity symbolized by the perfect wife.

Clearly, Zayas could not offer tales about women endowed with the subjective authenticity typical of her *Novelas amorosas* without relinquishing the chilling depths of her social critique: the lower the mimetic register of the stories, the more the innocent must suffer helplessly and die. Her passive, suffering, and virtuous characters do not represent the role that women should play in the world. They serve to draw out and display on their bodies the corruption around them, and their helplessness is an indispensable tool that Zayas wields to render the situation acutely.

On the other hand, had Zayas failed to articulate the notion that women can and should be active agents of their own destinies and resist oppression, the reader would have been left with the tales alone, risking their possible misinterpretation: women make good martyrs and inherently lack the subjective status necessary to alter the oppressive situation in which the perverse society leaves them. The appropriateness of empowering women is nullified by the author's need to represent a situation beyond hope, and the situation beyond hope necessitates the overt calls to female subjectivity positioned in the frame tales, a call that must lie outside the tales, but inside the book. True to the *concordancia de contrarios*, these concepts are mutually dependent and mutually exclusive.

The *Desengaños* are about the end of life, literal and symbolic, and Zayas's virtuous wives are by no means the only dead characters in the book. However, although many men die, only minor male characters die innocently, and each of them perishes in tandem with the wife whose fate he shares as a means to intensify the wrongness of her demise. Such, for example, are Elena's cousin, from whose skull her husband makes her drink (d4), and Magdalena's young servant, set up to look like her lover and killed for it (d10). Nor is death the only reason for the disappearance of nobly born characters in general. There are penitential protagonists of both sexes who retreat into convents and high-mimetic men who disappear into war, as well as women and men who end their lives in a convent for other reasons. The author's removal of these numerous characters from the world at large creates the same deep deficit in the secular social economy as the physically dead characters, if of a different kind. By the book's end, the final tally of high-mimetic characters who are gone creates an eerie loss. The dead wives, then, are one of several ways in which Zayas signifies the decrement of what is right in the *Desengaños*, and their deaths compound other disappearances that enhance the author's punishing removal of goodness and true nobility from human society. However, the fates of the perfect victims in that pattern are clearly the most dramatic.

Elisabeth Brönfren indicates that 'witnessing the death of the other means witnessing one's own limit and one's necessary return to the here and the self' (92). By forcing her readers to stand by as her nine perfect wives die, Zayas induces self-awareness and the critical distance crucial to baroque poetics and her narrative objectives alike. Both rely on the reader's taking a step back from the fiction to arrest the rapture of reading and turn to self-examination. Realizing that the perfect victims' deaths have no transcendent meaning and that they call the text back to earthly values, the reader can recognize that Zayas's God does not want perfect wives in life eternal, but rather in life on earth.

The removal of the good, innocent, and beautiful characters, with which the tales and the entire book ends, brings the corrupt social economy to its knees by taking away precisely what the nobility must have in order to endure. For a people who understood population as the base of wealth and power (Elliott 255), the price of ignoble behaviour as Zayas configures it is unbearably high. Making a bad situation worse, Zayas scripted yet another curtailment of the nobility's future, one that in the fictional ontology of the *Desengaños* signifies a living death. It is the convent.

Figure 4.1 *Infanta María Teresa*, Diego Velázquez, 1653. Kunsthistorisches Museum, Vienna, Austria. Erich Lessing / Art Resource, NY

4 Dead End: The Convent

There is a potential in goodbyes.
This may not be freedom,
but it feels like wine.

Imtiaz Dharker, 'Announcing the Arrival'

The characters in the *Desengaños* who die for the right reasons inscribe justice in the narrative, and the wrongly dead are a precious and select few. But not everyone dies. Carefully manipulating the ends of her characters' fictional lives, Zayas weaves a fragile thread that leads out of the dark labyrinth of misdeeds that block the paths of the innocent in the book. It is virtue, whose standards determine which characters attain the convent, her book's final ending. Whether virtuous by dint of innocence or repentance, all the virtuous characters in the *Desengaños* who reach the convent survive, at least in the flesh. However, the merits of survival, and the convent, are strictly relative and completely symbolic.

Because they are diegetically unsatisfying, the *Desengaños* move readers to determine how the ten lamentable stories could have been avoided. Zayas renders the answer particularly difficult because the end of the book – the female frame characters' retreat to the convent – constitutes a reaction to the problem, not its solution.[1] Examination of the convent motif in the *Desengaños* reveals how she musters that institution in the service of her negative aesthetics, which relies on what is not, but should be, for its foundational meaning. We must begin with the end, since characters go there reactively, in response to a failure. Those responses culminate in the final act of the book, when Lisis bedecks herself in symbols of purity, donning a white dress, lilies, pearls, and diamonds, and announces that she herself will enter the convent, after which the narrator confirms that she has done so (510).

Lisis's failure to attain her goal of marriage to Juan and her decision to enter the convent in disillusion provoke discomfort in the reader, for the young woman has neither a religious vocation nor does she plan to spend her life there: 'Lisis remained a secular member of the community' (Lisis se quedó seglar, 510). The story is not over; it has simply ended. Unwilling to subject Lisis to the dangerous world that she has crafted, Zayas has her retreat from it, making a bad decision for good reasons. The disjuncture between what the supposed heroine wants and deserves, and what she gets, leads the reader to a dead end.

The only option is to back up and try another route, which is to say, to review what has gone wrong and discern what must happen to get her, and the noble hegemony whose interests she represents, out of there. The answer is consistent with Zayas's other narrative strategies: enactment of the three reforms that she sets out in the book. The fact that it is not too late for the world to regain Lisis means it is not too late for the nobility to recover what the text defines as its members' true identity, synonymous with the virtue that moralist Juan de Costa defined in 1584 as 'a lit torch in a very dark place, so resplendent in the virtuous citizen that it shines light upon others that they might see their own vices' (una hacha encendida, en un lugar muy oscura, resplandeciendo en [el ciudadano virtuoso] tanto sus virtudes que dé luz a otros, para que vean sus vicios, 62).

Lisis crosses the threshold of the visible, secular world of Zayas's narrative into the invisible space of the convent precisely at the structural moment where a worldly marriage would have taken place had the author chosen to satisfy her character's desire to wed. In a non-religious text whose protagonists desire to marry human individuals, as do those of Zayas, the convent ending is the frustration of the marriage plot and signifies flawed human society's inability to attain a wedding or sustain a marriage.[2] Trapped in a fiction whose corrupt nobility makes marriage sure death, Zayas's frame tale protagonist chooses survival. To the extent that Zayas provides Lisis with an alternative to a marriage she does not want, she can grasp 'the importance of herself as [an] empowered agent of choice' (Boyer, 'War' 145).

Given her possibilities, however, it is a highly vexed choice. Entrance into the convent does not mean success in this context; it is a recoiling from danger – 'they save themselves' (se salvan, Foa, *Feminismo* 90). Here we consider how Zayas constructs this fictional non-space as a pseudo-sacred pointer to the way things should be in the world at large, in the same fashion she manipulates the saint's features to render what is wrong on the bodies of her perfect wives. Into the convent she draws her most treasured fictional artifacts, the virtuous female and male characters and their worldly wealth, using all to signify the prosperity and rightness that justice demands be removed from the corrupt world of noble dysfunction.

Zayas constructs flight to the convent in the *Desengaños* as the need of the virtuous to flee the world gone wild outside its walls, constructing a relationship between that space and the missing functional nobility, itself affiliated with God. For her disillusioned female characters, she creates a convent that is an invisible place controlled by a noble, empowered male who recognizes and protects their interests. To the virtuous male characters, the divinity whose order rules the convent offers protection from the death threats hanging over them in the secular world, and they are ushered through its doors under the patronage of a protective Virgin Mary. The convent, then, is a spatial signifier whose referent is an abstraction: in the *Desengaños* the offstage conventual interior means the hegemonic order (marriage) to which noble characters should rightly have access in the world, but do not. The consequence of human matrimony's failure is the end of life in the earthly social economy, either physical death in the world or symbolic death to the world in the convent. Neither is a happy ending.

To interpret the move of Zayas's characters into the convent as a negative act is at odds with the prevailing analysis of the place and its meaning, which critics universally celebrate as the author's idea of everything right for women. Critical esteem of the convent, usually in reference to the entirety of Zayas's fiction, began in 1922 with Sylvania: 'In all her literary work, Doña María reveals herself as an ardent Christian, to whom a religious life represents the perfect state ... There, at last, she [the heroine] finds true happiness and peace, and is content to remain in the shelter of the church for the remainder of her natural life' (15).

That esteem has continued unmitigated ever since. Ordoñez finds Zayas's convent ending to be 'a metonymic sign for the woman-authored text located beyond the confines of the erotic-executioner's plot' (9). For Boyer, it is the place where female desire is realized and liberation from the repressive patriarchy takes place ('Ravages'). Camino proposes that 'for [Zayas], convents were centres of feminine communal life where women could participate actively in private and public affairs' (532). Routt reads it as the only place for a female artist in the seventeenth century (620), and Alcalde says the author uses it as the place for women's intellectual enrichment and an escape from their families (116). For Edward Friedman, it means 'the company of God and her devout sisters in a community that operates in an alternate zone, that excludes men, and that denies value to beauty, wealth, gossip, and the honor code' ('María' 474). Greer allies the move to God's house with a conditional return to the house of the mother (*María* 147), whereas Romero-Díaz suggests that Zayas designs it as a space of social and sexual reformulation for women (*Nueva* 137). More recently, Hoffman refers to Zayas's 'penchant for a positive convent experience' (44).

My point is that there is no convent experience in the *Desengaños*. Although a clutch of named and unnamed characters finish their fictional lives there, the narrators never enter that space except in the most indirect and perfunctory statements, such as 'Octavia professed' (Octavia profesó, 195). Similarly, Inés ends her story in a convent 'with two servants who attend to her, sustaining herself on the large estate of her brother and husband, where she lives today leading the life of a saint' (con dos criadas que cuidan de su regalo, sustentándose de la gruesa hacienda de su hermano y marido, donde hoy vive haciendo vida de una santa, 288), and Juan 'went on to a stricter life, where he passed away in peace' (pasó a más estrecha vida, donde acabó en paz, 222).

Repeatedly mentioning that these characters live lives of 'great holiness,' Zayas says nothing about what that entails. Even Beatriz, whose tale is based on a saint's life, is abruptly dismissed at her story's end: 'she went to a convent where they all took the religious habit, the king giving her permission to do so, where she lived in holiness until a very advanced age' (se fue a un convento donde tomaron todas el hábito de religiosas dándole licencia el rey para ello, donde vivió santamente hasta que fue de mucha edad, 466). Of the frame tale characters, the narrator says merely, 'The next day, Lisis and Doña Isabel, with Doña Estefanía, went to her convent with great pleasure' (Otro día, Lisis y doña Isabel, con doña Estefanía, se fueron a su convento con mucho gusto, 510).[3] Although Kaminsky may be right that Zayas's happiest ending for women is the convent (493), that ending is a marker of what is wrong, not what is right.[4]

In the *Desengaños*, the absence of the convent in the narrative present is thematic as well as spatial, for inside the tales, not one character, male or female, enters a plot aspiring to life there. The invisibility of the place in which many characters of the *Desengaños* finish their fictional lives suggests a symbolic or at least formulaic function for the house of God, a resolution or lack thereof that marks a temporary giving up on the part of nobly born characters whose hopes for life in the world are dashed. Certainly in literary terms, it is a living death, a place where virtuous characters breathe but do not exist in terms of the narrative ontology, a haven in which to earn forgiveness or enjoy safety until the world is such that they can live in it. Thus, just before her religious profession Isabel sings a ballad that equates the remainder of her life with death, 'now only to die behooves me' (ya sólo morir conviene, 147).

Although it is now standard to idealize the convent in the works of Zayas, no one has done the same for the works of male authors, say those of Lope de Vega, dramas in which plenty of female characters end their lives there. This being said, Zayas's systematic recourse to the convent as an ending in the *Desengaños* cries out for attention in a way that its dispersed usage by other authors does not. Furthermore, her failure to say anything about what life in the convent is like leaves the reader in a silence at the book's end that begs for a hearing. Because her tales produce intense anguish, the reader longs for some place of release from the relentless power of wrong, in whose clutches she leaves the admirable characters writhing for prolonged periods of time. The convent, invisible in the *Desengaños* and inexorably aligned in the modern mind with high expectations, provides reprieve not only for the characters but also for the reader.

Recent decades of research into the female convent as a counterbalance to early modern society's repression of women has informed current understanding of Zayas's fictional convent as a place of fulfillment. Arenal and Schlau's 1989 study of the institution as a space of female creativity marks the starting line for subsequent research into nuns' activities. Investigations that followed in the wake of *Untold Sisters* enabled the idealization of the convent in general, leading readers to emphasize the enclosed religious life as one of opportunity, particularly for women. As Arenal and Schlau said early on, 'Nuns found a way of being important in the world by choosing to live outside it' (6). More broadly, Reuther has indicated how convent communities historically have not only allowed women to throw off traditional female roles, but also have offered community members the opportunity to 'pursue the highest self-development as autonomous persons' (73). Weber's work on Teresa of Jesus proves beyond the shadow of a doubt how a religious profession could catapult a woman to an enduring presence in history, and the importance of female convent life as a site of relative autonomy for women is now an accepted fact. However, the question of whether Zayas invokes the convent in the same fashion as religious writers did has not been posed.

Unlike Zayas's readers today, all members of her original Spanish public were Catholics for whom the convent was a familiar building, most often with zones through which the general public could access its interior, certainly the church or chapel, and, to greater and lesser extents, its inhabitants; the cloister was, as Lehfeldt indicates, permeable (*Religious Women*). This familiarity normalized the space and made it possible for Zayas to manipulate its meaning in a way that a twenty-first-century author might not, since many readers today are unfamiliar with the reality of convent life. Because research on the lives of early modern female religious has enhanced our understanding of the female convent as a space of women's empowerment, and perhaps because the convent today no longer serves the same social functions it did in Zayas's day, is it easy to project onto this literary space both the anxiety created by the fiction and our own relative lack of experience with it. Entering the text from inside the parameters of seventeenth-century religious culture, and from awareness of specific historical information about what the convent meant during that period, not only allows but requires us to read the claustration motif in the *Desengaños* in a period-specific fashion.

Zayas really does not want us, or her virtuous characters, in the convent, for she cloaks her fictional retreat to God in invisibility and keeps it at a far remove from her reader. As Merrim says, it is an 'elsewhere' (136). The fact that the narrative never goes there is evidence that the author's interest lies where she does take it, to urban centres around the imperial Hispanic world where she forces her readers to witness the horrible consequences of noble corruption. A close look at the *Desengaños* reveals that the historical reality of women-directed convents lacks a narrative presence. Zayas does not once mention the convent as a female-led community, nor does she celebrate the autonomy of women therein. She does not once affiliate the female convent with learning or artistic enterprise, and no character seeks or finds artistic or educational opportunities there. She does, however, relate the convent to physical survival for men and woman alike.

Furthermore, the fact that Zayas moves several female characters into women-only spaces must be reconciled with the fact that she moves male characters into men-only religious communities, which has never been mentioned as evidence of her support of male removal from the world, or celebration of an idealized community of men. The question of what the convent means, then, is larger than the question of gender. Just as the multiple calls to female agency sprinkled throughout the frame tale are nowhere enacted in the tales themselves, so the convent remains much invoked but never seen, a flickering light in a dark enclosure. Absenting the convent, then, is highly appropriate, because the dark aesthetics of the *Desengaños* demands the emphatic and intense representation of what is wrong without allowing the reader to lose sight of what is right. In accordance with this aesthetic imperative, that which is right must remain unseen and unattained, but consistently invoked.

Historically speaking, the convent in Zayas's day was primarily, and in theological terms exclusively, reserved for women and men who turned their backs on worldly concerns to serve the divinity: 'Standing at the threshold or entrance to the cloister, male and female religious renounced their ties to the world of family, community, and temporal attachments and proclaimed their acceptance of a new life no longer bound by these distractions. This ritual was often represented as the process by which monastics became "dead to the world"' (Lehfeldt, *Religious Women* 3). These nuns and monks made a life-long promise to reside in the convent as professional religious and endowed it with their resources, forming the core of the community and legitimizing the convent's existence.

The institution had other social functions: female convents were used as places to leave abandoned infants, for the education of girls by nuns, as residences for women aged sixteen and older who took solemn religious vows, as residences for women of all ages whose families considered them a burden, and as nursing homes for the elderly. Among convent residents who did not take solemn vows there were servants and slaves of the upper-class residents and women of the upper social echelons who merely resided there, including widows, and single and married women who did not need to promise to remain.[5] In the convents of exigent discipline, these multiple groups were not allowed to live.

Vigil describes convents as 'parking lots for women' (aparcamientos de mujeres, 215), and in spite of Tridentine directives against professions by force or fear, forced monachization remained a problem. Haliczer identifies the church, often attached to a convent, as a place of assignation, meaning the arrangement of a sexual rendezvous, solicitation (on the part of priests in particular), fornication, and masturbation (93). Male and female convents also served as asylums for individuals who had committed crimes; Zayas's character Juan hides in a convent of discalced religious men after he rapes Camila (193).

Seventeenth-century convents were as plagued by human debilities as other residences. For example, the Count-Duke of Olivares and King Philip IV himself were implicated in the sex scandal of the convent of San Plácido in Madrid, in which the Benedictine García Calderón had erotic conversations with the nuns, who swore they had been visited by the devil in the form of a man (García Carcel 56).[6] Bergmann calls attention to a passage from Padilla's *Nobleza virtuosa* in which the countess recommends that noblemen flee from women raised in the convent beyond the age of eight or ten. Young women there, she insists, were permitted to 'admit gallantries from married men and all men, gifts and letters, and I find no way to justify this, and if respect did not impose silence upon me, I would go on at length' (admitir galanteos de los casados, y de todos, dádivas y billetes, que no hallo camino para justificar esto, y si el respeto no me pusiera silencio, me alargara, 5; 65–6 in the original). Clearly, the historical record cautions against idealizing the conventual interior.

Among all these functions of the female convent, Zayas uses but one in the *Desengaños*: a secure place for the secular nobility, where goodness can find the refuge it needs to survive, something it cannot do in her fictional world outside its walls. This function may have a direct relationship to the use of the convent as a safe house in cases of litigation for divorce filed after the Council of Trent. To women accusing their husbands of abuse, the tribunal offered protection in a place of their choice, which was most often a family member's house but could also be a convent (Gil 182).

The historical realities of early modern Spanish conventual life can be distinguished from its use in fiction, whose historicity is most often tangential or metaphorical. Certainly Zayas is not alone in her employment of the convent as the ending place for a work of literature, for a veritable multitude of early modern Spanish plots end with a claustration.[7] In many of these, the convent is an extension of patriarchal power, an offstage space into which used female characters can disappear from a text with neither the means nor disposition to do anything else with them.

For example, in *El alcalde de Zalamea*, Calderón's honour-driven character Pedro Crespo describes his daughter Isabel, raped by the arrogant military officer Juan, saying, 'She has a convent already chosen / and has a husband / who closes his eyes to quality' (Un convento tiene ya / elegido y tiene esposo / que no mira en calidad, 2743–5). Would one say that Calderón's Isabel, as dishonoured as Zayas's characters, is exercising freedom of choice in entering the convent? In fact, in Calderón's play, Isabel does not signify herself, a young woman with her own ideas and desires, as much as she mediates her rapist's challenge to her father and all he represents. Her body supplies the canvas on which Calderón can dramatically paint the conflict between the two men, and her father's final word about where she will spend the rest of her life signals his victory over the captain who raped her and insulted him. This use of the female character was frequent if not the norm in dramas of honour in Spain and elsewhere; Stallybrass observes of Shakespeare's *Othello*, 'Woman's body could be imagined as the passive terrain on which the inequalities of masculine power were fought out' (141).

One would expect that María de Zayas, whose investment in women's subjective experience is deep, would depart from this representative practice. In a text that respects the validity of religious ontology, meaning that its author leaves the power and majesty of the divinity unchallenged – as Zayas does – a character's loss to the world is a consequence of whatever sad turn of events pushes that character into the convent, including that character's own bad behaviour.[8] In *El alcalde de Zalamea*, the need for Isabel to go there is evidence of Pedro Crespo's inability to safeguard his property, evidence that lingers beyond the resolution of the conflict between Pedro and Alonso and must be reconciled with the dominant notion that women belong with men for order to be re-established. She is married, then, to God. Even though she is not a virgin, this God will not disdain her, as Zayas's Isabel states in terms identical to Pedro Crespo's: her divine spouse is 'a husband who will not scorn me' (Esposo que no me despreciará, 167). The human interests driving the book inform the author's use of the convent motif, moulding it into the service of her objectives, which, as we have seen, are secular.

Literature that represents the convent possessed of its rightful religious meaning presupposes the inversion of earthly order with regard to sexuality (chastity is the norm), materiality (the material world is understood as insignificant in comparison with that of the spirit), and the exercise of human will (convent dwellers surrender themselves to the satisfaction of divine will and the service of others). It is a place associated with what Jeffrey studies as 'the delight of the sacred' (jouissance du sacré). All of the novellas in Cristobal Lozano's extremely popular *Soledades de la vida y desengaños del mundo* (*Solitudes of Life and Disillusions of the World*, 1658) privilege a religious ontology and can thus be called 'religious.' Before considering Zayas's figurative convent and her representation of the God who rules therein, it is revealing to see what a fictional text looks like whose author celebrates its function as the house of God. The convent as a literal referent endowed with its sacred function entails the crafting of a character who is born to or awakens to a religious vocation, which means a sincere devotion to the divinity, and the profound, transcendental shift of paradigm from the secular to the sacred that such a vocation requires.

Accessing the authentic religious meaning of the convent can be, and was, accomplished with the lightest of touches, but a touch that changes everything in a literary text. For example, among the novellas in Juan Pérez de Montalbán's 1624 collection *Sucesos y prodigios de amor* (*Love's Happenings and Prodigies*) is *La mayor confusión* (*The Greatest Confusion*). In that story, Fulgencia is dishonoured by Félix and, 'finding herself without pleasure and honour, gossiped about by her relatives and made a martyr by her parents, who were ever accusing her of flighty and lascivious behaviour, resolved to flee from it all to the refuge of a convent' (viéndose sin gusto y sin honra, murmurada de sus deudos y martirizada de sus padres, que a todas horas la acusaban de fácil y liviana, se resolvió a huir de todos en el sagrado de un convento, 144). At this point, Fulgencia is like any disgraced noblewoman of a seventeenth-century novella who enters the convent to escape her worldly dishonour.

Pérez de Montalbán, however, provides his character with another character – God – whose appearance in her life changes its entire meaning by confounding earthly paradigms, allowing her to shift her worldly desire to the desire for that which transcends human existence. The young woman finds not only salvation, but also a fulfilment unknown in the world in which she previously wanted to live. The narrator goes on to describe Fulgencia's life in the convent as the place, 'where, during the first year, she was so happy and *favoured by heaven* that she almost counted her error as good fortune for having been the means by which she found *a way of living so free from the misfortunes with which life in the world overflows*. And, indeed, having forgotten Don Félix, she made her profession and gave thanks to heaven *for having illuminated her soul*, the more *removed she was from worldly resources and pleasure'* (donde estuvo el primer año tan contenta y *favorecida del cielo,* que casi tuvo a ventura su yerro por haber sido causa de hallar *estado tan libre de las desdichas que suelen sobrar en el siglo.* Y en efecto, olvidada de don Félix, hizo su profesión y dio gracias al cielo de que la había *alumbrado el alma,* cuanto estaba más *ajena de remedio y de gusto,* 144, emphasis added).

Pérez de Montalbán has Fulgencia berate herself for having believed the lies of a man, thus delivering to his readers the requisite lessons: 'Men, do not lie'; 'Women, do not believe men's lies.' In what follows, he also proves Fulgencia to be a good person who deserves the very best option he can give her, which is profound fulfilment in a life in which she does not want or need Félix. He thus legitimizes the religious meaning of the convent and invokes God as the ultimate antidote to the flaws of humanity.

More specifically, Fulgencia's convent is a positive space ruled by an active, empowered divinity into which Pérez de Montalbán draws the reader, even if through indirect discourse, to behold the heroine finding an unexpected vocation as a nun. He arranges for his character to alter the paradigm of her life from the secular (pursuit of 'worldly resources and pleasure') to the sacred (she is 'happy and favoured by heaven'). This is one of the best ways to insult the defective human character, in this case Félix, because it renders him completely meaningless by invoking a religious ontology in which God, incontestably the superior authority, appreciates the merit to which the mortal man has been blind.

Zayas does not do this. Instead, she holds tenaciously to the secular paradigm while persistently invoking the holy one, refusing to enter into the sacred ontology and refusing to use God to transcend earthly meaning. She employs the convent as an ironic reflecting pool of features that the human world should have, but does not. These include safety for virtuous individuals, the opportunity to earn and attain forgiveness, and, most important, the rule of a benevolent, forgiving, faithful, and devoted male for the female characters, and the support of a mediating, loving but strict female for the males. Instead of entering the convent and allowing God to become a character in the fiction by deeply changing someone's life, Zayas delimits the male divinity to an object of female desire. This is an appropriate strategy in a book whose objective is not to celebrate the sacred in itself, but rather to signal the distance from God produced by human corruption, thereby pointing to the need for reform in the secular world.

Zayas represents the behavioural improvements she desires as consonant with divinely instated precepts, and divine will provides her with recourse to a superhuman authority to bolster her entire narrative agenda. She endows God and the Virgin with precisely those features whose lack in human men and women produce chaos in the fiction. In the *Desengaños*, in other words, the sacred functions as justification and support of the secular, and not vice versa. Zayas manipulates the sacred significance of the convent and the divinity, just as she manipulates the martyr figure to reinforce her text's tellurian foundation without relinquishing the theocentric function of those signifiers.

As Vasileski observes, in all twenty of Zayas's novellas, not one female character has a religious vocation (59). In a book whose admirable protagonists seek marriage, retirement to the convent is logically one among several signifiers the author uses to communicate that something has transpired that disenfranchises the functional nobility and leads to the removal of their bodies, merit, and beauty, like treasures buried during a war. It is, as Montesa Peydró indicates, a 'holding pattern' (solución de repuesto, 178).

An idealized refuge, the convent is an invisible locale that Zayas uses as a sad ending to a collection of already sad stories. In the *Desengaños*, the convent is not what anyone wants; it is what she or he settles for or is forced into. Characters go there for three reasons, all of which are negative: in response to worldly dishonour, out of fear for their lives, or in fear for their souls. Furthermore, there is a decided similarity between the dead wives' hyperbolically beautiful corpses and the high attractiveness and value of the characters who attain Zayas's convent.

Like other authors of her day, Zayas drives into the convent women whose social integrity has been violated, leaving them no other place to live. The most notable of these is Isabel, narrator and protagonist of the first tale, who clearly states the four reasons for her decision to become a nun, all secular: she cannot find Felipe (164); she would bring shame upon her mother were she to go home (165); Manuel is dead; and regardless, she does not trust men (166). Having unsuccessfully enslaved herself to a deeply flawed man, Isabel turns, in the end, not to freedom, independence, or the infinity of eternity in God's embrace, but to slavery to a better master: 'How much better it is to be God's slave and offer myself with the same name of Her Lover's Slave?' (¿Cuánto mejor es serlo [esclava] de Dios, y a Él ofrecerme con el mismo nombre de la Esclava de su Amante? 167).[9]

According to the social ethics of the *Desengaños*, Isabel's wayward lover Manuel has dealt shamefully with the young noblewoman, and he exemplifies the deceiving male from whom the female public should protect itself. Because Isabel failed to refuse contact with Manuel until married to him, she loses him and with him, her possibilities of marriage. The author has backed the young woman into a corner from which the only virtuous escape is up, into a world mimetically superior to the one in which she has lived. Retreating into the convent and the absent but longed-for order that it signifies, Isabel will theoretically find relief from the teeming disorder around her. The convent means that which she, and characters like her, cannot find in the world, but which should be there: a mutually desired relationship with a truly noble partner, the social foundation of the empire.

Likewise, Octavia's dishonour, in which she was an active agent, drives her to a religious profession after her unfaithful lover Carlos tricks her into entering the convent (d2). The fact that her brother swears to kill Octavia if she leaves it clearly problematizes her decision to stay there: 'Alonso replied to his sister that she should arrange to take the habit and be a nun, since she had acted as if she had lost her mind and behaved lightly, for there was no other recourse if she did not want to lose her life at his hands' ([Alonso] respondió a su hermana que tratase, pues había sido loca, y liviana, de tomar el hábito y ser religiosa, pues no había otro remedio, si no quería perder la vida a sus manos, 189–90).

Single women are not Zayas's only dishonoured convent dwellers. In desengaño 5, after Inés survives her six-year confinement in her house's chimney, the well-intentioned people who save her life put her in a convent (d5, 'a doña Inés pusieron … en un convento,' 288). The fact that Inés herself does not make the decision underscores her lack of vocation and magnifies her status as a virtuous and undone woman unwanted by the world. Because the convent in the Desengaños is a metonym of the functional nobility that is missing in the tales, were things aright, members of that nobility such as Inés would be able to protect themselves from malicious attempts to compromise them, which in turn would allow their continued residence in the world, outside the convent.

Zayas nests particularly harsh references to convent life in desengaño 8. While courting Mencía, Enrique describes his beloved's future life in the convent as 'the eternal captivity of religious life,' and the place where her father, inappropriately, will have her put (el eterno cautiverio de la religión, 373; 'os tiene para religiosa,' 373). These starkly negative articulations, highly appropriate given Enrique and Mencía's desire to wed, reinforce the relationship between a character's ingress to the convent and what is wrong.

Second, male and female characters retreat to the convent as a safe haven from threatening individuals or potentially dangerous situations: they go there out of fear, to remain there temporarily or permanently. Among those who seek such protection are Lisis (frame), Juan (d3), Enrique (d8), and Beatriz (d9). Several anonymous characters are also frightened into the convent by happenings in the world, shadow figures who reinforce its function as a zone of safety. These include Laurela's sisters who are terrified by their sibling's death at their father's hands (d6 331), and Ana's sisters, almost struck dead by a lightening bolt that clearly symbolizes the uncontrollable dangers of life in the corrupt world (d8 387). Zayas's fictional convent also realizes this function by a character's failure to attain it, which results in death. Called home from the convent by her husband, the raped wife Camila is poisoned by him (d2), and Blanca, terrified upon realizing that her husband's father has been party to his own daughter's death, asks permission to enter a convent, a request that is refused as a prelude to her murder by the same man (d7 358).

At the high-mimetic extreme of this retreat-for-fear motif, Zayas employs the convent as a place of rest from worldly trauma, a respite earned by Beatriz, the one female character who survives her husband's mistrust, rejects his attempt at reconciliation, and retires from the world. Two moments from Zayas's reworking of the St Beatriz story are particularly helpful in deciphering her fictional convent's significance. One is the protagonist's hermetic life that takes place between her third trial and her last one, and the other is her final entrance into the presumably sacred space.

Retreat from the world is an ancient Christian theme, derived from Christ's forty days in the desert, where he was driven by the Spirit and tested by Satan, the better to return to the world and act in it (Matthew 4:1–11; Mark 1:9–13; Luke 4:1–14). In this context it is important to distinguish a positive retreat like this, undertaken for spiritual exercise and fortification for life on earth, from its negative performance, undertaken as an escape from the tribulations of human life in a corrupt world. Christ, fully empowered as the divinity, never resorted to escape. In *desengaño* 9, Zayas invokes both, but affiliates only the negative motif with the convent.

After saving Beatriz from the false accusation that she had murdered the son of the emperor who had taken her in, the Virgin Mary removes her to an isolated, idealized locale where the protagonist is safe from the ongoing threats of Federico, who is stalking her and in league with the devil. Beatriz's protectress deposits her in a cave next to a small, clear spring shaded by a fruit-laden tree (454). Other items of hermetic décor, the Magdalen icons we saw in chapter 3, provide Beatriz with the apparatus necessary to lead a contemplative and disciplined life. In this protected refuge, Beatriz enjoys the company of God in a fashion similar to that of Pérez de Montalbán's Fulgencia, but without emphasizing transcendence: 'Let us leave her here now,' says the narrator, 'communicating with God at all hours' (Dejémosla aquí, comunicando a toda horas con Dios, 454).

Although Zayas added this woodland cave retreat to the romance vita of Beatriz she reworks in this tale, she reveals nothing about Beatriz's relationship with the divinity, nor does God signify in that relationship except as a type of status symbol for the rejected wife, whose merit that relationship proves. Significantly, Beatriz finds God while living in nature, not the convent, although she will ultimately retreat to one. This hermetic spot, in which objects of discipline figure prominently, recalls Christ's desert retirement before his trials in the world begin in earnest, as well as the narrative trappings of the lives of the desert Fathers in the Christian tradition. It is a positive experience. Zayas's Virgin Mary pulls Beatriz from this retreat, insisting on a very worldly topic: 'It is now time for you to leave here and go defend your honour' (Es ya tiempo que salgas de aquí y vayas a volver por tu honor, 460). The relationship between what the Virgin wants for Beatriz and what Zayas wants for women is clear.

At the story's end, the narrator explicitly states that Beatriz enters the convent, not to enjoy the continued presence of the divinity with which she became acquainted in her hermetic dwelling, but rather to escape the imperfect world that harassed her several times to the point of death. When her husband King Ladislao begs her to rejoin him in their marriage, she refuses. For Beatriz, 'there was by then neither kingdom nor spouse in the world for her, for she aspired only to the celestial Spouse and the kingdom of glory, [and asked] that he not try to convince her to return to more misfortunes than those she had already suffered' (ya no había reino, ni esposo en el mundo para ella, que al Esposo celestial y al reino de la gloria sólo aspiraba, que no la tratase de volver a ocasionarse más desdichas de las padecidas, 466). Zayas's world-weary Beatriz retreats from the earthly life she had hoped to lead, and the

Virgin Mary neither recommends that she go to the convent nor escorts her there. Yllera specifies that Zayas's female characters enter the convent out of spite or the desire for tranquillity ('María' 226), and Beatriz perfectly exemplifies the latter.

Beatriz's entrance into the convent is not good; it is simply less bad than what happens to the wives who do not make it to the convent doors. Were things right, King Ladislao would have credited his wife's virtue over his brother's false accusations in the first place, and the couple would have lived happily ever after. Ladislao's punishment is the realization of his wife's unblemished virtue, revealed to him just as she disappears from his life, in the same fashion that Zayas has Elena die exactly when her wrong-minded husband Jaime realizes that he has killed her for a wrong she did not commit (d4). Both endings entail the loss of a virtuous woman to upper-class society, a loss produced by the nobility's failures.

Finally, Zayas utilizes the convent as a place for repentance, where an individual who has committed grievous wrong can save her or his soul by turning from bad behaviour to good, as in the cases of Juan (d3) and Florentina (d10). Variants on the retreat-for-fear motif, Juan and Florentina's tales view the convent from the perspective of the wrongdoer. They display how men and women make terrible mistakes, and then use the convent as the penitential space in which they can right those wrongs by denying themselves access to the world whose principles they violated.

Florentina's final wealth and comfort in the convent appears to contradict her guilt, for she is ultimately responsible for more deaths in the book than anyone else. In his analysis of the final *desengaño*, Edward Friedman holds that her confession of that guilt is misleading and false, and that the story does not permit a clear transition from 'injustice toward women to the shelter of the convent' ('María' 474). In the story's denouement, the wretched woman hides from the officers of justice her role in the massacre that took place in her house and thus avoids punishment ('no culpándose a sí por no ocasionarse el castigo,' 484). Zayas ultimately rewards Florentina, who inherits the estates of her half-sister and her brother-in-law.

But if we read the convent as the place forced on sinners as punishment for wrongs committed, the minimum requirement for saving their souls, the ending becomes harsher and falls into line with the rest of the book. From her narrative's outset, Florentina berates herself for betraying her half-sister. She accepts responsibility for Magdalena's death (484), states that she let herself be lost beyond repair (486), and cries that she repaid Magdalena's love falsely and wrongly (486). By inserting a vigilant confessor who refuses to absolve Florentina if she fails to abandon her life of sin (492), Zayas clarifies the extreme at which Florentina is operating: she is going to hell, and she knows it.

Like Juan of *desengaño* 3, the finally repentant woman recognizes her guilt and hopes to regain her soul: 'I went into the street with the intention to seek out (seeing myself in the state in which I was) someone to confess me so that, since I was losing my life, I not lose my soul' (Salí a la calle con ánimo de ir a buscar [viéndome en el estado que estaba] quien me confesase, para que, ya que perdiese la vida, no perdiese el alma, 499). Zayas uses Florentina and Juan to exemplify what the guilty nobility should do, and Florentina's punishment is to live without everything she wanted, bereft of everyone she knows, since Dionís kills everyone in her house (500). The repentant woman's accounts are settled in the end, privately, as befits a member of her class, when Gaspar negotiates her release from public punishment with no less than the king, precisely because she recognizes herself to be 'the worst woman born to the world' (la más mala hembra que en el mundo ha nacido, 497). The king, God's agent on earth, enacts in the world the forgiveness that characters such as Isabel seek from God in the convent. He acts nobly: in light of her repentance, he forgives her ('dio piadoso el perdón de la culpa que Florentina tenía' [he mercifully forgave Florentina's guilt, 500]).

Like Juan, Florentina takes the necessary measures to protect the social body from her pernicious influence, removing herself from the secular world, a behaviour that may seem peculiar to postmodern readers. To Zayas's early modern public, whose identities were deeply invested in community and the mathematics of Catholic salvation, Florentina's final situation is the best for which she can hope, and Zayas draws a parallel between her, the repentant woman in the convent, and Juan, the repentant man in the same situation.[10] By having some deeply flawed characters enter the convent, Zayas clearly asserts the importance of reconciling themselves with the order in whose interests they should have controlled their lust before it was too late. The remainder of their lives is the price exacted of them for their failure to do so. The convent, then, is the space in which a recognized debt to hegemonic order can be paid, in alliance with a God who in Zayas's fictional construct is its safeguard. In this circumstance, life in the convent is negative in that it is a response to deeply wrong actions; it is positive in that it manifests the wrongdoer's rejection of her or his misguided will. In effect, Juan and Florentina die to the world in which they wanted to live.

Without validating a single religious vocation as such, Zayas crafts an association between what is right and her invisible convent's interior. It is not merely a resting, protective place for the innocent, because three very guilty, if repentant, characters end their lives there (Juan, Florentina, Ladislao). It is an absent but crucial spatial signifier of noble virtue, a virtue that demands repentance of the guilty and abandonment of the nobility's flawed ways on the part of all.

In this pattern of signification Zayas affiliates the invisible, absent space of the convent with survival in suspended time, and the world outside it – the only space visible in the narrative – with extreme danger. The logic of her convent trope, then, is perfect, because removing the virtuous and repentant protagonists there assures that they will not be exploited by the flawed, worldly social economy and guarantees that members of the functional nobility will remain alive to perpetuate the empire. As Romero-Díaz observes, the woman's body steps out of circulation when she enters the convent (*Nueva* 137). The same is true of a man's body. Leaving flawed members of the nobility in the world, and removing the virtuous from it condemns the corrupt to live with the corrupt. It brings the dominant sexual economy, reliant on purity of blood and honour, to a halt.

However, the life with which Zayas affiliates the convent is ironic – mere survival – because the characters there desired to live in the world, not removed from it. Sending them to the convent in violation of their will to marry and remain married permits Zayas to sustain her emphasis on the need for reform of that worldly society. Pérez de Montalbán's character Fulgencia's loving and fulfilling relationship with God validates religious life and thereby opens up an alternative to life in the world that is not only viable, but also superior. Zayas's emphasis lies squarely on life in the world, the signifying foundation of her narrative objectives, into the service of which she conscripts the convent and other sacred motifs.

God of the Convent, Wealth of the World

Zayas's association of convent life with an undesired solution rests uneasily with the reader accustomed to that institution's semantic affiliation with the other world, or life eternal. She employs it to point to what the secular world needs and does not have: honesty, respect for others, fidelity, forgiveness, the protection of innocence. One of the most potent ways she bolsters her metaphorical convent is her way of describing the divinity, the power that reigns over the place to which so many of her characters retreat. Not the countenance of an authentic god, the masculine as well as feminine face of Zayas's divinity gazes out at the reader with the features of what a right-behaving human being should look like.

Three main male characters in the *Desengaños* end their fictional lives by retiring permanently to a convent. The narrators describe them there as engaged in decidedly human concerns that draw the reader not to the spiritual realm, but back to the worldly reasons that drove them there. Juan, whose intention to have a sexual relationship with his best friend's wife was frustrated by the Virgin, confesses his misdeed to both his friend and his friend's wife, after which he enters a convent to devote his life to the correction of his mistake. Therein, Zayas describes him as rightly devoted to the Holy Mother: 'He went to a convent of religious discalced Carmelites and became a friar, taking the habit of that most pure Lady who had liberated him from such manifest danger' (Se fue a un convento de religiosos carmelitas descalzos, y se entró de fraile, tomando el hábito de aquella purísima Señora que le había librado de tan manifiesto peligro, 219). Like Juan, Enrique is threatened with a violent death in the world, from which he retreats with relief, also saved by the Virgin (d8). In his Franciscan convent, his only activity mentioned is his construction of an elaborate memorial chapel in which to bury his murdered wife (385). In *desengaño* 9, King Ladislao rejects his kingdom and his royal destiny in recognition of having wrongly discredited his wife and removes to a monastery, 'inspired by God' (inspirado de Dios, 466).

Bluntly put, these men devote their lives in the convent to toeing Zayas's line: honour women, and if you have not done so, regret it. Her aggressively interventionist Virgin Mary, modelled on the Virgin of romance hagiography and miracle tales, assures the placement of all three where they belong and earns their devotion thereafter. To reinforce the importance of heterosexual marriage in the world, Zayas does not represent her male characters as serving the male, Catholic God but instead uses them to reinforce the paradigm of human marriage by affiliating them with the female component of the Catholic divinity. In an inverted symbolism in which the divine represents the human, the Mother of God stands in place of the women these men should have served and respected all along. Juan, Enrique, and Ladislao are three ultimately rightly behaving men, two redeemed by repenting their failure to recognize female virtue and one saved for his fidelity to his wife. As such, they belong in Zayas's preserve of the virtuous: the convent.

On the other hand, Zayas consistently represents her female characters who find refuge in the convent as longing for a male whom they define very specifically as a man who lacks the flaws of the human man who wronged each of them. Isabel sings of her God at the conclusion of *desengaño* 6:

> I believe in only one man
> whose truth I esteem as my occupation.
> And this man is not on earth
> because *God is a man* whom heaven encloses.
> Yes, this man does not deceive;
> this man is beautiful and wise,
> and never offended any woman. (335–6, emphasis added)[11]

> (En sólo un hombre creo
> cuya verdad estimo por empleo.
> Y éste no está en la tierra,
> porque *es un hombre Dios*, que el cielo encierra.
> Éste sí que no engaña;
> éste es hermoso y sabio,
> y que jamás hizo a ninguna agravio.)

Lacking majesty, transcendental presence, and power, this figurehead God is the antidote to the flawed men who wreak havoc on the lives of the virtuous outside the convent. Unlike a true divinity that exists in its own infinite terms, Zayas's God signifies the inversion of human failings.

On the surface it appears that Zayas emphasizes 'the wisdom of rejecting men and of rejecting life in the predatory chaos of the secular world' (Clamurro 44). However, examination of the book's figurative divinity reveals that these convent dwellers do not reject men at all. Zayas steps into the tradition of identifying female religious as brides of the male divinity, a symbolic marriage that predates Christianity, using it to articulate the longing of her used female characters to wed a worthy man they cannot find on earth.[12] She defines her characters' relationship with God solely in terms of what they desire and cannot find

– a husband who abides by the precepts of the noble class – explicitly delimiting the sacred to a mirroring reinforcement of the human social economy outside the convent. The earthly nature of this paradigm is clear when the Virgin Mary declares to Beatriz that her son wants his wives to have good reputations ('quiere mi hijo que sus esposas tengan buena fama,' 460).

Zayas carefully has each victim character project qualities onto the God she seeks in the convent that invert her bad experiences with human men. In the first tale, Isabel wrongly believes Manuel's promise to marry her, even as he rejects her again and again, even when she stands before him wearing a Moorish slave disguise, materializing the degradation he thrust upon her. Not surprisingly, she describes the 'husband' she will find in the convent insisting, 'I have chosen a Lover who will not forget me and a Husband who will not disdain me, for I behold him now with his arms open to receive me' (Tengo elegido Amante que no me olvidará y Esposo que no me despreciará, pues le contemplo ya los brazos abiertos para recibirme, 167). Similarly, after Carlos betrays Octavia in the first part of *desengaño* 2, he tricks her into the convent so he can marry another woman. Thereafter, Octavia finds a God-husband whom the narrator describes as a male possessing precisely the heroic features that Carlos lacks: 'Octavia professed, being the most fortunate, for she traded for the true Husband the false and traitorous one who fooled her and left her deceived' (Octavia profesó, siendo la más dichosa, pues trocó por el verdadero Esposo el falso y traidor que la engañó y dejó burlada, 195).

These characters do not desire God, nor does Zayas activate God on their behalf once they attain the convent. They desire noble husbands who behave in consonance with prevailing precepts of social virtue. Like Isabel, Octavia is guilty of having made herself vulnerable to a lying man, and she is subsequently shut into the convent for the wrong reasons. Once there, however, she lives in material sufficiency and prospers, because the author associates the empowered, functional nobleman with the God who rules the convent, neither of whom is present in the book.

Zayas inverts and intensifies her negative troping of the convent in Octavia's counterpart, Camila, Carlos's wealthy and legitimate wife. Innocent of Octavia and Carlos's wrongdoing, Camila needs and deserves access to the domain of goodness beyond the reach of the corrupt world. After Octavia's enraged brother rapes her, she retreats into the convent to save herself from the avenging fury of her husband, who blames her for being the victim of his own moral affliction. To render her dark disorder more perfectly, Zayas dangles Camila over the threshold of the convent haven and the functional male who rules it, only to pull her from it and kill her at the hands of her deeply flawed human husband. Had Camila stayed in the convent, analogically accessing the functional nobility living in conformity with God's mandates, she would have survived, as does the noble wife Inés in *desengaño* 5.

The most vocal defendant of the functional man-divinity is Estefanía, the nun character in the frame tale, who describes herself as having 'sacrificed herself when a very young girl to a Husband who has never deceived me nor will do so' (me sacrifiqué desde muy niña a Esposo que jamás me ha engañado ni engañará, 409). The detail is telling, for Estefanía represents her 'vocation' as does Isabel, a self-sacrifice to a man whom she describes exclusively in terms of human failures, in terms of what noblemen in the world should be and are not: forthright and faithful.

Estefanía listens with the rest of the public to the story of Inés (d5). Although Zayas silences Inés after she is released from the chimney and receives confession, she arranges for Estefanía to describe the God Inés needed but was denied, a 'husband' who is precisely what Inés's husband was not, which is forgiving and uninterested in holding her responsible for the wrongdoing of others. To assure the comparison of this forgiving spouse with the unforgiving, earthly ones, Zayas slyly has Estefanía use a paralipsis to pose the very comparison she insists cannot be made: 'Oh my divine Spouse! And if every time we offend you, you were to punish us thus, what would become of us? *But I am foolish in making a comparison between You, merciful God, and the husbands of the world.* During the time since I consecrated myself to you, I never regretted it ... for although I might offend you, at the smallest tear you will forgive me and receive me with open arms' (¡Ay, divino Esposo mío! Y si vos, todas las veces que os ofendemos, nos castigarais así, ¿qué fuera de nosotros? *Mas soy necia en hacer comparación de vos, piadoso Dios, a los esposos del mundo.* Jamás me arrepentí cuanto ha que me consagré a vos de ser esposa vuestra ... pues aunque os agraviase, que a la más mínima lágrima me habéis de perdonar y recibirme con los brazos abiertos, 289, emphasis added). As a nun, Estefanía should have no occasion to offend God as did Isabel, Octavia, and Florentina, whose failure to live by Zayas's prescribed behaviour led them straight into the clutches of the corrupt world. Estefanía's offended 'God' is clearly the functional human nobleman, who rightly demands payment of morally errant women like Florentina, a man whose succour is just as rightly available to women who simply fail to safeguard their own interests, such as Isabel and Octavia, and who welcomes innocent women such as Beatriz.

By virtue of her religious profession and her life in the convent (when she is not outside it attending parties), Estefanía is key in understanding the meaning and function of the convent in the *Desengaños*. Zayas uses this character's exclamation to reveal that the God who rules her fictional convent is really a pseudo-divinity. Far from the ultimate Subject, the source of universal truth and power, this figurehead god is an object of female desire. Zayas constructs him as a heroic, fictional male designed to display the features of the perfect man sought by women who willingly and rightly sacrifice themselves to him. She dresses this functional human nobleman in the adjective *divino* to signal the distance between what should be and what is, on the one hand, and to exalt the man who possesses these desirable features, on the other.

Estefanía eschews the nun's rightful spatial and ideological affiliation with an authentic divinity by being seen exclusively in the secular world and describing with particular vehemence a God who does not exist in terms of a divinity but as the answer to secular society's defects and failures. A presumably religious woman, she identifies her profession in terms of the men who hunger for female flesh at the grate of the convent salon, the *locutorio*, expecting favours from the nuns whom Estefanía defines as *engañadoras*, 'deceivers,' for their sweet words and false promises of favours. She defines herself as a master of deceit ('maestra de engañar,' 409) and insists that the ladies of the world should be grateful to nuns for exacting vengeance of men by exercising this deceit, luring them to favours that will never be attained, returning tit for tat: 'The first inheritance of which we [nuns] take possession is the act of deluding, as is seen in all the ignoramuses who, clinging to the convent grates, without pulling themselves away, drinking like Ulysses the deceptions of Circe, live and die thus enchanted, without considering that *we are deceiving them with sweet words*, and that they will never accomplish what they seek' ([Es] la hacienda que primero aprendemos [las monjas] el engañar, como se ve en tantos ignorantes, como asidos a las rejas de los conventos, sin poderse apartar de ellas, bebiendo, como Ulises, los engaños de Circe, viven y mueren en este encantamiento, sin considerar que *los engañamos con las dulces palabras*, y que no han de llegar a conseguir las obras, 408–9, emphasis added). Describing her sisters as the legendary enchantress who transforms men into beasts, Estefanía establishes the nun of the *Desengaños* as a powerful, even threatening guardian intent on retaliating the wrongs done to noblewomen.

Even more remarkably, Estefanía describes her fellow nuns not as peace-minded intermediaries of the divine, but rather as avenging animals to whom she threatens to serve misbehaving men who do not heed her words: 'I will turn them over to a dozen or so of my companions, which will be like throwing them to the lions' (los entregaré a una docena de compañeras, que será como echarlos a los leones, 410). Her description of her convent companions as fierce intensifies the author's link between the revanchist power of the right-minded nobility and the convent. This description is completely inappropriate for nuns, whose professions, if authentic, would move them in a direction opposite to ferocious vengeance. It is completely appropriate, however, for the residents of Zayas's troped convent, the empowered and virtuous nobility whose members are rightly powerful and fierce indeed.

Given the patriarchal, even paternalistic nature of the God to whose protection the convent-seeking characters flee, it is difficult to sustain the argument that Zayas uses the convent as an alternative to the patriarchy, for her own alliance with patriarchal objectives would have rendered this alternative undesirable. Zayas's fictional convent is a literary device that indicates how human beings should amend their behaviour in the earthly sexual and social economy, not to alter that economy itself. By affiliating the ideal human man with God, in a book whose divinity is decidedly remote from humans floundering in their dysfunction, Zayas underscores the distance between the flawed ways of the nobility and the perfect qualities of the Godlike, flawless nobleman who has gone missing outside her fictional convent.

As a complement to the worldly power and rightness with which she invests the God whom her female characters seek, Zayas consistently relates the convent with a materialistic opulence that belies any spiritual function it might have, but speaks perfectly to the worldly meaning of the signifiers she imports from the sacred lexicon. In consonance with the baroque correlation of ostentation with merit and status, she regularly associates what is right with abundance and splendour, thereby glorifying the urban upper classes and their members' role as the sustaining power of order. These associations would have had particular meaning for a people who related merit to the conspicuous display of wealth and the accumulation of riches not only to passive wealth but to the capacity to control the economies of others, to broadly project oneself upon society and dispose of others (Maravall, *Culture* 117; *Poder* 221). The social and literary significance of material wealth as indicators of status reflects the class anxiety that, according to Romero-Díaz, permeates the Spanish novella (*Nueva*).

Zayas constructs a direct relationship between the material magnificence of the soirée, the visible enclosure where the truth is revealed, and that of the convent, the invisible enclosure in which that truth is protected. Relying on baroque esteem of material and financial weight, Zayas endows her fictional convent with the power to consistently draw the material resources of the rightly behaving into itself like a deep, dark vault. Those resources have two forms: the highly idealized bodies of right-minded female and male characters, and the material goods they bring into the enclosure with them. This placement of worldly magnificence is at odds with the emphasis on spiritual values with which the convent would be invested were it a truly sacred signifier.

Baroque Catholic culture mustered ritual complexity and material splendour in response to larger cultural aesthetics as well as starker Protestant aesthetics and relative iconoclasm.[13] The purpose of this opulence-laden cult was theoretically the inspiration of awe and adoration of the divinity, which in the political realm redoubled with the opulence used to inspire awe of the monarch. Sustaining her narrative gaze on the human world and not the divine, Zayas conscripts Catholic ritual in the *Desengaños* into the service of her aesthetics by limiting her use of that ritual to the moment of contrition and death – confession and last rites, the only sacraments in which characters participate in the present tense of the plots. This stark delimitation sustains her emphasis on loss.

Just as the female character who dies in the world, or to it, takes away from that world her beauty, described as highly compelling, so the male and female characters who retire to the convent take with them a bundle of wealth that defies spiritual significance but exalts the secular baroque relationship – certainly Zayas's – between material prosperity and what is right for the functional nobility. When the characters pass from the corrupt world into the invisible space of the convent, the author has them disappear in a cloud of opulence whose splendour cements her association between what is good and what the world outside the convent has lost. By the end of the book, the loss is huge.

Zayas associates the retreat to the convent with the removal of riches from the secular world in the first *desengaño* in the splendorous, jewel-laden attire of Isabel, and Lisis's offer to provide her friend with even more wealth should she need it to make her retreat from the world (166). The narrator describes Isabel as she emerges on the scene for the second evening's events as specifically displaying the costly jewels with which she will disappear from sight: 'Her adornments were most costly; so much so, that one could not judge what was more resplendent: her lovely face or her rich jewels, for this night she displayed those jewels which, on the previous night, she had said she was setting aside for the expenses of her religious life' (Su aderezo era costosísimo; tanto, que no se podía juzgar qué daba más resplandores: su hermoso rostro o sus ricas joyas, que esta noche hizo alarde de las que la pasada había dicho tenía reservadas para los gastos de su religión, 259). The financial bleeding of the corrupt world begins here and continues to the end of the book.

The affiliation of what is right, material goods, and the convent continues in *desengaño* 2, as Carlos throws lies and wealth at Octavia to shuffle her out of sight: 'I will be giving you jewels and cash' (te iré dando joyas y dineros, 186). He subsequently reveals that his true motive for gifting Octavia so extravagantly is to 'meet his obligation' to her by substituting assets for marriage to him, and those assets allow Octavia to live comfortably in the convent forever after (187). There is poetic justice in the fact that she makes off with a good portion of the estate that Carlos's greedy father sought to keep from her, to a place where he can never get it back.

Zayas repeatedly uses jewellery, money, and entire inheritances to signify retribution. The maligned Inés (d5), put in a convent once recovered from her traumatic years in her house's chimney, inherits the goods of her family members who tortured and tried to kill her and survives in the lap of justice and luxury 'sustaining herself with the large estate of her brother and husband' (sustentándose de la gruesa hacienda de su hermano y marido, 288). The much-maligned wife acquires hyperbolic beauty in tandem with this wealth to indicate the relationship between the resources of virtue and prosperity, both lost to the human world when the convent doors close around the beautiful young widow.

The association between ethical superiority and worldly abundance is equally clear. In *desengaño* 8, the Virgin mediates Enrique's fate through a vow he makes on his deathbed to serve her if he should survive, a vow to which he is faithful. Physically recovered, he enters a Franciscan convent. However, Zayas violates the spiritual significance of Franciscan poverty, using it instead as a canvas on which to paint her association between what is good and material prosperity, for when inserted into a poor community, Enrique's wealth has a high visibility by contrast. The young nobleman uses his riches to build a chapel with an ornate vault commemorating his dead wife, displacing the divinity as the object of devotion and disallowing a shift from human to divine values.

Zayas invokes wealth in the final *desengaño* with particular potency, yet again weighting down the convent with heavy human resources that belie a spiritual meaning. Her astounding character Florentina is directly responsible for the deaths of twelve individuals, including her half-sister Magdalena, whose husband and rightful position in the household Florentina usurped. It was Florentina who declared her desire to her brother-in-law Dionís, unleashing the disasters that follow, and given Florentina's culpability, it seems remarkable that Zayas retires her to the convent with the greatest abundance of all, in one of Lisbon's most sumptuous convents, where her every need is more than amply met: 'supplementing her dowry and allowances with the large estate she received from one side of her settlement and the other, where she lives a holy and most religious life today' (supliendo el dote y más gasto la gruesa hacienda que había de la una parte y la otra, donde hoy vive santa y religiosísima vida, 500).

Using the same words with which she describes the wealth that Inés takes with her from the world, Zayas reinforces the alliance between material prosperity, living a saintly life, and the convent, thereby reinforcing her link between the convent and right behaviour with Florentina's luxurious life in it. By repenting her misdeeds and removing herself from the world in payment for them, Florentina becomes a highly prized exemplar of the turn from wrong to right, and as such, Zayas rewards her lavishly. Throughout the *Desengaños*, the convent draws material wealth away from the dysfunctional world like a magnet.

The greatest loss to Zayas's fictional urban noble society is without doubt the retirement of Lisis from it. The ten tales told at her soirée hang from Lisis's decision to abandon the world like dark and weighty jewels on a necklace that clicks closed into a circle at the book's end. Appropriately, Zayas bedecks her character in clothing laden with symbolic meaning and aglitter with wealth, precisely at the moment when she is about to disappear into the convent. A living variant of the beautiful and dead woman, Lisis emerges onto the highly theatrical scene of her soirée's final evening dressed in signifiers of purity, victory, and eternity, having failed to don the clothing, jewels, or flowers sent to her by Don Diego and thereby indicating her rejection of his suit.[14] Accompanied by Isabel, who dresses as she does, Lisis emerges onto the scene

> with full skirts of *white* silk, with many *diamond* buttons that formed lovely sheens, farthingales, and white crepe at the neckline; their hair, instead of bearing ribbons, was braided with most *purely white pearls*, and at the top of their headdresses, as a finishing touch, two crowns of *lilies* made of *diamonds*, whose green leaves were emeralds, their jewels and clothing having been made with care before the festivities began; belt and collar likewise of *diamond*, and on the lining of their long skirts, many *lilies* like those on their heads, and atop the crowns, clustered feathers of heron, *whiter* than the untrodden *snow*. (405, emphasis added)

> (con sayas enteras de raso *blanco*, con muchos botones de *diamantes*, que hacían hermosos visos, verdugados y abaninos; los cabellos, en lugar de cintas, trenzados con *albísimas perlas*, y en lo alto de los tocados, por remate de ellos, dos coronas de azucenas de *diamantes*, cuyas verdes hojas eran de esmeraldas hechos ellas y los vestidos con cuidado, desde antes que se empezara la fiesta; cinta y collar, de los mismos *diamantes*, y en las mangas de punta de las sayas enteras, muchas *azucenas* de la misma forma que las que traían en la cabeza, y en lo alto de las coronas, en forma de airones, muchos mazos de garzotas y marinetes, más *albos* que la no pisada *nieve*.)

Not surprisingly, it is precisely when the men in the fictional audience behold this spectacle and realize what is about to disappear that they repent of their deceiving ways, with which Zayas fictionalizes the accomplishment of one of her objectives: 'Had the gentlemen beheld nothing more than their beauty, they would have repented of their deceitful behaviour, for in it they saw the greatest rude awakening from their trickery' (Cuando los caballeros no miraba más de su hermosura, fuera el arrepentimiento de sus engaños, pues en ella [la hermosura] veían el mayor desengaño de sus cautelas, 405). Lisis's retirement of her body from the world, bearing all the wealth that adorns her, also diegetically inscribes the realization of the author's goal to convince women to respect themselves. She will not risk losing her honour or her life, nor will she disperse her abundant wealth in the corrupt world, from which she retires instead. Implicitly, until the nobility improves its inept performance of its own standards, Lisis and everything she possesses will remain in hiding, and her withdrawal is but the final one of several in the book.

Zayas's coupling of material wealth with proper social ethics, both of which she deposits in the convent at her book's end, harmonizes perfectly with her larger objectives. Uninterested in exalting the spiritual, she is artistically invested in rendering the loss of the virtuous to the world outside the convent. That loss is great indeed when the stunningly beautiful bodies of young women, and the gallants who serve order, are removed from circulation in tandem with similarly stunning wealth; Zayas calculates her narrative resources such that the departure of any virtuous character from secular society is very expensive. The loss has meaning in the secular, not religious, ontology, and Zayas's ironic use of the convent to reinforce that celebration is extraordinary.

Unlike the marriage ending, the early modern convent finale sometimes marks a suspension versus a conclusion, for it constitutes a non-ending for characters who do not take permanent religious vows. Lisis, whom Zayas does not describe as planning a permanent life in the convent, calls her ingress there a retreat to a parapet (*talanquera*), the raised earth surrounding a trench on a battlefield, that offers her a position from which to safely observe the war being waged in and for the world: 'I am taking refuge in the sacred and shelter in the retired life in the convent, from where I plan [as from a parapet] to watch what happens to everyone else' (Me acojo a sagrado y tomo por amparo el retiro de un convento, desde donde pienso [como en talanquera] ver lo que sucede a los demás, 509). In the service of Zayas's dark aesthetics, Lisis reveals her reasons for this retreat in negative terms, using the same logic as did Isabel at the book's beginning. She explains to the disappointed Diego that she simply does not dare rely on her own luck to lead her to a happy ending: 'It is not right for me to trust in good fortune' (no es justo que yo me fíe de mi dicha, 508). The convent doors close behind Lisis and the book ends, leaving Zayas's fictional world echoing with emptiness.

In the *Desengaños*, entering the convent is less a decision, one option among several, than a last resort and survival strategy, a straightforward and stark compliment to the many worthy characters who are dead at the book's end. The dead inscribe the high cost of vice already exacted, whereas the women and men in the convent suggest even greater losses to come. Zayas uses the convent as the locked box into which she safeguards that which she represents as Spain's most precious resource: the chivalric, aggressive, wealthy, and honourable nobility of both sexes. It buttresses Catholicism as the church of the imperial state and affiliates the virtuous with God's plan for the present and future, as manifest in the past she so nostalgically renders in her book.[15]

Metonymically affiliated with the functional nobility, the convent in the *Desengaños* is a safe space. It is also a sterile space, a non-space, configured in the narrative as an absence to which the characters disappear in resignation. In taking up residence there, the admirable male and female characters reject contact with the opposite sex, contact proven to ignite unjust violence in Zayas's unreformed fictional world. That contact, however, is also the only way to assure the nobility's generations. Zayas configures the God of the female convent as an invisible object of female desire whose appearance in the world will coincide with the reforms for which she cries loudly in her book. Implicitly, Lisis will return to the world and when those reforms are accomplished, for that is where she wants to live the life of the nobility in whose hands the fate of the Spanish nation rested.

Women with religious devotion write of God as the guarantor of the self, whose power supports and sustains identity.[16] Zayas's characters seek neither individuation nor integration into that which is all. Their author crafted them to represent the desire to form a meaningful and esteemed part of human society, a community ruled successfully by the mandates of hegemonic nobility in which men have their role and women theirs. The convent is thus the holding space for the male hero and his rightly (according to Zayas) responsive partner, the unseen place of order to which men and women retreat until their class regains its grip on its own heroic destiny.

Zayas manipulates her pseudo-sacred space as would a resident of the urban centre, using it to reinforce her political agenda, an agenda impossible to separate from its Catholicism: in Zayas's fictional world, the convent is a Counter-Reformation solution that narratively integrates the monastic institution into the imperial image, an institution that distinguished Catholicism from Protestantism and as such forwarded Zayas's nationalistic ideology. At the far reaches of the convent's inherent power to signify what is right, Zayas waves her pen over her characters headed there as if casting a spell, and they simply disappear.

The silence their absence produces is very disquieting because of its contrast with the loud and violent narrative fugues that precede it. All of the main characters whose stories Zayas leads to the convent are active individuals. The most horribly abused character, Inés, is smart and articulate, even while cemented into the chimney of her own home. It is extremely telling that entrance into the convent silences her in a way that not even the torments visited upon her were able to accomplish.

For Zayas's female convent dwellers, who have no religious vocation but do long for a functional male, who are not able to live in the world but wish to do so, the convent is a kind of living death, benign but fatal in narrative terms, at odds with their perfectly legitimate desire.

In sum, the convent, Zayas's architectural rendering of what is right, is *not*. It is not, in the same fashion that the happy ending is not, that the hero is not, that the worldly space in which the virtuous woman and man who can exercise virtue is not. Teetering on the precipice of modernity, peering down into the dark abyss of a world she represents as having alienated the divinity, Zayas removes the house of God and the divinity itself to the very edges of meaning, sustaining her narrative emphasis squarely on the high drama of what is wrong, the better to intensify her reader's horror and provoke that reader's reform. Thus, the same dark pattern of meaning takes shape in all of the *desengaños*, whose finales crescendo in death to the world or death in it. The misbehaviour of the nobility, in collusion with wrongly empowered social inferiors, produces the removal from the earthly social economy of the virtuous and the wealth that signifies their worth. Zayas leaves her dysfunctional fictional elite to founder on the rocks of its own failure, or reform and thereby recover its rightful identity.

Figure 5.1 *Portrait of a Young Girl*, Diego Velázquez, 1649. With the kind permission of the Hispanic Society of America

Postscript: Laurela

The youngest victim character of the *Desengaños* is Laurela (d6), into whose house, life, and honour the vicious Esteban inserts himself, bringing lies and death in with him. The most horrifying of all Zayas's victims because of her age, Laurela is twelve years old when Esteban sees her for the first time, and is but fourteen when he enters her house disguised as a maid and becomes her intimate companion. She is fifteen when her family kills her. She is the only unwed noblewoman who dies as a consequence of social corruption, and her story is the only one in which Zayas blurs the boundaries between her perfect and imperfect victims, to great effect. The author manages to bring everything that can go wrong in a courtship and honour plot down on the head of her youngest protagonist, literally killing her. Seduced like an unmarried noblewoman, Laurela is punished like a perfect wife but not exalted like one.[1]

At the time when Esteban disguises himself as Estefanía and presents himself as the ideal candidate to be Laurela's maid because of his musical talent, the narrator specifies that Laurela does not know what love is or anything about it. Still a girl (*niña*), she is absorbed by her passion and talent for music, an interest on which Esteban plays by offering skills in precisely that area. Once he enters her family's house, the reader recalls the narrators' diatribes against servants and begins to prepare for the worst. The worst begins when Laurela's father starts to share his daughter's enthusiasm for Estefanía, albeit for different reasons.

Zayas paints Laurela into the corner in which all of her noblewomen characters die literally or figuratively, for she is not only deceived by a deeply flawed man but also related to flawed members of the nobility.

When Esteban reveals himself as a man to his presumed beloved, even at age fifteen the young woman knows she has been dishonoured and will be held responsible for his actions, although every other member of her family was completely deceived by his disguise as well. Like Isabel and Octavia before her, she seeks to solve her problem by marrying the man who has dishonoured her. She agrees to this because Esteban says he is a nobleman disposed to wed her, and it is under this pretext that she leaves her house with him, taking substantial jewels and money with her.

The narrator of Laurela's tale, Matilde, specifies that the protagonist falls in love with Esteban because she is too young to know about the tricks of the world. Matilde also insists that this is the worst thing that could happen ('Y lo peor es que se halló enamorada de don Esteban,' 321). Laurela's naivety is deadly because it justifies her father's fury at her leaving his house to marry without his consent, which she does after he had arranged her marriage to Don Enrique. To make things worse, Laurela had obediently acquiesced to that match. In the process and without meaning to, Laurela further makes a fool of her father by revealing the object of his desire to be a man, and shames the family by winding up disrobed and robbed of her literal and symbolic jewels in a public place, where Esteban abandons her after revealing himself to be a commoner and a married one at that.

The fact that Zayas produces the noble and wealthy Enrique as Laurela's faithful suitor evidences authorial manipulation of the plot to maximize her public's anguish. Enrique is one of the few heroic men in the entire book, and Zayas zealously keeps him in the text's background. He fails in his attempt to marry Laurela after Esteban has dishonoured her, because her father claims to want his daughter in the convent. Textual evidence such as this reveals the particular care with which Zayas heaps problems on Laurela, the weakest and most vulnerable of all her female characters, for those problems include many of the difficulties faced by the older noblewomen in the *Desengaños*. Among them are extreme naivety; an unforgiving, flawed father as unable as she to tell Esteban from Estefanía; a despicable, lying lover; a disempowered mother and sisters who do not dare challenge her father; and other family members who first beat her, and then are determined to do away with her because she embodies their dishonour.

Following her established pattern, Zayas kills Laurela *because* she is beautiful, young, and naive. Cruel but not entirely unjust – her family's dishonour is real – the young woman's death brings home like no other tale the high cost of simply living in the corrupt world.

However, the fact that Zayas abandons the girl at death reveals that Laurela is not a perfect victim. Her corpse does not glow, bleed, or speak, and it is not beautiful. According to the poetics of the *Desengaños*, God does not claim her because she was an agent in her own demise by responding to Esteban's desire, unable to imagine that he was deceiving her. The fact that she had no other solution does not matter, but rather makes her dilemma all the more perfect. Her conscious, willing decision to leave home with Esteban and marry him, although she was fully aware that she was formally engaged to another man, disqualifies her from female perfection, and she simply dies under the wall that her father, uncle, and aunt arrange to collapse on her. After the wall falls and people gather to try and save her, 'they found the hapless Laurela completely dead, because the wall had opened up her head, and the debris had finished her off by suffocation' (hallaron a la sin ventura Laurela de todo punto muerta, porque la pared la había abierto la cabeza, y con la tierra se acabó de ahogar, 330).

Zayas engineers this *desengaño* such that as soon as Esteban/Estefanía gains access to Laurela, things get very messy. Everyone involved is responsible for what happens: her father for being tricked by a commoner, her mother and sisters for their blind obedience of the father, Laurela herself for loving a man who had disguised himself as a woman (which in the gender ethics of the *Desengaños* signifies degradation), her aunt and uncle for colluding with her father's cruelty. Particularly compelling is how Zayas uses Laurela to reveal that once a noble-woman is dishonoured, even doing the right thing will be wrong. The young woman's decision to marry Esteban is in itself a good one; once he enters her house, she is in the same bind as the raped woman and has but one way to save her honour and her life, and that is it. Simultaneously, however, that very decision justifies her father's rage because his daughter has in fact dishonoured him. So fraught with contingencies, so entangled in wrong is this tale that no single character could have set things right.

The solution, then, is as multifarious as the problem and entails inverting each one. Importantly, Esteban is not the problem, for he behaves in accordance with the book's expectations for the lower class. He is the catalyst that reveals where the real problem lies: with the imperfect nobility. Laurela's father should not have been deceived by a lying, disguised, married member of the serving class. Laurela should not have fallen in love with a man she knew had deceived and dishonoured her as well as her family for months on end. Her mother and sisters should not have silently tolerated the father's rejection of his daughter. Her aunt, uncle, and father should have protected the young woman. The disorder of the story is perfect, because one party's role in Laurela's death is embroiled with that of another, including the young woman herself, of whom Zayas exacts responsibility. Only meeting all three of the book's objectives could have saved Laurela.

So as not to leave the *Desengaños* enveloped in their own gloom, and to solve the puzzle that this story presents to the reader, set forth in chapter 1, let us imagine a utopian fantasy of the author's ilk that envisions how Laurela's tale would have been different had the book's objectives been met. To begin with, Esteban's disguise would have been detected by Laurela's vigilant father, or by her equally vigilant mother and older sisters. Had Esteban entered the house and declared himself to Laurela, she would have told her father of the intruder's behaviour. That father would have made inquiries into Esteban's true identity, would have accepted his responsibility for a commoner's violation of his house, and would have recognized that since he himself had been deceived by Estefanía, it was no wonder that his young daughter had been, too. Esteban would have been quietly executed for defamation of a noble family, as was Diego, who pursued Inés in *desengaño* 5. Had the crisis been averted here, Laurela would have had her reputation and her father his, because the dishonour would have been contained.

Had Laurela eloped with Esteban and been dishonoured and robbed by him, and then left at the church, her aunt and uncle would have taken pity on her rather than punish her, taking her to a convent. They would have paid her convent dowry, had her father refused to do so. Her mother and older sisters would not have been cowering, helpless pawns of her father, but rather strong women in control of those who had access to the youngest member of the family and protective of her after she was lied to. Finally, all members of Laurela's family would have accepted the noble, generous, and sincere offer of Enrique to marry Laurela even after she had been dishonoured, recognizing as did Enrique, 'that if Laurela had been deceived, the deceit itself served to exculpate her' (que si Laurela había sido engañada, el mismo engaño le servía de disculpa, 328).

Not a single one of these changes alone would have sufficed to save Laurela from her fate. Had she denounced Esteban to her father the minute he revealed he was a man, her father would have killed her regardless had he not reformed his own multiple flaws. Had her mother and sisters arranged to secret the dishonoured young woman into a convent, that same unreformed father would likely have done away with them all for contradicting his wishes. The primacy of the patriarch in Zayas's domestic hierarchy is clear in the inability of virtue (Enrique) to reach Laurela through the thick wall of her father's dysfunction that radiates into the world around him. That wall kills her. The centrality of the patriarch in the reversal of Laurela's fate speaks to Zayas's faithfulness to her society's vision of an ordered hierarchy that was itself patriarchal. No one is going anywhere if the noblemen do not come along.

In Laurela's death, Zayas renders as nowhere else the importance of noble community in the rescue of the nobility itself. Her story illustrates better than any other that the reason things can go so very wrong all through the *desengaños* is because of the inexorable contingencies inherent in social life as Zayas envisions it. In the intricate web of inter-reliance that she spins between noblewomen and noblemen, Zayas stakes out new territory for women and men of her class, defining the noble woman as an indispensible player in the power politics of imperial Spain and the noble man as obliged to himself, to her, and their community to respect and protect their mutual interests.

Figure Conclusion 1 *Doña Inés de Zúñiga*, Juan Carreño de Miranda, c. 1669. With the kind permission of the Fundación Lázaro Galiano, Madrid

Conclusion

It is not a tragic ending,
but rather the happiest one that could be offered.

(No es trágico fin,
sino el más felice que se pudo dar.)

Narrator, Desengaños

Reading the *Desengaños* in light of Zayas's objectives not only reconciles the text with itself but also sheds light on two of its important features that are otherwise invisible. The first is how a female author positions herself in the Spanish honour code, a ritual system universally defined as one that objectifies and victimizes women. Second, illuminating the multiple but coordinated systems of meaning operative in the *Desengaños* makes it possible to see how influential the book was.

There is no evidence that the reform to which Zayas urgently calls her readers was heeded. If it was, it proved ultimately unsuccessful, and the Spanish empire collapsed under its own weight. The aesthetics of the *Desengaños*, however, ascended, wielding particular influence on British authors, and it is likely that Zayas's systematic blocking of transcendence opened the creaking door leading down into the dungeons of Gothic literature, in whose depths writers explored the realm of terror.

To evaluate the question of how a woman defending female subjectivity negotiates the honour code, it is helpful to step back and assess how it is traditionally analysed. Whether critics find honour's violent defence to be an artistic convention or the historical rule of the day, it is consistently defined as existing about and for men. McKendrick, one of honour's eminent theorists, affirms Larson's argument that men's rigorous defence of their honour on the early modern Spanish stage was designed to reassure the [male] public, whose members were emasculated by imperial decline ('Honour/Vengeance'; *Honor Plays*).[1] Dramatists articulated this political threat as men's obsession with what was thought *about* them, a problem they managed through their control of women.

After reviewing several other theories, McKendrick proposes her own, related to Larson's: what she aptly calls 'Spain's seizures of honour' are the mimetic transfer of Spanish obsession with purity of blood onto the female body (318). She finds that male fear of genealogical impurity resulted from the Spaniard's need to have a provable Christian bloodline untainted by Moorish or Jewish 'impurity' in order to be accepted as a member of the dominant group. One of the first theorists of honour, Américo Castro, defines that cohort as 'those believed to have the right and power to appear on the front line of the Spanish empire' (quién se creía con derecho y con poder para figurar en primera línea dentro del imperio español, *Edad* 35).

Whether McKendrick's thesis or any other is correct or not is not my question here. What is noteworthy in all of them is how they consistently define the female as specular and dispossessed of honour: 'The women's actions reflect upon the men' (McKendrick, 'Honour' 323). Successful male control of females is thus a metaphor for male social standing in general. In this system and its interpretation, there is no allowance for a woman possessed of her own honour, nor is it ever postulated that the noblewomen charged with bearing racial purity into the Spanish future would themselves have been deeply invested in that very enterprise. Most studies on honour, even a recent one such as Carrión's *Subject Stages*, position women among those repressed and objectified by the honour code.

However, the *Desengaños* provide evidence that the noblewoman in seventeenth-century Spain does indeed have honour, her own honour, a subjective esteem believed to display the regard of her self and her community. The noblewoman's role in the production of an honourable society provides women with a positive, productive role in the discourse of honour, whether an author chooses to enact that role or not.

Zayas clearly does. When Nisi recommends that a noblewoman kill whomever stains her honour, when Lisis insists that the noblewoman esteem her honour and act to defend it, when the Virgin Mary contends to Beatriz that Christ loves only women who defend their honour, the author provides evidence that honour is theirs for the defending, that it belongs to them. Had Zayas wanted to protest the honour code itself, she had a legitimate platform from which to do so because it systematically sanctioned the killing of women, and she could have done so by activating any of her characters against it. She did not.

What is more, the numerous calls to noblewomen's energetic defence of their honour in the *Desengaños* suggest that, as Zayas represents it, female honour not only contributed to the integrity of society as a whole but also was absolutely necessary for its proper functioning. This is the essence of her book's first and second objectives, which insist that noblemen must recognize and defend noblewomen's honour and allow it to play an active role in the production of order. For their part, by defending themselves and their honour, noblewomen perform their proper role in the imperial scheme of things and the empire itself. The pistol that Carreño de Miranda painted, dangling from a lovely ribbon at the waist of Doña Inés de Zúniga, presumably would help them do that (see fig. Conclusion 1). The text's goals to convince noblemen to respect noblewomen and to convince society to return to honourable behaviour are thus correlates. Zayas's book makes it clear that without honourable women whom men and society at large respect, the nobility will fail, and with it the nation.

As we have seen, Zayas presents noblewomen's honour as relational, in that it necessarily relies on the respect of men to exist. As we have also seen, this is an accurate assessment of women's historical reality during this period, one that harmonizes with Maravall's insistence that honour itself is a social condition, not a personal quality ('Función' 15). Thus it may be that standing definitions of the Spanish honour code set up a fallacious antagonist in woman, establishing her position as oppositional and/or threatening to male honour by definition whereas some early modern Spaniards conceived of the two as compatible. This relational dynamic not only allows but forces men to take responsibility alongside women for honour's staining. This is what the *Desengaños* are about, and Zayas's three objectives demand that all members of the nobility comply with the same hegemonic standards.

A woman who positions herself this way equalizes an economics of honour that otherwise is extremely unequal and expensive to her. The honour code exacts a high price from the sexually defiled woman, whereas the sexually defiled man does not even exist. Thus, the noblewoman would logically seek out a way to implicate the men around her in her honour by revealing it as something produced and maintained by women and men together, to the benefit of all.

Zayas is not unique in her understanding of women's honour. In the section of *Nobleza virtuosa* (*The Virtuous Nobility*, 1637) labelled as advice to her eldest daughter, Luisa de Padilla holds the young wife responsible for holding up her end of the marriage bargain: 'Any sane woman must behave such that her husband never find her lacking on point of decorum; this is not only *for her own reputation*, but also for the great obligation in which he put her on the day he trusted her and entrusted into her hands the greatest of all temporal treasures, which is honour, carefulness that for a thousand reasons must be much greater in great ladies; thus I charge you with doing so' (Cualquiera mujer cuerda ha de procurar no ocasionar a su marido para que la advierta punto de recato; esto no sólo *por su propia estimación* sino por lo mucho que él la obligó desde el día que se fió de ella, y dejó por su cuenta el mayor tesoro de los temporales, que es el honor, cuidado que por mil razones ha de ser en las grandes señoras muy mayor, así os lo encargo, 283–4, emphasis added).

Indeed, the honourable woman's defence of her honour was the perfect tool with which to justify punishment of the male aggressor in a system that otherwise allowed him to go free of responsibility. According to Pitt-Rivers, in cases of honour it is not the offending male but the *offended* male – the man whose wife was defiled by another man – who had the problem and needed to take violent action. This dynamic obviates the real problem, which is the man who does the violating of a woman who 'belongs to' another man. In the *Desengaños*, Zayas offers a clear vision of how important the distinction is by representing not only how useless it is to punish the person blamed for the dishonour rather than the one responsible for it, but how extremely costly that confusion is. Her insertion of female agency into the praxis of honour inflects the honour code's grammar in ways that contradict the understanding of woman as disorderly, and simultaneously sets society up to lose everything it holds dear when it dishonours her.[2]

In his prescriptive treatise *Diálogos de apacible entretenimiento* (*Dialogues of Pleasant Entertainment*, 1605), Hidalgo defines the difference between a man and a woman's honour as one of degree, but not of kind. Male honour, he says, is calculated with multiple factors, such as education, military prowess, political power, and the practice of virtue. Female honour, in contrast, is derived exclusively from a woman's virtue (309). Equating good women with virtue, and virtue as the key to empire, is what allowed Zayas to deliver the impact of the *Desengaños*. Her book displays how the corrupt community defiles and eliminates a perfectly virtuous and therefore honourable wife when it wrongly charges her for an entire network of wrongdoings. That behaviour creates a social deficit that accumulates to unbearable dimensions when the elimination is systematic. It is the noblewoman's power as virtue's essential embodiment that allows Zayas to fictionalize virtue's undoing as deftly as she does in the *Desengaños*.

The noblewoman's honour, however, is burdened with the contingencies of baroque social ideology that prescribe her virtuous submission to hegemonic determinations, thus constricting her range of motion and meaning. The *Desengaños* leave no doubt that noblemen, occupying the superior position in the social hierarchy, are guarantors of order and God's own representatives in the family/state microcosm, and consequently bear the greatest responsibility for disorder. Zayas thereby adheres to the gender politics of her age, according to which 'the husband was the state's representative in his own house' and 'a threat to marital honour was by implication a threat to the state' (Mc-Kendrick, 'Calderón' 140). In this hierarchy, if the noblewoman's subjection to the nobleman is an analogue of humanity's subjection to God, then when the nobleman misbehaves, he insults his divine counterpart. The insulted divinity is exactly what Zayas uses to articulate the final word in her tales, affiliating all of her wronged characters with a God who corrects the situation by depositing markers of sanctity on the virtuous dead and leading the virtuous survivors into the convent. Neither of these events should transpire, neither represents what is right. On the contrary, both events are the culminations of a long string of wrong actions.

Whereas the position of male dramatists regarding the murder of an innocent wife is subject to multiple interpretations, in part because of the ambiguities of theatre, Zayas's is not. She marshals an entire aesthetic system to state clearly that the dishonouring of noblewomen makes nothing possible except loss and its horribly compelling representation. In the hands of María de Zayas, the virtuous wife speaks in an authentic first person, endowing the meaning of marriage and honour with new life. The author protects that meaning by erasing the woman precisely when what is done to her is both avoidable and unbearable. She leaves behind her body, whose sole function is to reflect the wrongs of others, and then God's correction of them.

It is no surprise that Zayas systematically undoes the honour code's definition of dishonour as what is done *to* someone, to insist instead on dishonour as what someone does or fails to do. Her dead wives are the most powerful articulation of that undoing. The perfect victim qualities of these characters and the specular nature of their abused bodies deflect the image of wrongness off the woman wrongly defined as defiled, and back onto the wronging community. After the wife dies, the author exacts a steep price for her removal: impoverishment, sterility, and the ghostly silence that rings at the book's end. By exacting that price, Zayas calculates the loss as intolerable, thereby pressuring the community to recover its purchase on its own nobility.

Emptying her perfect victims of their ability to represent themselves provided Zayas with an extreme way to render the ruptures in meaning explicit at other levels of her text, such as the abyss between what characters say and what they do, and the expectation for a happy ending that never transpires. The book's disjunctures reflect the distance between what should be and what is, as the stories and the frame tale do not end as much as they simply stop, beckoning the reader to take over from there. If, as Mulvey insists, narrative 'can be conceived around ending that is not closure' and the feminist perspective 'should insist on the possibility of change without closure' (175), then Zayas is a good place to see this possibility played out in fiction at a very early date.[3]

Just as importantly, the *Desengaños* prove that it is not necessarily detrimental for an author to objectify a female character, for Zayas ultimately objectifies the virtuous wife, doing so at least as intensely as her male counterparts by using her to reveal the loss sustained by the community that defiles her. Separating the undone female character's meaning, her subjective identity, from her body at the moment when her familiars betray her is what allows the author to save her: she is *not* what is done to her, but rather her flesh is used to mean the wrongness around her. In this fashion, Zayas refuses to imbricate the dying or dead woman and male subjectivity. The *Desengaños* indicate that a writer can reduce a fictional woman to a visual object whose meaning is for others, and do so without demeaning her. This is a stunning achievement.

Zayas's reader beholds the female character negotiating what she desires with what is expected of her. As long as society is virtuous, the two are one. When human irresponsibility wreaks havoc on her, she vanishes, leaving only a mirror behind. Zayas thus makes an important break with the scopophatic exaltation of the used female body visible in sacred and secular narratives alike. This, I would argue, is what keeps her display of suffering, passive women from being even remotely pornographic: the pornographic text derives its power from the fictional complicity of the objectified individual with the subject's desire.[4] Zayas never does that, and instead uses the wife's corpse to signify exclusively what is wrong, thereby casting dishonour upon all involved in her death. It was a dangerous and daring move on her part.

The danger is explicit in the highly compelling image of the beautiful, helpless female victim that I would like to suggest Zayas provided European art, whose terribly beautiful dead body adorns the cover of this book (see fig. Conclusion 2). Within the context of the *Desengaños*, this figure is a secular sacrifice whose negative meaning must be derived from contrast with its authentic deployment in Catholic culture. If we remove Catholic belief from the *Desengaños*, the victim is simply and horribly dead, and God will not deposit corrective meaning using the signifiers of sanctity on her body. Erasing Catholicism, a litany of Gothic conventions appears like a palimpsest on the page before us: an aesthetic based on pleasurable fear, the disruption of the signifier from its signified, live burial as punishment for sexual shame, the poisonous effects of guilt and shame, the convent entered for the wrong reasons, feelings of helpless paralysis.[5] The list only begins there, for the *Desengaños* also blur the boundary between life and death, and include multiple narrative framing devices, enclosures within enclosures, a broad range of tone and focus, tropes of isolation and immobilization, sleeplike and deathlike states, the self walled off from its normal access to the world, and subterranean spaces. The retrograde vision of the *Desengaños* that nostalgically idealizes the nascent Spanish empire provided an appealing tone for subsequent Gothic fashion if, as Butler suggests, the Gothic novel that became popular in England at the end of the eighteenth century 'purported to revive old stories and beliefs' (xviii).

This being said, the distinction between the *Desengaños* and the Gothic text is crucial. In her essay 'On the Supernatural in Poetry,' Gothic author Ann Radcliffe (1764–1823) says terror is distinguishable by its obscurity, meaning the indeterminacy of horrible events, which makes possible the Gothic sublime, the plumbing of what Radcliffe calls 'the mystery of the human mind.' Like Radcliffe, Zayas exalts what Radcliffe's speaker Mr W. calls 'the extravagant and erring spirit' in human-

Figure Conclusion 2   *St Eulalia*, John William Waterhouse, 1895. © Tate, London, 2011

ity.[6] Although Zayas is magisterial at painting how errant human beings drive innocent characters into a corner from which there is no escape, she leaves no doubt that the failure of the nobility to perform nobly is the reason they are in that corner. There is nothing mysterious or unsolvable about the origins of the problems that Zayas represents, although the tales themselves do not represent the solutions to those problems. In the *Desengaños*, then, we see not the sublime, not the unfathomable mystery of the human psyche, but the workings of a depraved humanity unleashed on the innocent without the sanction of a superhuman power and without any relief in sight. The difference between the *Desengaños* and the Gothic aesthetic is the expectation deeply embedded in Zayas's text that things should be vastly different than they are, and there is nothing sublime about any of it.[7]

The compelling, helpless, and abused female figure that Zayas created for the *Desengaños* became a hallmark of the Gothic aesthetic, whose artists delighted in the forced enclosure of the heroine in a dark space, physical and/or psychological, where death paces around her. Gothic terms of enclosure are hauntingly familiar to those who know Zayas's second book. In Matthew Lewis's classic *The Monk* (1796), we come upon Agnes – whose name recalls Zayas's references to her perfect victims as lambs – forced into a convent dungeon where she is locked up and fed bread and water by a malicious nun. We descend the dungeon stairs with Lorenzo, following human moans, to find 'a creature stretched upon a bed of straw, so wretched, so emaciated, so pale, that he doubted to think her woman. She was half naked: her long dishevelled hair fell in disorder over her face, and almost entirely concealed it' (355). Lorenzo finds Agnes delirious with grief and almost blind, holding her dead newborn in her emaciated arms. The nearly dead woman recalls waking during her imprisonment to find her fingers 'ringed with the long worms which bred in the corrupted flesh of my infant' (396). The echo of Zayas's Inés (d5) is loud.[8] The unbearable oppressiveness of content and style that characterizes Charles Robert Maturin's *Melmoth the Wanderer* (1820), whose protagonist roams the earth unable to die and unable to live, is in many ways the perfect culmination of Zayas's dark aesthetics. The frequency with which Zayas's texts crossed the channel and the Pyrenees makes her influence a reasonable conjecture, some of whose parameters I would like to propose here in hopes of opening an avenue for future investigation.[9]

Experts in eighteenth- and nineteenth-century literary history find that Spanish participation in the vogue of European Gothic was reactive and minimal because the country's experience of the Enlightenment was highly vexed, and the political questions that the Gothic rehearsed were not central to Spanish intellectual and artistic concerns of the eighteenth century. As much of Europe marched into the future, Spain was still negotiating its past and the legacy of its fallen empire.[10] Precisely because of this, Spain provided British authors with a fertile 'primitivist discourse' (Curbet 161; 163). At the end of the eighteenth century, Zayas's homeland was not a stop on the Grand Tour, which aided in foreigners' construction of Spain as a non-enlightened space (Curbet 163). The nascent effects of the Black Legend worsened an already dark reputation,[11] and Europe's negative construct of Spain made the country a source of great fascination.

It is more productive and accurate to seek out Spanish Gothic at the other end of the literary chronology: Spain's contribution to that tradition may be the baroque novella, where the Gothic aesthetic itself may have had its origin in the agonizing demise of Europe's greatest Catholic state. Seventeenth-century Iberia provided the Gothic imagination with more than the literary lexicon of a power-hungry, perverse Inquisition, death-trap convents, sex-driven monks, malicious nuns, and an arrogant aristocracy. Juan Pérez de Montalbán's scandalous 1624 novella about incest, *La mayor confusión* (*The Greatest Confusion*) is the rarely recognized source of the equally scandalous play *The Mysterious Mother* (1768; Dixon). That play's author, Horace Walpole, wrote the Gothic prototype novel *The Castle of Otranto* (1769) which, as Varma indicates, is informed by chivalric principles (12), the very principles whose loss Zayas and her generation mourned.

Scholars such as van Praag and Amezúa state that Zayas's novellas were second in popularity only to those of Cervantes in all of Western Europe, a claim often repeated and never substantiated.[12] The question of how and when Zayas's tales circulated around Europe in time to influence Gothic writers is a study that remains to be done and promises rewards. It seems likely that female authors and translators such as Clara Reeve, Sophia Lee, and Charlotte Smith, working during the second half of the eighteenth century, resonated with Zayas's pro-women agenda. The Spanish author would have held special appeal to them because they were struggling with the rights of female writers in the same terms as Zayas, whose works contain acerbic attacks on the literary establishment that refused to equalize female and male authors. Hale studies the translation activities of these British women, pointing to the stricter standards to which their work was held regarding morality and concluding that their struggles were 'a continuing battle of the sexes which was really about the right of women to the financial remuneration and intellectual prestige of authorship in the widest sense' (19). They would have found a sympathetic precursor in Zayas. The interest of British women in Spanish letters is certainly evident in the frequency and enthusiasm with which they read *Don Quijote* (cf. Charlotte Lennox's *The Female Don Quixote*, 1752).

European awareness of Zayas as an author was conditioned by whether or not her readers knew that she was the author of novellas they were reading.[13] Three of Zayas's tales circulated in English very early in the eighteenth century as the work of Cervantes, which doubtless enhanced their influence but erased the name of María de Zayas. *A Week's Entertainment at a Wedding ... Written in Spanish by the Author of Don Quixot and now first translated into English* was published in London in 1709 and again in 1710.[14] It contains *desengaños* 10 (Tuesday's story; the Florentina tale) and 8 (Wednesday's story; the Mencía/Ana tale), as well as Zayas's seventh *novela amorosa, Al fin se paga todo* (*All Is Avenged in the End*). English readers would have had equally early access to *desengaño* 1, Isabel's tale, disguised as *A Letter from Madrid*, published in weekly supplements by John Stevens in the gazette *The British Mercury* in 1712–13. He does not attribute the story to Zayas, claiming that he simply came upon it in Madrid. In 1727, *desengaño* 5 (Inés) was adapted into English in volume 2 of P. Aubin's *The Illustrious French Lovers*, itself a translation of Charles Challes *Les illustres françaises* of 1713, which does not identify Zayas as the author of the story either. The fact that Aubin identifies his source as French rather than Spanish makes it possible that Zayas was ushered into England during the years when French literature was very popular there, via French translations of her fiction. At the same time, the high interest of some of these authors in Spain (Stevens was a Hispanophile) makes it just as possible that some of these translations came from the Spanish text.

Zayas was extremely popular and widely read in seventeenth-century France, as King and Klein indicate, and although translations of her works were more adaptations than accurate renditions, it is also likely that some French readers read them in Spanish.[15] *Desengaño* 9 (Beatriz's tale) was included in François le Métel de Boisrobert's *Les nouvelles héroïques et amoureuses* (*Novellas of Heroism and Love*) of 1657, highly adapted. All of Zayas's novellas were freely translated into French and published in 1680, and again in 1711.[16]

During the eighteenth century, when eleven editions of all twenty tales appeared, Zayas's works were published in Spanish more than any other time in history. This is telling of her popularity during the age that immediately followed her own, suggesting that she was perhaps ahead of her time (Senabre 163), and that her aesthetics had considerable resonance among European readers of pre-Romantic inclinations.[17] The commonalities of Zayas's second book and Gothic literature make that aesthetics a very likely source of inspiration for Gothic authors.

Indeed, without the expectation of transcendence that the Catholic reader brings to the *Desengaños*, Zayas's stories would be simply terrifying and, but for that, they would be Gothic. Fully reliant on that expectation, they instead mark a crucial historical step in the representational paradigms of Europe, for in them the author dissociates sacred signifiers from their sacred significance without releasing one from the other, and in so doing builds the bridge from pre-modern sacred to the modern desacralized. Outside of Spain after 1647, Zayas's Catholic signifiers point to perversion, the absence of what they were intended to mean. Even though Zayas uses both the sacred significance and the signifier, she separates them as a means to distinguish right from wrong: death for God is good but death for human error dressed up as death for God is not; the convent is good, but having to go there is not.[18] She remains firmly grounded in the integrity of the Catholic sacred, realized precisely in her use of the dead wives' bodies as the precious altar upon which a reluctant divinity inscribes an authentically sacred message: this is wrong. The function of the display is not to plumb the depths of humanity's nature but rather to paint in no uncertain terms humanity's wanderings from divine dictates.

Zayas's second book marks an important passage in the progression from prescriptive baroque fiction, which tells of bad deeds to inspire correction, to Gothic literature, which explores the negative human experience for its own sake. Zayas is a Catholic writer of imperial Spain who assumes her public's knowledge of and belief in models of religious transcendence to bring home the contrast between meaningful female sacrifice and the sacrifice that means less than nothing. Using their texts to point to the potentially abusive features of papism, Gothic writers turned Catholicism against itself, using the abused woman but removing the implicit contrast of her abuse with Zayas's holy models. That removal left only dread in the text, which Wilt defines as 'the father and mother of the Gothic' (5).[19]

True to form, the *Desengaños* rely absolutely and negatively on God, whose exclusion from the narrative as an agent of reordering casts a pall over the entire text. The divinity's signifiers have profound meaning, even though that meaning is invoked as an absence until the stories reach their endings, when divine justice and power are quickly and powerfully affirmed. Designed to instruct through the negative, the text sacrifices the innocent and withholds the divinity's intervention until the last possible moment, until the instant at which the existence of the divinity itself would be questioned were it any later. In fact, Enríquez de Salamanca finds that the *Desengaños* represent 'the erosion of religious orthodoxy,' and in them, 'doubt is raised regarding the meaning of Divine Providence' (250). We have seen, however, that Zayas's objective was not to challenge, much less sever, humanity's relationship with God. The *Desengaños* reveal the importance of that relationship by representing a society whose members compromise their relationship with God and are undone for it. That compromised relationship is both the cause and result of the terrible pressure Zayas manages to exert on her reader with her aesthetics, the better to realize her artistic and moral objectives.

The entrapping aesthetic of the *Desengaños* does announce, and perhaps inspired, the securing of male status as subject, studied by Brönfren in nineteenth-century literature as 'the use of the feminine body as trope for castration and mortality' (11).[20] Onto the backdrop of belief characteristic of imperial Spain, Zayas projects her sacred signifiers into inverted signification, relying on her readers' high literacy in the sacred and support of Catholicism to distinguish the text's form from its meaning, its signifiers from what they signify. As we have seen, such dissociations are standard manoeuvres of baroque poetics, although the specific referents that Zayas uses are not. After Zayas, the Gothic aesthetic empties of meaning the very lexicon that she had eviscerated while it was still alive, leaving the body of the wronged woman to signify human depravity that is not hers except insofar as her flesh is charged with it. This process both protests and betrays what later became 'our culture's need to ground theoretical and aesthetic representation on the displayed "erasure" of the feminine' (Brönfren 40).

Writing from within the believing community, Zayas could deploy the Catholic sacred to signify perversion and emptiness, as well as the ultimate right. Gothic literature constitutes a fictional world replete with the same signifiers whose hollowness is the point, and by the nineteenth century the female body was an established trope of a host of things that were not the person whose breath and soul gave it life. Remarkably, María de Zayas's dead wives and missing women prefigure the later intensification of the misguided practices she used them so effectively to protest.

With her *Desengaños*, María de Zayas offers us a brilliant, complex work that marks a sea change not only in literature by women but in literature as a whole. Her second book provides readers today with difficult challenges and important lessons in interpretation, which when met are rewarding and instructive about what is required to approach a text on its own terms. The *Desengaños* teach us, for example, that the question of whether any author objectifies a female character or not cannot be answered with a simple yes or no. Zayas's perfect victims begin their stories as apparent objects, even patriarchal fantasies. Their subjective status is in a sense objectified by their nature: they do not resist the way the dominant group expects them to be, and on the contrary, desire only to fulfil that group's expectations. Does this mean that a character such as Inés (d5), virtuous, lovely, wealthy, and desirous of pleasing her husband, is an object?

Thereafter, as their stories take their downward spiral, Zayas's perfect victim characters' subjective status, problematic from the outset, is completely obliterated as they are pushed into a dark abyss by overwhelming corruption, only to be flown to invisible heights by overwhelming goodness. Seen from within a contemporary subject/object paradigm, Zayas's perfect victims are doubly cursed, for they begin their stories as subjects conforming to an objectifying tradition and end them with no identities of their own at all. Nonetheless, they are the author's most compelling tool in the accomplishment of her pro-noblewomen agenda. These complexities lead us to a different question: when a self-aware female author's female characters display precisely the features prescribed by a potentially repressive ideology, does it necessarily signify conformity to repression?

The *Desengaños* make it clear that it does not, and that Inés and characters like her may be objectified but they are not mere objects. This distinction can open up broad avenues of rereading of texts by women and men. Zayas's second book reveals that when confronting a work of art that appears to represent characters in an alienated state from their own identities and best interests, it is crucial to interrogate the text with care and read from within its own parameters: which characters (female and male) are objectified, how, and to what end? These questions free female artists to work with and within repressive traditions without sacrificing their awareness of those traditions as such. It gives them the power, essentially, to play with fire, and thereby create powerful art. The *Desengaños*, aflame with Zayas's indignation over the disintegration of the world as she wanted it to be, confound the repressive ideologies that kept noblewomen from full participation in their world by walking straight into the horrible and dangerous consequences of that repression, and then leading the way out. It is easy to see the horrible consequences. It is more important to see the way out, for in struggling to acquire that vision we train ourselves to enjoy great art at its full potential, thereby responding to María de Zayas's call for her readers' furtherance of their own best interests.

Plot Summaries

All main characters are members of the nobility.
Titles added by an editor in 1734 are in brackets.

FIRST EVENING

Frame tale
Lisis, recovering from an illness, organizes a soirée at her Madrid house. Enamored of Don Juan, who desires her cousin Lisarda, Lisis nonetheless accepts the proposal of the noble Diego, and the soirée is to culminate in their nuptials. After stipulating that all storytellers be women, and all tales serve the purpose of delivering a rude awakening (*desengaño*), Lisis presides over three nights of entertainment, at which ten stories are told.

d1
Her Lover's Slave
Isabel / Manuel, failed courtship
Zaragoza, Murcia, Alicante, Sicily, Algiers, Cartagena, Zaragoza
Isabel, courted, raped, and abandoned by Manuel, dresses and brands herself as a Moorish slave and follows him around the Mediterranean in an attempt to convince him to marry her. Manuel alternately promises to do so and refuses to make good on that promise. Years later, Isabel, Manuel, her other suitor Felipe, and Manuel's intended Moorish bride Zaide return to Manuel's house where the story began. There, Felipe definitively refuses to marry Isabel, Felipe kills Manuel, and Zaide kills herself. Isabel sells herself into slavery once more, and winds up as

Lisis's own slave. Having told her story at Lisis's soirée, and unable to find Felipe, Isabel decides to enter the convent.

d2

[*The Most Infamous Revenge*]
(Octavia / Carlos, failed courtship
+ Carlos / Camila, failed marriage ⇨killed wife)
Milán

Octavia believes the false promises of Carlos to marry her and sleeps with him. When Carlos's father pressures his son to wed the wealthy Camila, Carlos tricks Octavia into the convent and marries Camila. Octavia's brother Juan avenges his sister's dishonour by raping Carlos's young wife, in response to which Carlos poisons Camila, who dies after a prolonged period of suffering. Octavia becomes a nun, and Carlos disappears in search of Juan.

d3

[*His Wife's Executioner*]
Pedro / Roseleta, failed marriage ⇨killed wife
Sicily

Part one: Juan and Pedro are best friends. Pedro weds Roseleta, with whom Juan falls passionately in love. When Juan reveals his desire to Roseleta, she tells Pedro and together they plot Juan's death by having Roseleta invite him to a rendezvous, where Pedro will kill him. On his way to meet Roseleta, Juan prays to the Virgin, as is his custom. When he comes upon the body of a hung criminal who speaks to him, Juan releases the body from the noose and the grateful criminal insists on taking Juan's place at the upcoming tryst. Pedro kills the criminal, whom he thinks is Juan. Juan, who witnesses the vengeance from afar, begs forgiveness of Pedro and Roseleta and becomes a devout Carmelite monk.

Part two: Juan's former lover, Angeliana, whom Juan had dishonoured, ingratiates herself with Pedro, and the two have an affair. When Roseleta threatens to have Angeliana killed, Angeliana convinces Pedro that Roseleta and Juan did indeed have a relationship. In response, Pedro has Roseleta bled to death, and then weds Angeliana, unaware that she had been Juan's lover and that she lied to him about his wife's guilt.

d4
[*Disillusion Arrives Too Late*]
Jaime / Lucrecia, failed courtship
+ Jaime / Elena, failed marriage ⇨killed wife
Grand Canary Island

Shipwrecked off the Canary Islands, Martín swims to shore and finds shelter in the house of Jaime, where he is witness to a spectacle in which a beautiful, deathly thin and pale white woman, whom Jaime keeps locked in a wall cage, is sent to eat crumbs beneath the table while a black slave, dressed in jewels and finery, occupies the position of mistress at the same table. After the meal, Martín's host Jaime explains the situation by telling his story:

> *embedded narration, part 1:*
> While a soldier in Naples, Jaime is literally captivated by the beautiful and wealthy Lucrecia, who singles him out as her lover. Nightly, Jaime is blindfolded and led to the inner sanctum of Lucrecia's chambers, where she regales him with sex and wealth, asking only that he keep the secrecy of their relationship. When he fails to do so, Jaime is stabbed to the brink of death and sent back to Spain to recover, heartsick over having lost Lucrecia.

> *embedded narration, part 2:*
> Jaime falls in love with Elena, weds her, and adores her. When a black slave accuses Elena of having an affair with her young cousin, Jaime believes the slave, kills the cousin, exiles his wife to a cage in the wall from which he lets her out to eat under the table, and treats the black slave as his wife.

When Jaime finishes his story, the black slave, in the throes of death, confesses that she lied about Elena and her cousin out of jealousy. Jaime stabs her to death. They go to free Elena from her cage, but find she has died. Jaime loses his mind. Martín returns to Spain, where he marries.

SECOND EVENING.

d5
[*The Punishment of Innocence*]
Inés / Alonso, failed marriage ⇨killed wife
Seville and environs

Part one: Inés is married to Alonso. Diego falls in love with Inés and pursues her openly, without success. A former servant of Inés's offers to access Inés for him, and the woman sets up a scam in which she presents Diego with a prostitute wearing Inés's dress, which she has borrowed, and the ruse continues for some time. When the former servant ends the arrangement, alleging that Inés's husband is suspicious, Diego confronts the real Inés in church about their trysts. Inés responds by calling him to her house, where she hides a magistrate and has Diego recite his claim. The law intervenes and the former servant is punished, but Diego wants Inés more than ever. Resorting to a magic candle made for him by a Moorish necromancer, Diego finally enjoys nightly sex with Inés, who is powerless under the candle's spell and goes somnambulant to his house, unaware of what she is doing. When Inés's brother and the magistrate come upon her on the street in her petticoat, headed to Diego's house, they follow her and the candle is discovered. Diego is imprisoned by the Inquisition and is never heard of again; the Moor disappears.

Part 2: After feigning to accept Inés's innocence, her husband, brother, and sister-in-law cement her into the chimney of their house, hoping she will die a slow death. Inés endures six years in the chimney, until a neighbour hears her cries and her decrepit body is freed from the wall and then recovers its beauty in the care of her kindly neighbours. Her family members are executed, and Inés, blind but beautiful, is put into a convent, where she inherits all their wealth.

d6
[*To Love Only to Conquer*]
Laurela / Esteban, failed marriage
Madrid

Part 1: Esteban desires the young Laurela, the darling of her family. To gain access to her, he dresses as a woman and becomes her lady's maid. Laurela's father pursues Esteban, now known as Estefanía, and Laurela innocently accepts her/him into her life. When Laurela's father arranges a marriage for his daughter with the noble Enrique, Esteban comes out as himself and Laurela realizes she is trapped, for Estefanía has been with her night and day. She convinces herself to love Esteban, believing he is a nobleman, and runs off with him. He takes her virginity and the jewels she had brought from home, reveals himself as a low-class man who is already married, and abandons her at the church, where her uncle finds her.

Part 2: Laurela's father refuses to allow his daughter to come home or to marry Enrique, who is still willing to marry her. She spends a year in isolation with her aunt and uncle, who mistreat her. After taking her niece to church and confession, the aunt leaves her in a room whose wall her father and uncle arrange to fall on her, killing her. Laurela's sisters enter the convent shortly thereafter, where their mother joins them after Laurela's father dies.

d7
[*A Bad Omen, to Marry Far*] ·
Blanca / Prince of Flanders, failed marriage ⇨killed wife
Madrid, Flanders
Blanca is promised in marriage to the Prince of Flanders, whom she insists spend a year courting her so she can be sure of him. The prince obliges her and enamours her. Immediately before their wedding, Blanca finds out that her oldest sister was crippled attempting to escape her Portuguese husband's attempt on her life, and her middle sister was killed by her Italian husband, who also killed their child. Blanca's wedding takes place amid these presages of doom. When Blanca and the prince arrive in Flanders, he turns against her in collusion with his wicked father, who hates Blanca for being a Spaniard. As the tension and violence between Blanca and her husband mounts, her father-in-law kills his own daughter, Blanca's only friend, on a feigned suspicion of infidelity to her husband. Shortly thereafter, Blanca comes upon her husband in bed with his male advisor. She responds by having the bed burnt and accepting the fact that her own death is immanent. Her husband and his father stand by as she is bled to death. According to the narrator, the Spanish Duke of Alba's ravaging of the Netherlands (a historical event) was in part a response to Blanca's death.

d8
[*The Traitor of His Own Blood*]
Mencía / Enrique, failed marriage ⇨killed wife
Jaén
Part 1: Mencía and Alonso are the offspring of the cruel and avaricious Don Pedro, who wants Mencía in the convent to save money on her dowry. Mencía, however, loves Enrique, the two wed in secret, and Enrique visits his wife nightly at her window, which causes some scandal in the neighbourhood. Clavela, whom Enrique had abandoned for Mencía, informs Alonso of his sister's clandestine relationship with Enrique. Alonso catches his sister writing a letter to Enrique, locks her in her room, insists that a priest confess her, and then stabs her to death. When Enrique arrives, the grates at Mencía's window fling open and

he beholds the bloody body of his wife, from which an unnatural light emanates. Mencía's voice warns him to flee, but her brother catches him as he does so, stabs him, and leaves him for dead. Enrique recovers and becomes a Franciscan, in whose monastery he builds an ornate sepulchre for his wife's body.

Part 2: Alonso flees to Naples, where he befriends the vicious Marco Antonio. In spite of his father's designs on a wealthy match for him, Alonso weds the poor but noble and virtuous Ana, whom he loves, and they have a child. When his father finds out about the union, he disinherits Alonso, who immediately regrets his marriage. With Marco Antonio, he draws Ana out of their house to the garden of Marco Antonio's, where he beheads her. They stuff Ana's body down a well and bury her head in a seaside cave. The two are caught stealing stockings in Genoa and brought to justice in Spain. On the scaffold, Alonso reveals the location of his wife's head, which is brought to him, miraculously still bleeding. He repents of his misdeeds before being hung, whereas Marco Antonio remains arrogantly unrepentant in the face of death. Ana and Alonso's son inherits all of his greedy grandfather's wealth.

THIRD EVENING

d9
[*The Persecuted Woman Triumphs*]
Beatriz / Ladislao, failed marriage
Hungary, Germany
Princess Beatriz of England is married to King Ladislao of Hungary, whose brother Federico desires her. When Ladislao goes off to war, leaving Beatriz and Federico in charge of the country, Federico aggressively pursues the queen. She locks him in an elaborate cage inside the palace, where he remains until his brother returns from war. When Federico insists to his brother that Beatriz locked him up for failing to satisfy *her* desires and take over the realm, the king believes him and orders his wife taken into the woods and her eyes put out.

trial 1: The deed is done, but a mysterious Lady appears immediately, restores the Queen's sight and leaves her in a meadow where she is found by Duke Octavio of Germany and welcomed into his household, where she is known as Rosimunda. In Hungary, Ladislao becomes aware of his error and Federico goes off, presumably to recover Beatriz, but planning to rape and murder her. He meets up with an ugly Doctor who identifies himself as an enchanter and promises to bring Beatriz to him so he can violate her, provided Federico never betray him to any-one, and Federico agrees.

trial 2: The Doctor provides Federico with a ring that renders him invisible and a letter that will make Beatriz look like a traitor of state to Duke Octavio. Federico enters the palace unseen and plants the let-ter on Beatriz, where it is discovered. The duke must execute her but, moved by her beauty and apparent virtue, instead returns her to the meadow where he found her. Federico meets her there and is about to rape her when the Lady appears and magically replaces Beatriz with a fierce lion from whose claws Federico escapes barely alive, with the Doctor's help.

trial 3: The Lady whisks the queen away to some shepherds, in whose company she is seen by the emperor, empress, and their child. Cap-tivated by her beauty, they invite her to live with them as their son's caretaker, and she does so. The Doctor provides Federico with a sleep-ing potion and instructs him to kill the child and place the bloody knife in the hands of Beatriz while she is unconscious, which he does. Accused of murder, Beatriz is stripped and taken back to the place she was found for execution, but the Lady uses magic to whisk her away once more. At the emperor's palace, the dead child comes back to life and vindicates Beatriz, who by then has disappeared.

The Lady deposits the queen in a cave stocked with penitential and contemplative objects, where Beatriz spends eight happy years alone. The Lady then reappears, and assigns the reluctant Beatriz the task of curing the plague that is ravaging the land, dressing her as a man to do so. Beatriz is brought to cure Federico, which she does in exchange for his promise to reveal his sins in the presence of his brother and Beatriz herself (still dressed as a man). The truth comes out, Federico's evil Doctor disappears in a cloud of smoke, the Virgin is recognized as the Lady, and Beatriz is restored to her exact appearance the day her husband discredited her. Ladislao asks his queen to rejoin him, but she refuses and plans a life in the convent. Ladislao bestows his king-dom on the now virtuous Federico, married to Beatriz's sister, and then retires to a monastery.

d10
[*The Ruination that Comes of Vice*]
Magdalena / Dionís, failed marriage ⇨ killed wife
Lisbon
The Spanish gentleman Gaspar establishes a relationship with a lady

of easy virtue in Lisbon, where he serves Philip III. Entering this lady's building one night, Gaspar hears moans from a dead body left in a storage room, a body he has properly buried and prayed for. Afraid of this portent, Gaspar abandons the lady and falls in love with Florentina, whom he knows to be of noble blood and believes to be virtuous. One night he finds Florentina, bathed in blood, outside the house where she lived with her sister and brother-in-law. He takes her to his rooms, where she recovers and tells him her story.

> *embedded narrative*: Florentina and Magdalena are half-sisters and grew up happily together. When Magdalena weds Dionís, Florentina joins their household, where she falls madly in love with her half-sister's husband. After unsuccessfully attempting to control herself, she declares her affections to Dionís, who responds passionately and the two have a secret affair for four years. When a confessor refuses to absolve Florentina of her sins, she realizes something has to change and reveals her problem to her maid, who suggests murdering Magdalena as the only way for Florentina to marry Dionís. Florentina accedes to the plan and the maid sets Magdalena up with her young page, whom Dionís comes upon in his wife's bedroom. The enraged husband kills his wife and the page, stabs Florentina and kills everyone in the house before impaling himself on his own sword. It was when Florentina had dragged herself out the door that Gaspar had found her.

Gaspar, repulsed by Florentina's behaviour, urges her to repentance and into the convent, to which she agrees. She retires there having inherited the estates of both Dionís and Magdalena. Gaspar returns to Toledo, where he marries.

Frame Tale: Conclusion

After reciting the final tale, Lisis declares that she will not wed Diego after all but will enter the convent as a lay resident, to her mother's initial distress as well as Diego's. Don Juan, rejected by Lisarda who weds a foreigner, dies in a frenzy. Isabel's avenger Felipe is discovered to have died at war. Lisis's mother eventually joins her daughter in the convent, where they are residents, not nuns.

Notes

Introduction: Setting the Interpretative Baseline

1 Yllera relates Zayas's title to the ban (Introducción 68). Printers responded to the ban by publishing outside of Castile, as did Zayas, by falsifying frontispieces and dates on books, and using conservative titles. See Moll, Pacheco-Ransanz, Cayuela ('La prosa'), Cruickshank, and Ripoll.

2 Yllera, 'María' 223, n. 7. On the textual history of Zayas's works, see Yllera (Introducción) and Olivares (Introducción).

3 Citations are from Alicia Yllera's edition of the *Desengaños*.

4 Here and throughout, I use the term 'baroque' to connect the cultural production of Spain to the dynamics of its empire, as 'the cultural superstructure of a non-capitalist and non-Protestant modernity' (Beverly 19, 17), whose episteme is hegemonic, literate, and aristocratic. Beverly analyses current definitions and applications of the baroque. Robbins defines seventeenth-century emphasis on interpreting versus living reality similarly, in reference to Gracián's *El Criticón* (70). The essays in *Barroco* (ed. P. Aullón de Haro et al.) provide the most recent and thorough investigation of the term.

5 In *La burlada Aminta* (*Arminta Deceived*) and *Al fin se paga todo* (*Just Deserts*), *La fuerza del amor* (*The Power of Love*), and *El juez de su causa* (*The Judge of Her Case*), respectively (*Novelas amorosas*).

6 Maiorino, following Levin, considers the title to be a seminal version of the work itself. Cayuela analyses the title's literary politics in light of Genette's notion that it establishes a generic contract (*Paratexte*). Williamsen cites Lanser when making her case for the importance of titles in works by women ('Questions' 106).

1 The *Desengaños* at a Distance

1 12 July 1658 approbation of Cristobal Lozano's novellas, *Soledades de la vida y desengaños del mundo* (*The Solitudes of Life and Disillusions of the World*), np.

2 See Finaldi's informative article on Pereda's painting.

3 See Place (*Bosquejo*), Pabst, Bourland, Laspéras, and Rabell on how the novella developed in Spain.

4 The full text reads: 'I find it full of models to reform behaviour and worthy to be printed, since in it (given that women's leisure has expanded the number of useless books), she who devotes her time to reading it will find examples to use to flee the risks into which some inattentive women precipitate themselves' (Le veo lleno de ejemplos para reformar costumbres y digno de que se dé a la estampa, que en él [ya que el ocio de las mujeres ha crecido el número a los libros inútiles] la que se ocupase en leerle tendrá ejemplos con que huir los riesgos a que algunas desatentas se precipitan, dated 8 Oct. 1646, n.p.). The Ginovés approbation appeared in the first edition of the *Desengaños* in 1647; it is in the Ruíz-Galvez Priego edition of Zayas's *Obra narrativa completa* (386–7). Rabell supports Pabst's contention that censors did not read the texts they were censoring (37, n. 36). This makes it difficult to explain the novellas that were prohibited, such as Lope de Vega's censorship of Pérez de Montalbán's *La mayor confusión*, which Rabell cites (31, n. 25). While censors' attentiveness to texts probably varied, the specificity of their observations suggests that they did read them.

5 'Despertadores violentos para los vicios [y] maestros perpetuos que enseñan como han de intentarlos y proseguirlos' (Joseph de Jesús María 168; cited in Pacheco-Ransanz, 420, n. 30).

6 'Fruto y provecho común.' From Gil Fernández's citations of the decree issued by Philip IV on 13 June 1627, which also prohibited publications that were 'unnecessary or inappropriate' (no necesarios o convenientes, 625).

7 Early modern Spanish texts that overtly seek to define moral categories are beginning to receive attention. In her revealing study of casuistic morality, Río Parra rightly stresses that in any confessional society, pastoral and canonical literature is crucial to understanding that society (21).

8 As Merrim observes, in Zayas's works, 'moralistic literature subsumes and obviates the category of feminist discourse' (78). See Beverly's exact assessment of the relationship between morality and literature during the period, in which he points to the moral objectives of the most highly wrought baroque poetry and contrasts modern fixation on *Don Quijote* with the fact that Mateo Alemán's highly moralistic *Guzmán de Alfarache*

was by far the preferred reading of seventeenth-century Spaniards (1–53). Cayuela specifies the moralistic terms of seventeenth-century Spanish censorship ('La prosa'), while Felten as well as Foa ('María') identify the social morality that Zayas shared with other writers of her generation.

9 I use the term 'ideology' as Giddens defines it: 'shared ideas or beliefs which serve to justify the interests of dominant groups' (583).

10 'They are domestic animals and unavoidable enemies whom we regale and on whom we spend our patience and estate and in the end, like the lion who turns against the lion keeper weary of raising and feeding it, and kills him, so do they, in the end, kill their masters and mistresses, telling what they know about them and what they do not know, never wearying of gossiping about their lives and habits. And the worst thing is that we are unable to get along without them, out of vanity, or our foolish little honour' (Son animales caseros y enemigos no excusados, que los estamos regalando gastando con ellos nuestra paciencia y hacienda, y al cabo, como el león, que harto el leonero de criarle y sustentarle, se vuelven contra él y le mata, así ellos, al cabo, matan a sus amos, diciendo lo que saben de ellos y diciendo lo que no saben, sin cansarse de murmurar de su vida y costumbres. Y es lo peor que no podemos pasar sin ellos, por la vanidad, por la honrilla, 508). According to Mariscal, this passage indicates a lack of solidarity among women, 'a sign that racial and class affiliations, rather than gender, usually provided the sites of subject formation of preindustrial women' (61). Parr makes important qualifications (15).

11 Herrero reviews other passages in Camos's book that construct the figure of man as microcosm such that servants are the body's waste (882).

12 Zayas's conservative representation of servants as inherently disruptive to aristocratic interests is different from the way her friend and fellow author Ana Caro treats social class. In her play *Valor, agravio y mujer* (*Valour, Offence and Woman*), Caro proffers the heroine's servant Ribete as a sympathetic, witty, and able ally for that heroine, a means to reinforce her challenge to the dominant social hierarchy, a challenge absent from *Desengaños*.

13 It is not known if Zayas knew Gracián, although the striking affinity between their ideological positions and that of Countess Luisa de Padilla suggests they may have known each other. Bergamann indicates that the Countess was a close friend of Gracián's.

14 Rodríguez fully reviews the theory of the novella in seventeenth-century Spain. Pons offers what she called an oblique, readerly interpretation of *La fuerza del amor* (*The Power of Love*), the fifth story of Zayas's *Novelas amorosas*. Premodern fiction, certainly Zayas's, scripts the prescribed meaning even though the reader must discern it: the text is the teacher,

the reader is the learner, and the lesson is encoded in the text. According
to Keep, McLaughlin, and Parmar, this is the nature of all readerly texts:
'They do not locate the reader as a site of the production of meaning, but
only as the receiver of a fixed, pre-determined, reading. They are thus
products rather than productions and thus form the dominant mode of
literature under capitalism.'

15 Ife cites a variety of entertaining examples of readers' indiscriminate
absorption in fiction (49–50).

16 Bordwell and Thompson eloquently discuss this cognitive practice and its
importance in art (54–6). See also Crawford and Chaffin, and Richardson
and Crane's website, *Literature, Cognition and the Brain*.

17 There were many treatises written in seventeenth-century Europe defending difficulty as intellectual pleasure and moral betterment, especially in
poetry; see Parker, 30–2, and Robbins, 'Challenging the Mind' in *The Challenges of Uncertainty* (98–116).

18 May suggests a meaning of 'elicit' or 'bring out' (271–2); see also Blanco,
who nicely refers to such techniques of compression as drawing a concept
into a point.

19 Levisi identifies the source of this portion of the story as tale 32 of Mar-
garite de Navarre's *Heptaméron* (Place identified it as 28, 'María'); both
acknowledge it was in Bandello. In both the Italian and French versions,
however, the wife is guilty and is pardoned by her husband, whereas in
Zayas's tale she is innocent and dies regardless.

20 On Caro's status as the first professional writer of Spain, see Luna, 'Ana.'

21 The most complete biographical information about Zayas is in Greer,
who sees Zayas's identification with aristocratic values in conflict with
her unconscious awareness that women socialized to those values were
doomed to fail (*María* 17–35).

22 As Fuchs has nicely put it, echoing McKendrick (*Woman* 217) and Smith
(*Body* 14), cross-dressing is 'a catalyst for the re-ordering of the patriarchal
world when something has gone amiss' (22). Bravo-Villasante's typology
of the cross-dressed woman in Golden Age theatre is applicable to the
novella as well, although I would observe, with Felten, that the device
does not have a single valence but rather is a function of the context in
which each author uses it (76–7). Arguments such as Compte's, which find
Isabel's disguise to be liberating, obviously take the opposite tack and, I
would argue, necesarily ignore the protagonist's very negative assessment
of her self-defilement as well as the complete failure those actions produce
in all but the narrative sense (they make for a dramatic story).

23 The problematic of social ascendency, particularly given the crown's grow-

ing practice of selling patents of nobility for revenue, also intensified the financial difficulties of the country because members of the nobility did not pay taxes. Philip IV (1621–65) sold over 130 certificates of nobility to raise money (Kamen, *Spain* 245). On sentiments against social mobility during this time, see Casey ('Consolidation') and Domínguez Ortiz.

24 Vollendorf finds this to be the case for works by Zayas and Mariana de Carvajal, another baroque novella author ('Future').

25 Cf. Jesuit Gaspar de Astete's insistence that a husband behave with his household as a king does with his subjects ('Háse de haber el padre de familias con los suyos [como dice Santo Tomás] así como el Rey se ha con los de su reino,' 50). As Truman summarizes, during the early modern period, 'The order posited by earthly society is seen as part of a larger pattern of structures and purposes extending through the whole created universe' (221).

26 According to Martínez Gil's assessment of pertinent sources, the souls of the mad went to limbo (498). This option became unavailable to Catholic souls after 22 April 2007, when Pope Benedict XVI abolished it.

27 Most deaths happened at home, where corpses were prepared for burial by the women of the house. Martínez Gil cites seventeenth-century sources about the difficulties posed by a sudden death and the direct relationship between sin, illness, and pain. A life of extreme virtue was prescribed as the soul's only protection against dying unconfessed (152–4). Eire's study of death in Madrid is based on wills written 1529–99 and focuses on the upper class. On *ars moriendi* in casuistry, see the interesting details summarized in Río Parra, 86–8.

28 In seventeenth-century Spain, suicide was still considered the worst of sins because it discounted the power of divine grace and forgiveness; see Martínez Gil (157–60).

29 On the intellectual politics of what the early modern public actually read in contrast to the canon, see Beverly, Rhodes ('Spain's Misfired Canon'), and E. Davis ('Épica').

30 Walsh identifies the parallels between chivalric and hagiographic romance, both in vogue in the late fifteenth and early sixteenth centuries in Spain.

31 Levisi suggests that interest in Christian martyrdom during Zayas's lifetime was renewed by the discovery of the Roman catacombs in 1578 (454).

32 McKendrick (*Woman* 173); see also Rodríguez-Arango Díaz (751) and Foa (*Feminismo* 53). Carrión finds marriage to be a vehicle through which seventeenth-century Spanish dramatists interrogated the institution and its economic impact.

33 Among those who find that Zayas rejects marriage as a literary device

and/or as an institution are Camino, Kaminsky (489), Greer (*María* 340), Montesa Peydró, and Yllera ('María' 221). Tomás y Valiente provides no evidence to support his assertion that Zayas's was a society 'generally horrified by marriage' (con general horror al matrimonio, 47).

34 Poska regularly reminds her readers that early modern Spanish women's prospects improved if they could sustain a relationship with a man, even though marriage was the least productive of relationships for peasant women of Galicia, for reasons particular to their region and their class.

35 Cited in Elliott (55). Infant mortality in post-Tridentine Spain ranged from 44 to 55 per cent (Martínez Gil 323).

36 Moncada's *Restauración política de España* (*Political Restoration of Spain*) was first published in 1619. Elliott provides more statistics on his report and others (241–62).

37 'Marriage … is holy and good, and as such is received in the law of God, and one should not attribute to it the errors born of the little sanity and discretion of he who weds lacking the prudence required to know how to select the woman he takes' (El matrimonio … es santo y bueno, y como tal es recibido en la ley de Dios, y no se han de atribuir a él los errores que nacen de la poca cordura y discreción de el que se casa, no teniendo la prudencia que se requiere en saber escoger la mujer que toma, *Gobierno* 308). Foa puts it somewhat differently, saying that Zayas never rejects the sacrament of marriage, although her characters reject getting married ('María' 130–3).

38 See Atienza Hernández, who uses data about the noble dynasty of the Osunas to reconstruct the role of noblewomen during the period.

39 For example, 'It is God's will that men marry' (Es voluntad de Dios que se casen los hombres, Costa, *Gobierno* 309).

40 Cf. the confessional questions in Ledesma (*Consejero cristiano*, 1678) and Ciruelo (*Confesionario* 1541, 49v–51r). Many early modern confessors' manuals in Spanish are elaborations of Dueñas's very popular *Remedio de pecadores* (*Sinners' Remedy*), first published in 1545. The book provides its original readers with a list of questions to consider before confession; it informs readers today about a wide variety of surprising human behaviours from the early modern period. Martín de Azpilcueta's *Manual de confesores*, more officially influential, was written specifically for priests and was first published in 1549. The 1567 edition specifies that if a married couple did not want more children, they could legitimately stop having sexual relations (176).

41 Distinctions of all these categories are in early modern Spanish codes of civil and canon law. Of particular interest to readers of Zayas is Pradilla's

Suma de las leyes penales (*Summary of Penal Laws*), 1639. The effects of class on when and how (and if) sex crimes committed by the nobility were tried and documented have yet to be studied.

42 A historical study of the rape of noblewomen in early modern Spain, the only women whose violation Zayas fictionalizes, remains to be written. See Baines's astute assessment of this historiographic situation and Ruff's excellent assessment of data (140–7). On the literary context, see Casa (207), Maravall (*Culture* 62), McKendrick ('Calderón'), O'Connor, and Welles (*Persephone's Girdle*).

43 If the raped woman did not want to marry the man, he was to completely dower her. Failure to comply in theory led to whipping followed by penance, 'but such punishment is not used any more, rather he should marry her or give her a decent dowry' (pero tal pena ya no está en uso, sino que case con ella o la dote decentemente, Pradilla 3v). Interestingly, raping a woman in an uninhabited area (*yermo*) was punishable by death, regardless of the woman's status or class (3v), a practice Pradilla does not say had fallen out of usage.

44 Zayas's version of this popular novella plot is a clear response to Masuccio's tale III. 26, which makes light of the man's betrayal of the woman. On the frankly erotic content of some novellas, including those written by priests, see Rey Hazas.

45 On such violent outbursts, see Wardropper, 'Horror.'

46 Recent studies include Barahona and Taylor. MacKay concludes that the supposed Spanish obsession with honour in literary sources does not represent reality, whereas Casey's *Family and Community in Early Modern Spain* uses data from Granada to conclude that honour was an overpowering ideal that played a dominant role in shaping the choices made by early modern Spaniards.

47 Moralists and theologians alike make this distinction. Cf. Alonso de Vega's 1606 *Suma llamada Nueva Recopilación y práctica del fuero interior, utilísima para confesores y penitentes* (*Summary Called the New Rendition and Practice of Inner Law, Most Useful for Confessors and Penitents*).

48 The practice of painting Spanish royalty with divine attributes or representing them directly as saints, studied by Marín Cruzado, underscores the importance of the absolute monarchy during this period. Feros traces its development into the seventeenth century.

49 Pradilla is glossing jurist Gregorio López's 1587 own gloss of the famous thirteenth-century law code by King Alfonso X of Castile, *Las siete partidas*. In a subsequent chapter, Pradilla cites multiple circumstances in which a judge might lessen the adulterous woman's penalty, such as if she com-

mitted the crime as the result of feminine weakness (116v), or under the power of love's passion (117v). Sánchez, citing an autograph treatise by lawyer Antonio de la Peña, quotes details of the wife murder law. Heiple, citing moralist treatises but not legal codes, finds that moralists' refusal to sanction wife murder suggests that it did happen. I would add that the question of what was done about it was subject to local precedence, in the case of civil courts, and private determinations, in the case of mortal sin. Carrión cites some other civic and ecclesiastic sources in her review of early modern marriage (17–31).

50 Azpilcueta adds that a woman sins if she refuses to subject herself to her husband, wants to control him, or disdains his request that she cast aside superfluous vanities and illicit habits (138). Casuistic sources summarized by Río Parra come to the same conclusion (153–5).

51 A similar smart remark by Zayas's contemporary María de Guevara (d. 1683) is refreshing: 'Queen Dido killed herself because a Trojan Prince dishonoured her, as did Lucrecia. They were great idiots, for it would have been better to kill the men than to kill themselves' (la reina Dido se mató porque la burló un príncipe troyano, lo mismo hizo Lucrecia, ellas fueron grandísimas majaderas, que mejor fuera matarlos a ellos que no matarse ellas (cited in Romero-Díaz, 'Revisiting' 175).

52 Gottlieb cites sources indicating that across early modern Europe, violence against servants was completely unchallenged, whereas violence against wives was theoretically limited (170).

2 Attending the Soiree

1 Griswold enumerates these objectives more generally: 'to defend women, to reform men, and to change the way of the world,' and defines the essential conflict of the book as one between will and reason (110). Amezúa defines them as defending women and teaching a moral lesson ('Doña María,' 21); Brownlee says that Zayas's 'only ambition is to illustrate the blamelessness of her sex' ('Moral' 216), whereas for Alcalde, it is to prove that discrimination against women is baseless and that men are cruel (80). For other explanations of the shifting addressees and registers of the Desengaños, see Greer's analysis of Zayas as a subaltern writer (María 80–1). The idea that the Desengaños are anti-male and anti-establishment, 'a bleak picture of the battle of the sexes' (Armon 158), is now commonplace and is manifest in such recent analyses as Robbins (33), Gamboa Tusquets, and the essays in Escenas de transgresión (Albert and Felten, eds). I suggest a reading that allows for female authors to be authentically invested in and

supportive of dominant social structures, including male power, even as they criticized negative features of both.

2 'Volver,' literally 'to return,' also means 'to defend or protect someone or something' (defender o patrocinar a alguien o algo, *DRAE*).

3 If the deceived woman was of a social class inferior to that of the man who deceived her, that discrepancy of class sufficed to prove that the man did not intend to marry her (Azpilcueta 429). Ledesma states: 'When the promise is made with such dissimulation that he who is making the promise is not motivated to make it, nor to keep his promise, nor to oblige himself, said promise lacks validity as an obligation to wed … If he is motivated to make the promise and oblige himself, but is not motivated to keep the promise, said promise has true validity as an obligation to wed' (Cuando la promesa se hace tan disimuladamente que el que promete no tiene ánimo de prometer, ni de guardar lo prometido, ni de obligarse, la tal promesa no tiene verdadera razón de desposorio … Si uno tiene ánimo de prometer y de obligarse pero no tiene ánimo de guardar lo prometido, la tal promesa tiene verdadera razón de desposorio,' *Primera parte* 15). In their analyses of honour, Chauchadis and Río Parra cite some of these sources, as well as others, to arrive at different conclusions.

4 Interestingly, Ledesma's confessor's manual refers specifically to a man's sending a 'lascivious letter or message' to a woman 'with the intent to attract her and provoke her to badness' as a sin of fornication (Si envió billetes lascivos ó recaudos con ánimo de atraer y provocar a mal, *Primera parte* 115).

5 In his 1610 dictionary, Covarrubias defines 'fácil' as 'an inconstant man, he who is little firm in his opinion and voice, such that anyone can change his mind' (532). On fixedness as an early modern virtue, see Rhodes, 'Gender and the Monstrous.'

6 Armon proposes an analysis of this dedication (153–62).

7 A *prado* during this period was a tree-lined, grassy area in or close to a city where people went for recreation (*Aut*. 3:345a).

8 The fullest collection of protests against male effeminacy is in Cotarelo y Mori. On the changing standards of masculinity during the early modern period, see Donnell and Strasser. There is much scholarship on the crisis of the early modern Spanish nobleman, generally presented as a 'crisis of masculinity.' For precise and fascinating data on what constituted early modern manhood, see Behrend-Martínez; on the masculinity crisis, see Cartagena Calderón, Donnell, Lehfeldt, Perry, and Velasco. I find scholarly endorsement of this presumed crisis (which implicitly endorses conservative notions about masculinity) less important in the *Desengaños* than that of the nobility as a whole.

9 Hernández y Sánchez-Barba elaborates on the relationship between Spanish political and geographic aggression and Spain's mythology of chivalric virtues.

10 Kamen's refinement of Spain's so-called decline makes the distinction between Castile and the rest of what we today call 'Spain,' a country still in formation in the seventeenth century. He suggests that Castile was in fact in decline and points out that a decline supposes a rise, but 'Spain never rose' ('Decline' 25).

11 Zayas reminds her readers of precisely this in her *Novelas amorosas*: 'Whoever insults women is ungrateful, for he fails to acknowledge the lodging they gave him on his first journey' (Quien las ultraja [es] ingrato, pues falta al reconocimiento del hospedaje que le hicieron en la primer jornada, 161).

12 Ferdinand the Catholic, husband of Isabel of Castile, lived from 1452 to 1516. Because he ruled during Spain's most expansive imperial age, he was highly idealized throughout Europe as a model of the ideal king. Machiavelli used him as one of his models for *The Prince* (1515) and he is central in Gracián's *El héroe* of 1637.

13 The word 'valor' is not in the Covarrubias dictionary. The 1737 *Diccionario de autoridades* defines it as 'the quality that constitutes something worthy of estimation and appreciation' (la calidad, que constituye una cosa digna de estimación ú aprecio, 3:417b) and also disdain of fear, constancy in action, power, and the essence of qualities that produce results (3:418a).

14 The others include *estupro* (the deflowering of a female virgin by a man outside of marriage), incest (sex within four generations of relations), *rapto* (removing a woman from her rightful place of residence), sacrilege (sexual intercourse with a person of religious profession), and crimes against nature (orgasm with no procreative potential; because women were believed to produce the equivalent of sperm with orgasm, mutual orgasm was believed necessary for conception).

15 The sexual relationship between Blanca's husband and his male servant in *desengaño* 8 qualifies as sodomy, a separate civil crime punishable by death under Spanish law and defined as a mortal sin by ecclesiastical law (Vega 2:960; Pradilla 6v–7r).

3 Dressed to Kill: Death and Meaning in the *Desengaños*

1 Mencía qualifies as a wife because she and Enrique exchange vows *de presente*, before witnesses (376) and thereafter refer to each other as *esposos* (spouses), as does the narrator (377; 382; 385).

2 Greer finds Zayas's 'macabre surfeit of blood, pathos and beautifully incor-

ruptible feminine cadavers' to be 'a masochistic fantasy of love and honor for the beautiful, martyred flesh after death' (*María* 281, 285). Brownlee ('Moral'), Avedaño, and Vila, in contrast, find it sadistic.

3 Alcalde, in contrast, interprets Zayas's dead women as authentic martyr characters whose lives and deaths imitate Christ.

4 On noblewomen and litigation, see Ellen Friedman's important study ('Estatus jurídico') and the essays in *Power and Gender.*

5 Barahona's surprise that families did not claim the dishonour of deflowered women in his court data from Vizcaya (119–71) can be countervailed by acknowledging the dishonour explicit in using the law to address such offences.

6 The young girl survived, physically. On current upper-class wife murders, see Keith O'Brien.

7 Bomli points to this historical account (81). Yllera signals that authors Lope de Vega and Rojas Zorilla used the same plot detail for eliminating stained women ('María,' 330, n. 22)

8 Sources of Zayas's stories continue to emerge. See Rubiera Mata's interesting study of the influence of the *1001 Nights* on two of Zayas's *Novelas ejemplares* and Salstad's study of sacred oratory's influence on another of them.

9 The romance legend of Queen Beatriz has its origins in ancient eastern folklore; it derived from the same source as the Crescentia legend, but developed separately from it (Wallensköld). Bibliographers attribute the 1497 Spanish *Leyenda de los santos* to Jacobus de Voragine, although it differs from Voragine's *Golden Legend.* The ?1497? edition of the *Leyenda* is the only one that contains all the saints' lives from which Zayas borrows in the *Desengaños.* On the complex history of hagiographic texts in early modern Spain, see the studies by Aragüés Aldaz.

10 In Western culture, it is more acceptable for women to express pain than men, as it is for lower-class individuals over those of the upper class (Cohen 2–4).

11 Cohen studies the meaning of pain in the medieval context (18–19). Mâle's classic book on religious art addresses the same question in early modern culture, as do the essays in *Saints and Sinners* (ed. Mormando). Levisi relates baroque gusto for martyr accounts to the paintings of martyrs by Spanish artists José de Ribera, Juan de las Roelas, and Pedro Orrente (454).

12 Parker-Aronson suggests that Zayas physically metamorphosizes raped women such as Camila to signify the social stigma attached to their bodies. Camila's poisoning echoes Cervantes' courtship novella, *La española inglesa* (*The Spanish Englishwoman*), in which the mother of the heroine's

rejected suitor poisons the heroine Isabel and her body acquires a grotesque appearance, including her face. Cardaillac-Hermosilla points to the frequency of poisoning in European politics, domestic and state, in the sixteenth and seventeenth centuries (365–6).

13 During the early modern period, female sinner saints in the Spanish *Flos sanctorum* are not prostitutes. They are women who openly indulge in the pleasure of the flesh, to the ruination of the men around them (Rhodes, 'Saint for One Season').

14 Pedro de Rivadeneira was the compiler of the most influential and popular Counter-Reformation *Flos sanctorum*, whose Part I was first published in 1599. On how the conflation of three biblical Marys into the Magdalen played out in early modern Spanish literature, see E. Davis ('Woman').

15 Baroque representations of the prostitute saints run the gamut from Rivera's relatively chaste paintings that emphasize the penitential phases of their lives to the highly sexualized images of them that superimpose their eroticized bodies onto their tearful regret of that past. The furniture of repentance is always present: the skull, a crucifix, harsh landscape, etc. As Boyarin indicates, female virgins trope male concerns with male bodies and their spiritual states (67), and the female sinner saints accomplish the same thing, if in a different way. According to Gamboa Tusquets, Elena's dress is that of a prostitute and refers to Jaime's false accusation of her (53).

16 Zayas's borrowing ends there, but the story continues, telling how Theodore is falsely accused of fathering a child, whom he raises at the door of the monastery until his community readmits them both, after which he dies and is recognized to be a woman, to the astonishment of all. In his *Flos sanctorum* published from 1599 on, Rivadeneira replaces this Theodora with another, 'a holy and most pure virgin' (una santa y purísima doncella, 1623, 226b). Problems of verisimilitude and sources aside, the idea that an unfaithful wife could be a saint was likely unpalatable for the seventeenth-century Spanish Catholic establishment.

17 See also Inés, 283; Blanca, 349; Beatriz, 431 and 453.

18 Smith elaborates a theory about the other meaning of 'blanca,' a coin ('Writing'), an objectification on which Williamsen elaborates ('Re-writing'; '"Death"').

19 Blanca's 'daring' is her bold action against her husband and his male lover, whom she caught in a sex act: she has their bed dragged outside the palace and burnt. In early modern Spain, convicted sodomites were burned alive (Berco 337), and Blanca's symbolic action is highly condemnatory of him and dishonouring. Gamboa Tusquets also points to how Zayas displaces the penalty for sodomy onto the bed burning (138).

20 The word 'humour' here refers to the four humours of Galenic medical

theory, according to which health was determined by the body's balance of blood, yellow bile, black bile, and phlegm. Blood prodigies were attributed to male and female saints of the Catholic tradition. Incorruptibility, in contrast, was more typical for female saints; see Thurston (*Physical* 283–93 and 'Blood Prodigies'). When St Agueda is in prison, the great light her body emits strikes her jailors with fear (Voragine 61v). St Engracia's body shines 'more than the sun' after torture because God does not want his grace to be hidden from earthly sight' (no quiso Dios que su lumbre fuese escondida, Voragine 265v).

21 The resurrected thief who saves Juan's life is a variant on a miracle that Zayas likely found in a vita of the Virgin Mary in some *Flos sanctorum*. It is in the *Cantigas de Santa María*, a thirteenth-century songbook in praise of the Virgin Mary attributed to King Alfonso X. Cantiga 13 relates the hanging of an evil-doing thief who always commended himself to the Virgin in prayer. As he is dying on the scaffold, the Virgin places her hands beneath his feet and raises him up, allowing him to survive for three days. Found alive, he is hung again but survives once more. After loudly attributing his salvation to the Virgin Mary, to the edification of all, he is freed and immediately enters a religious order, as does Zayas's repentant Juan (*Cantigas* 32–3).

22 The inherent beauty of virtue was defined as intrinsic to the noble person in prescriptive social and political literature of Spain's early modern period. For example, in his 1595 treatise on nobility, Pedro López de Montoya insists: 'It is appropriate to teach nobles in conformity with their station, revealing to them the beauty and being of virtue that they might become devoted to it' (Lo que conviene es enseñarlos [a los nobles] conforme a lo que pide su natural, descubriéndoles la hermosura y ser de la virtud para que se aficionen a ella, 94r–v). In a broader context, see *Virtue and Beauty*, the catalogue of a 2001–2 exhibit of Renaissance female portraits at the National Gallery of Art.

23 This passage echoes romance martyr death scenes such as that of Catherine of Alexandria, whose 1497 Spanish vita concludes with young Catherine – about to be beheaded – insisting she will not renege, at which point, 'A voice from heaven came to her saying, "My very beloved spouse, come unto me" … And she saw the door of paradise open' (Vino una voz del cielo a ella diciéndole, 'La mi esposa muy amada, vente para mi' … [Y vio] la puerta del paraíso abierta, Voragine 1497, 272r).

4 Dead End: The Convent

1 I use the word 'convent' to include what English calls the 'convent' (for women) and the 'monastery' (for men), because Spanish does so.

2 I say 'non-religious' to signal that distinguishing between 'religious' and 'secular' sets up a presentist dichotomy in reference to early modern texts, written when the difference between the two was less meaningful than their seamless totality. In the seventeenth century, religion served not only to relate people to God, but also to each other and to the state, since from the age of Isabel and Ferdinand, Spanish rulers used Catholicism for purposes of political cohesion (Tomás y Valiente 886). This is especially evident in society's use of the convent for religious and worldly functions, although I support Lehfeldt's thesis that early modern society's predominant understanding of the convent's rightful function was 'religious' (*Religious Women*). I use the words 'religious' and 'secular' reservedly, to indicate emphasis, precisely because Zayas is unusual in pushing the distinction between the two to the verge of a true dichotomy.

3 Zayas used the convent in other ways in her *Novelas amorosas.* In *Aventurarse perdiendo (Taking a Risk as Losing)*, a nun secretes her husband, whom she had believed dead, into the convent for sexual relations.

4 Merrim's presentation of the convent as a script (103–20) provides an analytic lens similar to mine, although my interpretation of how Zayas writes it differs from hers.

5 On the historical reality of female convents and convent life during this period, see Vigil (208–61), Sánchez Lora, and Sánchez Hernández. Comparable research on early modern male convents remains to be done.

6 Imirizaldu presents other cases of religious fraud.

7 In his study of the baroque Spanish novella, Laspéras lists those published between 1493 and 1637 (*Nouvelle* 226–32).

8 I use the term 'in the world' in the fashion that privileges its religious meaning, as a contrast to 'the convent,' which rhetorically exists 'out of it' in the sense that life there rejects secular society's anthropomorphism.

9 Isabel's reference to herself as a slave lacks the sado-masochistic tones it may appear to have today. Covarrubias defines the slave as 'a servant, a captive,' adding, 'he is a shadow in that he cannot constitute a person' (el siervo, el cautivo; es sombra por cuanto no puede representar persona, 538); of the female slave, 'esclava,' he says simply 'the servant' (la sierva). Cervantes' feisty character Dorotea describes her desire to wed the inconstant Don Fernando in the same terms: 'Let me be your slave, for in belonging to you I will consider myself both blessed and fortunate' (admíteme por tu esclava, que como yo esté en tu poder, me tendré por dichosa y bien afortunada, 1:36, 428).

10 In *desengaño* 9, the evil-doer Federico does not have to purge his sins by abandoning the world, and instead is allowed to marry and live happily

ever after, in spite of having repeatedly shattered the life of the innocent protagonist. This can happen, I would argue, because Beatriz purges Federico's sins for him, in the same fashion as Mira de Amescua's ill-fated character Lisarda does penance for the wrongdoings of Gil, so he does not have to; see Rhodes, 'Economics.'

11 The contrast between men and the heavenly spouse is a staple of female saints' lives. When a Roman demands the 'love' of thirteen-year-old St Inés, she counters, 'Yo he otro entendedor mejor que tú y que es más hijo de algo, y más rico y más fuerte y más poderoso que tú, ca estas cosas deben demandar las esposas a los esposos' (I have another suitor better than you who is superior to you in status and richer and stronger and more powerful than you, for these are things that wives should demand of husbands, Voragine 40v). The comparison of Christ to the human spouse is a staple in Juan Luis Vives's *Instrucción de la mujer cristiana* (*Instruction of the Christian Woman*), and Schwartz cites verses in the male voice, by Pedro Soto de Rojas from his 1625 *Desengaño de amor en rimas* (*Disillusion of Love in Rhymes*), identical to these sung by Isabel (311).

12 For example, 167 (2), 195, 289, 409, 466. McNamara indicates that the metaphor of the bride of Christ was intended to repress early Christian women, citing the exclamations of Tertullian (a second-century church leader): 'Be veiled, virgin ... for you are wedded to Christ. To him, you have surrendered your body. Act as becomes your husband's discipline' (44).

13 Abad's synthesis of theories of baroque summarizes this aesthetics. Sebastián finds that the decorative exuberance typical of baroque Catholicism reflects the Catholic struggle with Protestantism and was not a perversion of taste (145).

14 The colour code of early modern literature differs from its modern counterpart; Gutierre de Cetina's sonnet 'Es lo blanco castísima pureza' ('White means the most chaste purity') is the best de-coder available (206). See Kenyon's and Chamberlin's elaborations.

15 The argument – my argument – that Zayas is not simply pitting women against men in the *Desengaños* is difficult to assimilate because current readers are accustomed to this approach to the text. In the case of her wealthy female convent dwellers, for example, it is tempting to see an association with the Petrarchan tradition of objectifying women as jewels, which Zayas might be seen as using for vengeance: the woman takes her valuables, representing her self, out of circulation. This is perhaps part of the story. But because a male character also retires with wealth to a convent, and because the book's objectives are by no means limited to correctives of the male nobility, the association is more about politics than

gender, celebrating noble wealth as evidence of virtue and merit. On the underside of this celebrated consumption on the part of early modern Spaniards, see Vilches.

16 See, for example, the religious poetry of Cecilia del Nacimiento (Rhodes, 'Gender in the Night').

Postscript: Laurela

1 In her study of this *desengaño*, Boyer observes that it reworks the second tale of Zayas's *Novelas amorosas* ('War'). El Saffar finds a subversion of the honour code in this tale ('Ana/Lisis/Zayas'); Gorfkle offers a psychoanalytic reading of Laurela's story. For Greer, the cross-dressed Esteban is evidence of Zayas's evasiveness in gender positioning (*María* 222).

Conclusion

1 Theories about Spanish honour begin with the work of Américo Castro (1885–1972) and Ramón Menéndez Pidal (1869–1968). Castro's 1961 *De la edad conflictiva* (*From the Age of Conflict*) is his correction of his own 1916 study of the issue. McKendrick addresses honour in *Woman and Society,* 'Celebration,' and 'Calderón.' Other pertinent theorists of honour include Caro Baroja, Mandrell, Maravall ('La función del honor'; *Poder*), and McCrary. Pitt-Rivers and Moxnes analyse Mediterranean honour.

2 Whether this was an innovation in seventeenth-century Spain will only be discernable in light of continued archival discoveries and analyses of works by women which, as Vollendorf points out, are altering long-standing interpretations of the early modern world ('Transatlantic').

3 Dunn finds this lack of closure in texts as early as Cervantes, and he identifies lack of narrative closure with modernity rather than feminism.

4 For elaboration, see Rhodes, 'Women on Their Knees.' Brownlee offers another interpretation, related to female desire as Zayas represents it ('Moral').

5 Sedgwick's 'Coherence of Gothic Conventions' (1975) continues to be one of the most important texts about Gothic literature, and these are among the features of Gothic she identifies (8–58). See also the resources in *Approaches to Teaching Gothic Fiction*. To date, reference to the Gothic features of Zayas's fiction have been made in support of Welles's initial mention of them ('María').

6 Shakespeare's *Hamlet* speaks these words (1.1.136). Radcliffe's essay, published in the *New Monthly Magazine* in 1826, is a fictional dialogue between

two travelling companions, Mr S. and Mr W. Mishra provides a thorough analysis of the Gothic sublime.

7 The word 'sublime' in seventeenth-century Spain did not yet have the meaning of 'overwhelming grandeur' that it acquired in the 1700s (see ·OED 'sublime'), and certainly not the amplified significance it acquired in Gothic literature. It meant simply 'moral,' or 'eminent.' Cf. Gracián's definition of the sublime observation: 'its perfection consists more in the sublimity of what is known than in the delicacy of the artifice' (consiste su perfección más en la sublimidad del conocimiento que en la delicadeza del artificio, *Agudeza* 2:119).

8 Lewis's debt to Zayas may be greater; many of his descriptors are identical to hers. His narrator insists, for example, that 'possession, which cloys man, only increases the affection of women' (237). Matilda's magical enchantment of the innocent Antonia that puts her into a 'death-like slumber' (275) recalls the Moor's enchantment of Inés. Like Zayas, Lewis insists on women's fated misfortune: 'Antonia was born under an unlucky star' (303).

9 Yllera summarizes previously published information about translations of Zayas in her 'Introducción' (82–91). Important sources for that information include Place (*Bosquejo* and 'María'), Bourland, van Praag, Senabre, Serrano Poncela, and especially Williams.

10 Juárez positions works of five early-1800 Spanish texts by male authors, which she calls Gothic, within Romanticism. Bertsche does likewise, working with canonical authors of nineteenth-century Spain. Curbet marks a greater distinction between Gothic and Romantic.

11 On the Black Legend, the negative characterization of Spain begun during the age of Spanish imperial decline, see *Rereading the Black Legend* (ed. Greer et al.).

12 Van Praag's 1952 declaration lacks evidence, if not enthusiasm (43). In the prologue to his 1950 edition, Amezúa uses evidence of translations and wide plagiarism of Zayas's novellas by French authors to justify his celebration of the author's 'triumphal career' (Prólogo xxiv); he provides a list of Spanish editions and translations into French, English, Dutch, and German in his article, 'Doña María' (30–2), which Yllera repeats (Introducción 70–93). Although the argument that Zayas and Cervantes are the novella authors of preference for literary critics after 1980 is undeniable, Zayas's popularity with her peers needs qualification. Her novellas were published separately or together in the seventeenth century some ten times. Juan Pérez de Montalbán's 1624 *Sucesos y prodigios de amor* (*Love's Happenings and Prodigies*) were republished at least nineteen times in the

seventeenth century and were quickly translated into Italian and French (Guiliani xlviii–xlix).

13 On the appropriation of one of Zayas's *Novelas amorosas* by Paul Scarron, see Meding. In what follows, I refer only to the translations I have seen myself.

14 The book is now catalogued under the name of Pérez de Montalbán, who wrote three of the six stories in the book. According to the *Eighteenth Century Collections Online* bibliographer, the translation was by Edward Ward.

15 One wonders, with Zuili, about the historical accuracy of the narrator's claim in Cervantes' *Persiles y Segismundo* (1617) that 'in France neither man nor woman fails to learn Spanish' (en Francia ni varón ni mujer deja de aprender la lengua española, 567). Zuili provides evidence of a lively interest in things Spanish on the part of the French.

16 On these adaptations and translations, see Place and King. Klein determines that Zayas is Boisrobert's primary source.

17 Antoine Le Metel translated the *Novelas ejemplares* into French individually in the 1650s and in a single volume in 1656. Paul Scarron adapted some of them in his *Nouvelles tragi-comiques* (1655), from which John Davies translated them into English in 1657 (Place, 'María').

18 The *Desengaños* may presage the change that came about at the end of the seventeenth century, when a religious vocation, particularly the claustration of daughters, stopped being a socially acceptable option for Spain's upper classes (Hernández 192).

19 This is intentionally simplified on my part. As Wilt says, the Gothic dichotomy is between God and church, and in the end, Gothic leaves religion 'untouched, even strengthened' (32). Zayas's dichotomy is between God and the Catholic state, on the one hand, and the ignoble nobility, on the other, and likewise uses the dichotomy to strengthen the former.

20 Guthke finds that medieval and Renaissance affiliation between woman and the devil led to the gendering of death as feminine (38–127). The *Desengaños* suggest that even positive troping of the dead woman contributed to this process.

Works Cited

(sources are print unless otherwise indicated)

Abad, Francisco. 'Semiótica y 'barroco': Un concepto y una palabra.' *Epos* 6 (1990): 225–41.

Aladro, Jorge. 'Algunos aspectos de la sociedad de los Siglos de Oro vistos desde el púlpito.' *Memoria de la palabra: Actas del VI Congreso de la Asociación Internacional del Siglo de Oro. Burgos, La Rioja 15–19 de junio 2002.* Ed. Francisco Domínguez Matito and María Luisa Lobato. Madrid; Frankfurt: Iberoamericana; Vervuert, 2004. 169–81.

Albert, Irene, and Uta Felten, eds. *Escenas de transgresión: María de Zayas en su contexto literario-cultural.* Madrid; Frankfurt: Iberoamericana, Vervuert, 2009.

Alcalde, Pilar. *Estrategias temáticas y narrativas en la novela feminizada de Mara de Zayas.* Newark, DE: Juan de la Cuesta, 2005.

Alemán, Mateo. *Guzmán de Alfarache.* Ed. Francisco Rico. Barcelona: Planeta, 1983.

Alfonso X. *Cantigas de Santa María. Códice Rico de El Escorial. Ms. escurialense T.I.1.* Ed. José Filgueira Valverde. Castalia: Madrid, 1985.

– *Las siete partidas del sabio rey don Alonso el Nono / nuevamente glosadas por el licenciado Gregorio López.* Madrid: Boletín Oficial del Estado, 1974.

Amezúa y Mayo, Agustín G. de. Prólogo. *Desengaños amorosos, Parte segunda del sarao y entretenimiento honesto de doña María de Zayas y Sotomayor.* Ed. Agustín G. de Amezúa y Mayo. Madrid: Real Academia Española, 1950. vii–xxiv.

– 'Doña María de Zayas, notas críticas.' *Opúsculos histórico-literarios.* Vol. 2. Madrid: CSIC, 1951–3. 1–32.

Approaches to Teaching Gothic Fiction: The British and American Traditions. Ed. Diane Long Hoeveler and Tamar Heller. New York: MLA, 2003.

Aragüés Aldaz, José. 'Tendencias y realizaciones en el campo de la hagiografía en España (con algunos datos para el estudio de los legendarios hispánicos.' *Memoria Ecclesiae* 24 (2004): 441–560.

– 'Para el estudio del *Flos Sanctorum Renacentista* (I): la conformación de un género.' *Homenaje a Henri Guerreiro. La hagiografía entre historia y literatura en la España de la Edad Media y del Siglo de Oro.* Ed. M. Vitse. Madrid: Iberoamericana, 2005. 97–147.

Arenal, Electa, and Stacey Schlau. *Untold Sisters: Hispanic Nuns in Their Own Works.* Trans. Amanda Powell. Albuquerque: U of New Mexico P, 1989.

Armon, Shifra. *Picking Wedlock: Women and the Courtship Novel in Spain.* Lanham, MD: Rowman & Littlefield, 2002.

Astete, Gaspar de. *Tratado del gobierno de la familia, y estado de las viudas y donzellas.* Burgos, 1603.

Atienza Hernández, Ignacio. 'Las mujeres nobles: clase dominante, grupo dominado. Familia y orden social en el antiguo régimen.' *Ordenamiento jurídico y realidad social de las mujeres: Actas de las cuartas jornadas de investigación interdisciplinaria.* Ed. María Carmen García-Nieto París. Madrid: Seminario de Estudios de la Mujer, 1986. 149–66.

Aubin, P. 'The History of Monsieur Des Frans and Silvia; or, The Cruel Husband, and Innocent Adultery.' *The Illustrious French Lovers, Being the True Histories of the Amours of Several French Persons of Quality.* London: printed for D. Midwinter et al., 1727.

Aullón de Haro, Pedro, et al., eds. *Barroco.* Madrid: Conde Duque; Editorial Verbum, 2004.

Avedaño, Nadia. 'La violencia masculina en los *Desengaños* de María de Zayas.' *South Carolina Modern Language Review* 5.1 (2006): 38–52.

Ayala, Lorenzo de. 'Al lector.' Trans. Lorenzo de Ayala. *Historias trágicas.* By Mateo Bandello. Madrid: Editiones Atlas, 1943. 7.

Azpilcueta Navarro, Martín de. *Manual de confessores y penitentes, que contiene casi todas las dudas que en las confesiones suelen ocurrir, de los pecados, absoluciones, restituciones, censuras e irregularidades.* Barcelona: Claudio Bornat, 1567.

Baines, Barbara J. 'Effacing Rape in Early Modern Representation.' *ELH* 65.1 (1998): 69–98.

Bandello, Mateo. *Historias trágicas.* Trans. Lorenzo de Ayala. Madrid: Editiones Atlas, 1943.

– *Histoires tragiques.* Trans. Pierre Boaistuau. Paris: H. Champion, 1977.

Barahona, Renato. *Sex Crimes, Honour and the Law in Early Modern Viscaya. 1528–1735.* Toronto: U of Toronto P, 2003.

Behrend-Martínez, Edward. 'Manhood and the Neutered Body in Early Modern Spain.' *Journal of Social History* 38.4 (2005): 1073–95.

Benjamin, Walter. *The Origin of German Tragic Drama*. 1928. New York: Verso, 1998.

Berco, Christian. 'Social Control and Its Limits: Sodomy, Local Sexual Economies, and Inquisitors during Spain's Golden Age.' *Sixteenth Century Journal* 36.2 (2005): 331–58.

Bergmann, Emlie. 'A Maternal Gracián? Luisa de Padilla's Advice to Aragonese Nobility.' *(Re)Capturing the Female Hispanic Body: Cultural Representations and Discourse*. Third Annual Conference on Women Writers of Medieval and Early Modern Spain and Colonial Latin America. Loyola Marymount University, Los Angeles. Oct. 1998.

Bertsche, Allen Parker-Suárez. 'The Unseen Spectre: The Gothic Mode in Nineteenth-Century Spanish Narrative.' PhD Diss. U of Wisconsin, Madison, 2000.

Beverly, John. *Essays on the Literary Baroque in Spain and Spanish America*. Woodbridge: Tamesis, 2008.

Blanco, Mercedes. *Les Rhétoriques de la Pointe: Baltasar Gracián et le conceptisme en Europe*. Paris: Librairie Honoré Champion, 1992.

Boisrobert, François le Métel. *Nouvelles heroiques et amoureuses*. Paris: P. Lamy, 1657.

Bomli, P.W. *La femme dans l'Espagne du siècle d'or*. The Hague: M. Nijhoff, 1950.

Bordwell, David, and Kristin Thompson. *Film Art: An Introduction*. 8th ed. New York: McGraw Hill, 2008.

Botero, Giovanni. *Della ragione di stato, libri dieci*. Milan, 1598. 2007. Digital Library of the Catholic Reformation. Web. 19 Feb. 2010.

Bourland, Caroline B. *The Short Story in Spain in the Seventeenth Century, with a Bibliography of the Novela from 1576 to 1700*. New York: Burt Franklin, 1973.

Boyarin, Daniel. 'Thinking with Virgins: Engendering Judaeo-Christian Difference.' *Dying for God: Martyrdom and the Making of Christianity and Judaism*. Stanford: Stanford UP, 1999. 67–92.

Boyer, H. Patsy. Introduction. *The Enchantments of Love: Amorous and Exemplary Novels of María de Zayas*. Berkeley: U of California P, 1990. xi–xxxix.

– '"The Ravages of Vice" and the Vice of Telling Stories.' *Voces a ti debidas: In Honor of Ruth Anthony El Saffar*. Ed. Marie Cort Daniels et al. Colorado Springs: Colorado College, 1993. 29–34.

– 'The War between the Sexes and the Ritualization of Violence in Zayas's *Disenchantments*.' *Sex and Love in Golden Age Spain*. Ed. Alain Saint-Saëns. New Orleans: UP of the South, 1996. 123–45.

Bravo-Villasante, Carmen. *La mujer vestida de hombre en el teatro español, siglos XVI–XVII*. Madrid: Revista de Occidente, 1955.

Brönfen, Elisabeth. *Over Her Dead Body: Death, Femininity and the Aesthetic.* Manchester: Routledge, 1992.

Brownlee, Marina S. '"Moral Pornography": Angela Carter and María de Zayas.' *Marriage and Sexuality in Medieval and Early Modern Iberia.* Ed. Eukene Lacarra Lanz. New York: Routledge, 2002. 214–31.

– 'Postmodernism and the Baroque in María de Zayas.' *Cultural Authority in Golden Age Spain.* Ed. Marina S. Brownlee and Hans Ulrich Gumbrecht. Baltimore: Johns Hopkins UP, 1995. 107–25.

– Preface. *The Cultural Labyrinth of María de Zayas.* Ed. Marina S. Brownlee. Philadelphia: U of Pennsylvania P, 2000. xi–xvi.

Buser, Thomas. 'Jerome Nadal and Early Jesuit Art in Rome.' *Art Bulletin* 58.3 (1976): 424–33.

Butler, Marilyn. Introduction. *Northanger Abbey.* By Jane Austen. 1995; London: Penguin, 2003. xi–l.

Calderón de la Barca, Pedro. *El alcalde de Zalamea.* Ed. Angel Valbuena Briones. 12th ed. Madrid: Cátedra, 1992.

Camino, Mercedes Maroto. 'Spindles for Swords: The Re/dis-covery of María de Zayas's Presence.' *Hispanic Review* 62.4 (1994): 519–36.

Camos, Marco Antonio de. *Microcosmia: Gobierno universal del hombre cristiano para todos los estados y cualquiera de ellos.* Madrid: Casa de la Viuda de Alonso Gómez, 1595.

Cardaillac-Hermosilla, Yvette. 'La magia en las novelas de María de Zayas.' *La creatividad femenina en el mundo barroco hispánico: María de Zayas, Isabel Receba Correa, Sor Juana Inés de la Cruz. Actas del Congreso internacional La creatividad feminina y las trampas del poder.* Ed. Barbara Potthast et al. Vol. 1. Kassel: Reichenberger, 1999. 351–83.

Caro, Ana. *Valor, agravio y mujer.* Ed. Lola Luna. Madrid: Castalia, 1993.

Caro Baroja, Julio. 'Honour and Shame: A Historical Account of Several Conflicts.' *Honour and Shame: The Values of Mediterranean Society.* Ed. J.G. Peristiany. Chicago: U Chicago P, 1966. 79–138.

Carrasco, Rafael. 'Loin des enfers: littérature hiagiographique et propagande dans l'Espagne classique (XVIè et XVIIè siècle).' *Enfers et damnations dans le monde hispanique et hispano-américain.* Ed. Jean-Paul and Annie Molinié-Bertrand Duviols. Paris: Presses Universitaires de France, 1996. 363–80.

Carrión, María M. *Subject Stages: Marriage, Theatre and the Law in Early Modern Spain.* Toronto: U of Toronto Press, 2010.

Cartagena Calderón, José. *Masculinidades en obras: El drama de la hombría en la España imperial.* Newark DE: Juan de la Cuesta, 2008.

Casa, Frank P. 'El tema de la violación sexual en la comedia.' *El escritor y la escena: Actas del I Congreso de la Asociación internacional de teatro español y novo-*

hispano de los Siglos de Oro (18–21 March 1992, Ciudad Juárez, México). Ed. Ysla Campbell. Ciudad Juárez: U Autónoma de Ciudad Juárez, 1993. 203–12.

Casey, James. 'The Consolidation of an Aristocracy.' *Early Modern Spain: A Social History*. London: Routledge, 1999. 138–64.

– *Family and Community in Early Modern Spain: The Citizens of Granada, 1570–1739*. Cambridge: Cambridge UP, 2007.

– 'Household Disputes in Early Modern Andalusia.' *Disputes and Settlements: Law and Human Relations in the West*. Ed. John Bossy. Cambridge: Cambridge UP, 1983. 189–217.

Castan, Nicole. 'La criminal.' *Historia de las mujeres: Del Renacimiento a la Edad Moderna*. Ed. Reyna Pastor. Trans. Marco Aurelio Galmarini. Vol. 3. *Historia de las mujeres*. Madrid: Taurus, 2000. 511–24.

Castillo, David R. 'Horror (Vacui): The Baroque Condition.' *Hispanic Baroques: Reading Cultures in Context*. Ed. Nicholas Spadaccini and Luis Martín-Estudillo. Nashville: Vanderbilt UP, 2005. 87–104.

Castro, Américo. 'Algunas observaciones acerca del concepto del honor en los siglos XVI y XVII.' *Revista de filología española* 3 (1916): 1–50; 375–86.

– *De la edad conflictiva*. Madrid: Taurus, 1961.

Cayuela, Anne. *Le paratexte au siècle d'or: Prose romanesque, livres et lecteurs en Espagne au XVIIe siècle* Geneva: Droz, 1996.

– 'La prosa de ficción entre 1625 y 1634: Balance de diez años sin licencias para imprimir novelas en los reinos de Castilla.' *Mélanges de la Casa de Velázquez* 29.2 (1993): 51–78.

Ceballo, Gerónimo. *Arte real para el buen gobierno de los reyes y príncipes y de sus vasallos*. Toledo: Diego Rodríguez, 1623.

Cervantes Saavedra, Miguel de. *Don Quijote de la Mancha*. Ed. Francisco Rico and Joaquín Forradellas. 2 vols. Barcelona: Crítica, 1998.

– *Don Quijote*. Trans. Raffel Burton. Ed. Diana de Armas Wilson. New York: W.W. Norton, 1999.

Cetina, Gutierre de. *Sonetos y madrigales completos*. Ed. Begoña López Bueno. Madrid: Cátedra, 1990.

Chamberlin, Vernon A. 'Symbolic Green: A Time-Honored Characterizing Device in Spanish Literature.' *Hispania* 51.1 (1968): 29–37.

Chauchadis, Claude. *Honneur, morale et société dans l'Espagne de Philippe II*. Paris: Editions du CNRS, 1984.

Ciruelo, Pedro. *Confesionario*. Zaragoza, 1541.

Clamurro, William. 'Ideological Contradiction and Imperial Decline: Toward a Reading of Zayas's *Desengaños amorosos*.' *South Central Review* 5 (1988): 43–50.

Cohen, Esther. 'The Animate Pain of the Body.' *The American Historical Review* 105.1 (2000): 36–68.

Compte, Deborah. 'The *mora* as Agent of Power and Authority: María de Zayas's "La esclava de su amante."' *Hispanic Journal* 24.1–2: 53–64.

Connor (Swietlicki), Catherine. 'Marriage and Subversion in Comedia Endings: Problems in Art and Society.' *Gender, Identity and Representation in Spain's Golden Age*. Ed. Anita K. Stoll and Dawn L. Smith. Lewisburg: Bucknell UP; Associated UP, 2000. 23–46.

Coolidge, Grace E. 'Choosing Her Own Buttons: The Guardianship of Magdalena de Bobadilla.' *Power and Gender in Renaissance Spain: Eight Women of the Mendoza Family, 1450–1650*. Ed. Helen Nader. Chicago: U of Chicago P, 2004. 132–51.

Coontz, Stephanie. *Marriage, a History: From Obedience to Intimacy, or How Love Conquered Marriage*. New York: Viking, 2005.

Costa, Juan. *Gobierno del ciudadano … de cómo se ha de regir a sí, su casa, y república*. 1578. Zaragoza: Joan de Altarach, 1584.

Cotarelo y Mori, Emilio. *Bibliografía de las controversias sobre la licitud del teatro en España*. Madrid: Revista de Archivos, Bibliotecas y Museos, 1904.

Covarrubias Orozco, Sebastián de. *Tesoro de la lengua castellana o española*. Ed. Martín de Riquer. Barcelona: Editorial Alta Fulla, 1987.

Crawford, Mary, and Roger Chaffin. 'The Reader's Construction of Meaning: Cognitive Research on Gender and Comprehension.' *Gender and Reading: Essays on Readers, Text, and Contexts*. Ed. Patrocinio P. Schweickart and Elizabeth A. Flynn. Baltimore: Johns Hopkins UP, 1986. 3–30.

Cruickshank, Donald W. 'Literature and the Book Trade in Golden-Age Spain.' *Modern Language Review* 73.4 (1978): 799–824.

Curbet, Joan. '"Hallelujah to Your Dying Screams of Torture": Representations of Ritual Violence in English and Spanish Romanticism.' *European Gothic: A Spirited Exchange 1760–1960*. Ed. Avril Horner. Manchester: Manchester UP, 2002. 161–82.

Davis, Elizabeth B. 'Épica y configuración del canon en la poesía española del Siglo de Oro.' *En torno al canon: Aproximaciones y estrategias*. Ed. Begoña López Bueno. Seville: U de Sevilla, 2005. 317–32.

– '"Woman, Why Weepest Thou?": Re-Visioning the Golden Age Magdalen.' *Hispania* 76.1 (1993): 38–48.

Davis, Nina Cox. 'Re-framing Discourse: Women before Their Public in María de Zayas.' *Hispanic Review* 71.3 (2003): 325–44.

Dharker, Imtiaz. *I Speak for the Devil*. Tarset, Eng.: Bloodaxe Books, 2001.

Diccionario de autoridades. 3 vols. Madrid: Gredos, 1990.

Diccionario de la Real Academia Española. Web. 20 Feb. 2010.

Dixon, Victor. 'La mayor confusión.' *Hispanófila* 3 (1958): 17–26.

Domínguez Ortiz, Antonio. 'El estamento nobiliario.' *Las clases privilegiadas del Antiguo Régimen.* 1973. Madrid: Ediciones Istmo, 1985. 19–200.

Donnell, Sidney. *Feminizing the Enemy: Imperial Spain, Transvestite Drama, and the Crisis of Masculinity.* Lewisburg: Bucknell UP, 2003.

Dopico Black, Georgina. *Perfect Wives, Other Women: Adultery and Inquisition in Early Modern Spain.* Durham: Duke UP, 2001.

Dueñas, Juan de. *Remedio de pecadores, por otro nombre llamado confesionario.* Valladolid: Juan de Villacirán, 1545.

Dunn, Peter. 'Shaping Experience: Narrative Strategies in Cervantes.' *MLN* 109.2 (1994): 186–203.

Dyer, Abigail. 'Seduction by Promise of Marriage: Law, Sex, and Culture.' *Sixteenth Century Studies* 34.2 (2003): 439–55.

Eagleton, Terry. *Sweet Violence: The Idea of the Tragic.* Oxford: Blackwell, 2003.

Eighteenth Century Collections Online. Web. 6 Feb. 2010.

Eire, Carlos M.N. *From Madrid to Purgatory: The Art and Craft of Dying in Sixteenth-Century Spain.* Cambridge: Cambridge UP, 1995.

El Saffar, Ruth. 'Ana/Lisis/Zayas: Reflections on Courtship and Literary Women in María de Zayas's *Novelas amorosas y ejemplares.' María de Zayas: The Dynamics of Discourse.* Ed. Judith A. Whitenack and Amy R. Williamsen. Madison: Fairleigh Dickinson UP; Associated UP, 1995. 192–216.

– *Rapture Encaged: The Suppression of the Feminine in Western Culture.* London, New York: Routledge, 1994.

Elliott, John H. *Spain and Its World, 1500–1700: Selected Essays.* New Haven: Yale UP, 1989.

Enríquez de Salamanca, Cristina. 'Irony, Parody and the Grotesque in a Baroque Novella: "Tarde llega el desengaño."' *María de Zayas: The Dynamics of Discourse.* Ed. Amy R. Williamsen and Judith A. Whitenack. Madison: Fairleigh Dickinson UP, 1995. 234–53.

Escrivà, Francisco. *Discursos de los estados de las obligaciones particulares del estado y oficio, según las cuales ha de ser cada uno particularmente juzgado.* Valencia: Juan Cristóstomo Garriz, 1613.

Estruch Tobella, Joan. 'La situación social del escritor en la España del siglo XVII.' *Cuadernos hispanoamericanos* 477–8 (1990): 337–40.

Felten, Hans. *María de Zayas y Sotomayor: zum Zusammenhang zwischen moralist. Texten und Novellenliteratur.* Frankfurt am Main: Klostermann, 1978.

Feros, Antonio. 'Art and Spanish Society: The Historical Context, 1577–1623.' *El Greco to Velázquez: Art during the Reign of Philip III.* Ed. Ronni Baer and Sarah Schroth. Boston: MFA Publications, 2008. 15–39.

Finaldi, Gabriele. 'A Pereda Discovery in North Wales: A Kitchen Scene at Penryhn Castle.' *Apollo* 141 (1995): 10–13.

Foa, Sandra M. *Feminismo y forma narrativa: Estudio del tema y las técnicas de*

María de Zayas y Sotomayor. Valencia: Albatros Hispanófila Ediciones, 1979.

– 'María de Zayas: Visión conflictia y renuncia del mundo.' *Cuadernos Hispanoamericanos* 331.1 (1978): 128–35.

Friedman, Edward H. 'Afterword: Redressing the Baroque.' *Hispanic Baroques: Reading Cultures in Context*. Ed. Nicholas Spadaccini and Luis Martín-Estudillo. Nashville: Vanderbilt UP, 2005. 283–305.

– 'María de Zayas's *Estragos que causa el vicio* and the Feminist Impasse.' *Romance Languages Annual* 8 (1997): 472–5.

Friedman, Ellen G. 'El estatus jurídico de la mujer castellana durante el antiguo régimen.' *Ordenamiento jurídico y realidad social de las mujeres: Actas de las cuartas jornadas de investigación interdisciplinaria*. Ed. María Carmen García-Nieto París. Madrid: Seminario de Estudios de la Mujer, 1986.

Frye, Northrop. *The Anatomy of Criticism: Four Essays*. 1957. Princeton: Princeton UP, 1971.

Fuchs, Barbara. 'Border Crossings: Transvestism and "Passing" in *Don Quijote*.' *Cervantes* 16.2 (1996): 4–28.

Gamboa Tusquets, Yolanda. *Cartografía social en la narrativa de María de Zayas*. Madrid: Biblioteca Nueva, 2009.

García Cárcel, Ricardo. *Las culturas del Siglo de Oro*. Madrid: Historia 16, 1989.

Giddens, Anthony. *Sociology*. 3rd ed. Cambridge: Polity Press, 1997.

Gil, Antonio. 'Mujeres ante la justicia eclesiástica: Un caso de separación matrimonial en la Barcelona de 1602.' *Las mujeres en el antiguo regimen: Imagen y realidad*. Ed. Marta Vicente Valentín et al. Barcelona: Icaria, 1994. 169–202.

Gil Fernández, Luis. *Panorama social del humanismo español (1500–1800)*. Barcelona: Alhambra, 1981.

Giuliani, Luigi. 'La novela corta del siglo XVII.' *Sucesos y prodigios de amor*. By Juan Pérez de Montalbán. Ed. Luigi Giuliana. Barcelona: Montesinos, 1992. ix–lv.

Góngora y Argote, Luis de. *Obras completas*. Ed. Juan Millé y Giménez and Isabel Mille Giménez. 4th ed. Madrid: Aguilar, 1956.

Gorfkle, Laura J. 'Seduction and Hysteria in María de Zayas's *Desengaños amorosos*.' *Hispanófila* 115 (1995): 11–26.

Gottlieb, Beatrice. *The Family in the Western World from the Black Death to the Industrial Age*. Oxford: Oxford UP, 1993.

Gracián, Baltasar. *Agudeza y arte de ingenio*. Ed. Evaristo Correa Calderón. 2 vols. Madrid: Castalia, 1969.

– *El criticón*. Ed. Santos Alonso. Madrid: Cátedra, 1980.

– *El héroe, El discrete: Oráculo y arte de prudencia*. Ed. Luys Santa Marina. Intro. Raquel Asún. Barcelona: Planeta, 1996.

Greer, Margaret R. *María de Zayas Tells Baroque Tales of Love and the Cruelty of Men*. University Park: Pennsylvania State UP, 2000.

– 'Who's Telling This Story, Anyhow? Framing Tales East and West: *Panchatantra* to Boccaccio to Zayas.' *Echoes and Inscriptions: Comparative Approaches to Early Modern Spanish Literatures*. Ed. Barbara A. Simerka and Christoher B. Weimer. Lewisburg: Bucknell UP; Associated UP, 2000. 33–45.

Grieve, Patricia E. 'Embroidering with Saintly Threads: María de Zayas Challenges Cervantes and the Church.' *Renaissance Quarterly* 44.1 (1991): 86–106.

Griswold, Susan C. 'Topoi and Rhetorical Distance: The "Feminism" of María de Zayas.' *Revista de estudios hispánicos* 14.2 (1980): 97–116.

Guevara, María de [Condesa de Escalante]. *Warnings to the King and Advice on Restoring Spain*. Ed. and trans. Nieves Romero-Díaz. Chicago: U of Chicago P, 2007.

Guillén, Felisa. 'El marco narrativo como espacio utópico en los *Desengaños amorosos* de María de Zayas.' *Revista de Literatura* 60.120 (1998): 527–36.

Guthke, Karl S. *The Gender of Death: A Cultural History in Art and Literature*. Cambridge: Cambridge UP, 1999.

Hale, Terry. 'Translation in Distress: Cultural Misappropriation and the Construction of the Gothic.' *European Gothic: A Spirited Exchange 1760–1960*. Ed. Avril Horner. Manchester and New York: Manchester UP, 2002. 17–38.

Haliczer, Stephen H. 'Sexuality and Repression in Counter-Reformation Spain.' *Sex and Love in Golden Age Spain*. Ed. Alain Saint-Saëns. New Orleans: UP of the South, 1996. 81–93.

Heiple, Daniel L. 'The Theological Context of Wife Murder in Seventeenth-Century Spain.' *Sex and Love in Golden Age Spain*. Ed. Alain Saint-Saëns. New Orleans: UP of the South, 1996. 105–21.

Hernández, Mauro. *A la sombra de la corona: Poder local y oligarquía urbana (Madrid, 1606–1808)*. Madrid: Siglo XXI, 1994.

Hernández y Sánchez-Barba, Mario. 'La influencia de los libros de caballeros sobre el conquistador.' *Estudios americanos* 19 (1960): 235–56.

Herrero, Javier. 'Renaissance Poverty and Lazarillo's Family: The Birth of the Picaresque Genre.' *PMLA* 94.5 (1979): 876–86.

Hidalgo, Gaspar Lucas. *Diálogos de apacible entretenimiento, que contiene unas carnestolendas de Castilla* (1605). *Curiosidades bibliográficas*. Ed. Adolfo de Castro. Biblioteca de autores españoles, vol. 36. Madrid: M. Rivadeneyra, 1855. 279–316.

Hoffman, Joan M. 'Ruecas into Espadas, Almohadillas into Libros: Subversion in María de Zayas' "La fuerza del amor."' *Hispanic Journal* 27.1 (2006): 37–46.

Ife, B.W. *Reading and Fiction in Golden Age Spain: A Platonist Critique and Some Picaresque Replies*. Cambridge: Cambridge UP, 1985.

Imirizaldu, Jesús. *Monjas y beatas embaucadores*. Madrid: Editora Nacional, 1977.

Jeffrey, Denix. *Jouissance du sacré: Religion et postmodernité*. Paris: Armand Colin, 1998.

Jehenson, Yvonne, and Marcia L. Welles. 'María de Zayas's Wounded Women: A Semiotics of Violence.' *Gender, Identity, and Representation in Spain's Golden Age*. Ed. Anita K. Stoll and Dawn L. Smith. Lewisburg: Bucknell UP, 2000. 178–202.

Joseph de Jesús María, Fray. *Primera parte de las excelencias de la virtud de la castidad*. Alcalá: Viuda de Juan Gracián, 1601.

Juárez, Leonor. 'Ghostly Traces: Gender and Genre in Popular Gothic Fiction of Early Nineteenth-century Spain.' PhD Diss. U of Miami, 2005.

Kagan, Richard L. 'A Golden Age of Litigation: Castile, 1500–1700.' *Disputes and Settlements: Law and Human Relations in the West*. Ed. John Bossy. Cambridge: Cambridge UP, 1983. 145–66.

Kahiluoto Rudat, Eva M. 'Ilusión y desengaño.' *Letras femeninas* 1.1 (1975): 27–43.

Kamen, Henry. 'The Decline of Spain: A Historical Myth?' *Past and Present* 81.1 (1978): 24–50.

– *Spain, 1469–1714: A Society of Conflict*. 2nd ed. London: Longman, 1991.

Kaminsky, Amy. 'María de Zayas and the Invention of a Women's Writing Community.' *Revista de estudios hispánicos* 35 (2001): 487–509.

Keep, Christopher, Tim McLaughlin, and Robin Parmar. 'Readerly and Writerly Texts.' *The Electronic Labyrinth*. 1993–2000. Web. 6 Jan. 2010.

Kenyon, Herbert A. 'Color Symbolism in Early Spanish Ballads.' *Romanic Review* 6 (1915): 327–40.

King, Katherine S. 'Boisrobert's *Nouvelles heroiques et amoureuses* and the *Histoire indienne*: His Prose Adaptations from the Spanish.' PhD Diss. Louisiana State U, 1979.

Klein, Andras. 'Une tragi-comédie française sur un sujet hongrois: Boisrobert: "Théodore, Reine de Hongrie."' *Revue d'Études françaises* 2 (1997): 178–209.

Lagreca, Nancy. 'Evil Women and Feminist Sentiment: Baroque Contradictions in María de Zayas's "El prevenido engañado" and "Estragos que causa el vicio."' *Revista canadiense de estudios hispánicos* 28.3 (2004): 565–82.

Langer, Ullrich. 'The Renaissance Novella as Justice.' *Renaissance Quarterly* 52 (1999): 311–41.

Lanser, Susan S. *The Narrative Act: Point of View in Prose Fiction*. Princeton: Princeton UP, 1981.

Lara, M.V. 'De escritoras españolas – II, María de Zayas y Sotomayor.' *Bulletin of Spanish Studies* 9 (1932): 31–7.

Larson, Donald. *The Honor Plays of Lope de Vega*. Cambridge, MA: Harvard UP, 1977.

Laspéras, Jean-Michel. *La nouvelle en Espagne au siècle d'or*. Perpignan: Editions de Castillet, 1987.

– 'La novela corta: hacia una definición.' *La invención de la novela*. Ed. Jean Canavaggio. Madrid: Casa de Velázquez, 1999. 307–17.

Ledesma, Pedro de. *Adiciones a la primera parte de la Suma: Trátase con diligencia todo lo moral tocante al sacramento del matrimonio*. Salamanca: Antonio Ramírez, viuda, 1614.

– *El consejero cristiano, político y moral, muy necesario para cualquier estado de personas*. Valencia: Francisco Mestre, 1678.

– *Primera parte de la Suma, en la cual se cifra y suma todo lo que toca y pertenece a los sacramentos, con todos los casos y dudas morales resueltas y determinadas*. Salamanca: Antonio Ramírez, viuda, 1614.

Lehfeldt, Elizabeth. *Religious Women in Golden Age Spain: The Permeable Cloister*. Aldershot, UK: Ashgate, 2005.

Lennox, Charlotte. *The Female Quixote, or The Adventures of Arabella*. New York: Oxford UP, 1970.

Levin, Harry. 'The Title as a Literary Genre.' *Modern Language Review* 72 (1977): xxii–xxxvi.

Levisi, Margarita. 'La crueldad en los desengaños amorosos de María de Zayas.' *Estudios literarios de hispanistas norteamericanos decidados a Helmut Hatzfeld con motivo de su 80 aniversario*. Ed. Josep M. Sola-Solé et al. Barcelona: HISPAM, 1974. 447–56.

Lewis, Matthew G. *The Monk*. Intro. John Berryman. New York: Grove Press, 1993.

Lilio, Martín de. *Segunda parte del Flos sanctorum*. Alcalá: Juan Brocar, 1558.

López, Gregorio. *Las siete partidas del sabio Rey Don Alonso el Nono, nuevamente glosadas por el licenciado Gregorio López*. Valladolid: Diego Fernández de Córdoba, 1587.

Lopéz de Montoya, Pedro. *Libro de la buena educación y enseñanza de los nobles, en que se dan muy importantes avisos a los padres para criar y enseñar bien sus hijos*. Madrid: Viuda de P. Madrigal, 1595.

López Pinciano, Alonso. *Philosophia antigua poética*. Ed. Alfredo Carvallo Picazo. Vol. 2. Madrid: CSIC, 1973.

Lozano, Cristóbal. *Soledades de la vida y desengaños del mundo, corregidas y enmendadas en esta segunda impresión*. Madrid: Andrés García de la Iglesia, 1664.

Luna, Lola. 'Ana Caro, una escritoria "de oficio" del Siglo de Oro.' *Bulletin of Hispanic Studies* 72 (1995): 11–26.

Machiavelli, Niccolo. *The Prince*. Trans. Harvey C. Mansfield. Chicago: U of Chicago P, 1998.

MacKay, Ruth. *'Lazy, Improvident People': Myth and Reality in the Writing of Spanish History*. Ithaca: Cornell UP, 2006.

Maiorino, Giancarlo. *First Pages: A Poetics of Titles*. University Park: Penn State UP, 2008.

Mâle, Emile. *L'art religieux de la fin du XVIe siècle, du XVIIe siècle et du XVIIIe siècle: Étude sur l'iconographie après le Concile de Trente, Italie-France-Espagne-Flandres*. Paris: A. Colin, 1951.

Mandrell, James. *Don Juan and the Point of Honor: Seduction, Patriarchal Society, and Literary Tradition*. University Park: Penn State UP, 1992.

Manero Sorolla, María Pilar. 'On the Margins of the Mendozas: Luisa de la Cerda and María de San José (Salazar).' *Power and Gender in Renaissance Spain: Eight Women of the Mendoza Family, 1450–1650*. Ed. Helen Nader. Chicago: U of Chicago P, 2004. 1–26.

Maravall, José Antonio. *Culture of the Baroque: Analysis of a Historical Structure*. Trans. Terry Cochran. 1975; Minneapolis: U of Minnesota P, 1986.

– 'La función del honor en la sociedad tradicional.' *Ideologies and Literature, a Journal of Hispanic and Luso-Brazilian Studies* 2.7 (1978): 9–27.

– *Poder, honor y élites en el siglo XVII*. Madrid: Siglo XXI, 1984.

– *Teatro y literatura en la sociedad barroca*. Ed. Francisco Abad. 2nd ed. Barcelona: Editorial Crítica, 1990.

Marguerite de Navarre. *L'Heptameron*. Ed. Renja Salminen. Geneva: Droz, 1999.

Marín Cruzado, Olga. 'El retrato real en composiciones religiosas de la pintura del siglo XVI: Carlos y Felipe II.' *El arte en las cortes de Carlos V y Felipe II*. Madrid: CSIC, 1999. 113–26.

Mariscal, George. *Contradictory Subjects: Quevedo, Cervantes, and Seventeenth-Century Spanish Culture*. Ithaca and London: Cornell UP, 1991.

Martínez de Portal, María. 'Estudio preliminar.' *Novelas completas de María de Zayas*. By María de Zayas. Barcelona: Bruguera, 1973. 9–30.

Martínez Gil, Fernando. *Muerte y sociedad en la España de los Austrias*. Cuenca: U Castilla-La Mancha, 2000.

Masuccio, Salernitano. *Il novellino, con appendice di prosatori napletani del '400*. Florence: Sansoni, 1957.

Maturin, Charles Robert. *Melmoth the Wanderer*. Ed. Victor Sage. London: Penguin, 2000.

May, Terence E. 'Notes on Gracián's *Agudeza*.' *Wit of the Golden Age*. Kassel: Reichenberger, 1986. 270–83.

McCracken, Peggy. 'Engendering Sacrifice: Blood, Lineage, and Infanticide in Old French Literature.' *Speculum* 77 (2002): 55–75.

McCrary, William C. 'The Theatricality of Male Orientation in the Comedia.'

Studies in Honor of William C. McCrary. Ed. Robert Fiore et al. Lincoln: U of Nebraska P, 1986. 27–33.

McKendrick, Melveena. 'Calderón and the Politics of Honour.' *Bulletin of Hispanic Studies* 70 (1993): 135–45.

– 'Celebration or Subversion? *Los comendadores de Córdoba* Reconsidered.' *Bulletin of Hispanic Studies* 61 (1984): 352–60.

– 'Honour/Vengeance in the Spanish "Comedia": A Case of Mimetic Transference?' *Modern Language Review* 79.2 (1984): 313–35.

– *Woman and Society in the Spanish Drama of the Golden Age: A Study of the Mujer Varonil*. Cambridge: Cambridge UP, 1974.

McNamara, Jo Ann Kay. *Sisters in Arms: Catholic Nuns through Two Millennia*. Cambridge, MA: Harvard UP, 1996.

Meding, Twyla. 'Translation as Appropriation: The Case of María de Zayas's *El prevenido engañado* and Paul Scarron's *La Précaution inutile*.' *The Shape of Change: Essays in Early Modern Literature and La Fontaine in Honor of David Lee Rubin*. Ed. Russell Ganim and Anne L. Birberick. Amsterdam: Rodopi, 2002. 91–118.

Menéndez Pidal, Ramón. 'Del honor en el teatro español.' *España y su historia*. Vol. 2. Madrid: Ediciones Minotauro, 1957. 357–71.

Merrim, Stephanie. *Early Modern Women's Writing and Sor Juana Inés de la Cruz*. Nashville: Vanderbilt UP, 1999.

Mihaly, Deanna. 'Socially Constructed, Essentially Other: Servants and Slaves in María de Zayas' *Desengaños amorosos*.' *Romance Languages Annual* 10.2 (1999): 719–25.

Mira de Amescua, Antonio. *El esclavo del demonio*. Ed. James Agustín Castañeda. 2nd ed. Madrid: Cátedra, 1984.

Mishra, Vijay. *The Gothic Sublime*. Albany: State U of New York P, 1994.

Moll, Jaime. 'Diez años sin licencias para imprimir comedias y novelas en los reinos de Castilla: 1625–1634.' *Boletín de la Real Academia Española* 54 (1974): 97–103.

Moncada, Sancho de. *Restauración política de España*. Ed. Jean Vilar. Madrid: Instituto de Estudios Fiscales, 1974.

Montesa Peydró, Salvador. *Texto y contexto en la narrativa de María de Zayas*. Madrid: Dirección General de la Juventud y Promoción Sociocultural, 1981.

Morant Deusa, Isabel. *Discursos de la vida buena: matrimonio, mujer y sexualidad en la literatura humanista*. Madrid: Cátedra, 2002.

Moxnes, Halvor. 'Honor and Shame.' *The Social Sciences and New Testament Interpretation*. Ed. Richard L. Rohrbaugh. Peabody, MA: Hendrickson, 1996. 19–40.

Mujica, Barbara. 'María de Zayas y Sotomayor: ¿Protofeminista o *marketing genius* por excelencia?' *Women Writers of Early Modern Spain: Sophia's Daughters*. Ed. Barbara Mujika. New Haven: Yale UP, 2004. 126–36.

Mulvey, Laura. 'Visual Pleasure and Narrative Cinema.' *Screen* 16 (1975): 6–18.

Nader, Helen. Introduction. *Power and Gender in Renaissance Spain: Eight Women of the Mendoza Family, 1450–1650*. Ed. Helen Nader. Chicago: U of Illinois P, 2004. 1–26.

Nahoum-Grappe, Véronique. 'The Beautiful Woman.' *A History of Women in the West*. Vol. 2, *Renaissance and Enlightenment Paradoxes*. Ed. Natalie Zemon Davis and Arlette Farge. Trans. Arthur Goldhammer. Cambridge: Cambridge UP, 1993. 86–100.

O'Brien, Eavan. *Women in the Prose of María De Zayas*. Woodbridge: Tamesis, 2010.

O'Brien, Keith. 'Why Do Men Kill Their Wives?' *The Boston Globe* 2007. Web. 16 Jan. 2010.

O'Connor, Thomas Austin. 'The Politics of Rape and Fineza in Calderonian Myth Plays.' *The Perception of Women in Spanish Theater of the Golden Age*. Ed. Anita K. Stoll and Dawn L. Smith. Lewisburg: Bucknell UP, 1991. 170–83.

Olivares, Julián. Introducción. *Novelas amorosas y ejemplares*. By María de Zayas. Ed. Julián Olivares. Madrid: Cátedra, 2000. 9–148.

Ordoñez, Elizabeth. 'Woman and Her Text in the Works of María de Zayas and Ana Caro.' *Revista de Estudios Hispánicos* 19 (1985): 3–15.

Orlin, Lena Cowen. 'Three Ways to be Invisible in the Renaissance: Sex, Reputation, and Stitchery.' *Renaissance Culture and the Everyday*. Ed. Patricia Fumerton and Simon Hunt. Philadelphia: U of Pennsylvania P, 1999. 183–203.

Ortega López, Margarita. 'El período barroco (1565–1700).' *Historia de las mujeres en España*. Ed. Elisa Garrido González. Madrid: Editorial Síntesis, 1997. 253–344.

Oxford English Dictionary. Web. 23 Feb. 2010.

Pabst, Walter. *La novela corta en la teoría y en la creación literaria: Notas para la historia de su antinomia en las literaturas románicas*. Madrid: Gredos, 1972.

Pacheco-Ransanz, Arsenio. 'Varia fortuna de la novela corta en al siglo XVII.' *Revista canadiense de estudios hispánicos* 10.3 (1986): 407–21.

Padilla, Luisa María de [under name of Fr. Pedro Henrique Pastor]. *Noble perfecto y segunda parte de la Nobleza virtuosa*. Zaragoza: Pedro Lanaja y Quartanet, 1639.

– *Lágrimas de la nobleza*. Zaragoza: Pedro Lanaja y Lamarca, 1639.

– [under name of Henrique Pastor]. *Nobleza virtuosa dada a la estampa*. Zaragoza: Pedro Lanaja y Quartanet, 1637.

Parker, Alexander A. Introducción. *Fábula de Polifemo y Galatea*. By Luis de Góngora. Madrid: Cátedra, 1983. 1–130.

Parker-Aronson, Stacey L. 'Monstrous Metamorphoses and Rape in María de Zayas.' *Revista canadiense de estudios hispánicos* 29.3 (2005): 525–47.

Parr, James A. 'Review of George Mariscal's *Contradictory Subjects: Quevedo, Cervantes, and Seventeenth-Century Spain*.' *Cervantes* 12.1 (1992): 129–32.

Pecoraro, Rosilie Hernández. '*La fuerza del amor* or the Power of Self-Love: Zayas' Response to Cerventes' *La fuerza de la sangre*.' *Hispanic Review* 70.1 (2002): 39–57.

Pérez de Montalbán, Juan. *Sucesos y prodigios de amor en ocho novelas ejemplares: Obra no dramática*. Ed. José Enrique Laplana Gil. Madrid: Biblioteca Castro, 1946. 1–304.

– (attributed to). *A Week's Entertainment at a Wedding. Containing Six Surprizing and Diverting Adventures*. London, 1710. *Eighteenth Century Collections Online*. Web. 20 Feb. 2010.

Perry, Mary Elizabeth. *Gender and Disorder in Early Modern Seville*. Princeton: Princeton UP, 1990.

Pitt-Rivers, Julian. 'Honour and Social Status.' *Honour and Shame: The Values of Mediterranean Society*. Ed. J.G. Peristiany. Chicago: U of Chicago P, 1966. 19–78.

Place, Edwin B. *Bosquejo histórico de la novela corta y el cuento durante el Siglo de Oro con tablas cronológico-descriptivas de la novelística desde los orígenes hasta 1700*. Madrid: Biblioteca Española de Divulgación Científica Suárez, 1926.

– 'María de Zayas, an Outstanding Woman Short-Story Writer of Seventeenth-Century Spain.' *University of Colorado Studies* 13.1 (1923): 1–56.

Pons, Margalida. 'Extrañamiento e identidad en *La fuerza del amor* de María de Zayas.' *Romance Languages Annual* 7 (1995): 590–6.

Poska, Allyson M. *Women and Authority in Early Modern Spain: The Peasants of Galicia*. Oxford: Oxford UP, 2006.

Power and Gender in Renaissance Spain: Eight Women of the Mendoza Family, 1450–1650. Ed. Helen Nader. Chicago: U of Chicago P, 2004.

Pradilla, Francisco de la. *Suma de las leyes penales*. Madrid: Imprenta del Reino, 1639.

Rabell, Carmen R. *Rewriting the Italian Novella in Counter-Reformation Spain*. Woodbridge: Tamesis, 2003.

Radcliffe, Ann. 'On the Supernatural in Poetry.' *New Monthly Magazine* 16.1 (1826): 145–52. Web. 23 Feb. 2010.

Rereading the Black Legend: The Discourses of Religious and Radical Difference in the Renaissance Empires. Ed. Margaret R. Greer et al. Chicago: U of Chicago P, 2007.

Ruether, Rosemary Radford. 'Mothers of the Church: Ascetic Women in the Late Patristic Age.' *Women of Spirit: Female Leadership in the Jewish and Christian Traditions.* Ed. Rosemary Radford Ruether and Eleanor McLaughlin. New York: Simon and Schuster, 1979. 72–98.

Rey Hazas, Antonio. 'El erotismo en la novela cortesana.' *Edad de Oro* 9 (1989): 271–88.

Rhodes, Elizabeth. 'Gender and the Monstrous in *El burlador de Sevilla.*' *MLN* 117.2 (2002): 267–85.

– 'Gender in the Night: Juan de la Cruz y Cecilia del Nacimiento.' *Studies on Women's Lyric Poetry of the Golden Age: Tras el espejo la musa escribe.* Ed. Julián Olivares. Woodbridge: Tamesis, 2009. 202–17.

– 'The Economics of Salvation in *El esclavo del demonio.*' *Bulletin of the Comediantes* 59.2 (2007): 281–302.

– 'Redressing Ana Caro's *Valor, agravio y mujer.*' *Hispanic Review* 73.3 (2005): 309–28.

– 'A Saint for One Season: Hagiography and Religious Politics in Early Modern Spain.' Renaissance Society of America Conference. Florence, Italy. March 2000.

– 'Spain's Misfired Canon: The Case of Fray Luis de Granada's *Libro de la oración.*' *Journal of Hispanic Philology* 15 (1990): 3–28.

– 'Women on Their Knees: Pornography and Female Religious Discourse in Early Modern Spain.' Center of Cultural and Literary Studies, Harvard University. Dec. 1993.

Richardson, Alan, and Mary Crane. *Literature, Cognition and the Brain.* Boston College. Web. 6 Jan. 2010.

Río Parra, Elena del. *Cartografías de la conciencia española en la Edad de Oro.* Mexico: Fondo de Cultura Económica, 2008.

Ripoll, Begoña. *La novela barroca: Catálogo bio-bibliográfico (1620–1700).* Salamanca: U de Salamanca P, 1991.

Rivadeneira, Pedro de. *Flos sanctorum o libro de las vidas de los santos.* 2 vols. 1599–1601; Madrid: Luis Sánchez, 1616.

Robbins, Jeremy. *The Challenges of Uncertainty: An Introduction to Seventeenth-Century Spanish Literature.* London: Duckworth, 1998.

Rodríguez, Evangelina. Introducción. *Novelas amorosas de diversos ingenios del siglo XVII.* Madrid: Castalia, 1987. 9–88.

Rodríguez-Arango Díaz, Crisanto. 'El matrimonio clandestino en la novela cervantina.' *Anuario de historia del derecho español* 35 (1955): 732–74.

Rodríguez de Montalvo, Garcí. *Amadís de Gaula.* Ed. Juan Manuel Cacho Blecua. 2nd ed. Vol. 1. Madrid: Cátedra, 1991.

Romero-Díaz, Nieves. *Nueva nobleza, nueva novela: Reescribiendo la cultura urbana del barroco*. Newark DE: Juan de la Cuesta, 2002.

– 'Revisiting the Culture of the Baroque: Nobility, City and Post-Cervantine Novella.' *Hispanic Baroques: Reading Cultures in Context*. Ed. Nicholas Spadaccini and Luis Martín-Estudillo. Nashville: Vanderbilt UP, 2005. 162–83.

Routt, Kristin. 'El cuerpo femenino y la creación literaria en *La inocencia castigada.' Romance Languages Annual* 7 (1995): 616–20.

Rubiera Mata, María Jesús. 'La narrativa de origen árabe en la literatura del Siglo de Oro: El caso de María de Zayas.' *La creatividad femenina en el mundo barroco hispánico: María de Zayas, Isabel Rebeca Correa, Sor Juana Inés de la Cruz*. Ed. Barbara Potthast et al. Vol. 1. Kassel: Edition Reichenberger, 1999. 335–49.

Ruff, Julius R. *Violence in Early Modern Europe 1500–1800*. Cambridge: Cambridge UP, 2001.

Ruíz-Gálvez Priego, Estrella. Introducción. *Obra narrativa completa de María de Zayas*. By María de Zayas. Madrid: Fundación José Antonio de Castro, 2001. xix–xlvi.

Saints and Sinners: Carvaggio and the Baroque Image. Ed. Franco Mormando. Chestnut Hill, MA; Chicago: McMullen Museum of Art; U Chicago Press, 1999.

Salstad, M. Louise. 'The Influence of Sacred Oratory on María de Zayas: A Case in Point, *La fuerza del amor.' MLN* 113.2 (1998): 426–32.

Sánchez, Galo. 'Datos jurídicos acerca de la venganza del honor.' *Revista de filología española* 4 (1917): 292–5.

Sánchez Hernández, María Leticia. *Patronato regio y órdenes religiosas femeninas en el Madrid de los Austrias: Descalzas Reales, Encarnación y Santa Isabel*. Madrid: Fundación Universitaria Española, 1997.

Sánchez Lora, José L. *Mujeres, conventos y formas de la religiosidad barroca*. Madrid: Fundación Universitaria Española, 1988.

Schwartz, Lía. 'Discursos dominantes y discursos dominados en textos satíricos de María de Zayas.' *La creatividad femenina en el mundo barroco hispánico: María de Zayas, Isabel Rebeca Correa, Sor Juana Inés de la Cruz*. Ed. Barbara Potthast et al. Vol. 1. Kassel: Edition Reichenberger, 1999. 301–21.

Scribner, Robert W. 'Demons, Defecation and Monsters: Luther's "Depiction of the Papacy" (1545).' *Popular Culture and Popular Movements in Reformation Germany*. London: Hambledon, 1987. 227–300.

Sebastián, Santiago. *Contrarreforma y barroco: Lecturas iconográficas e iconológicas*. Madrid: Alianza, 1981.

Sedgwick, Eve Kosofsky. 'The Coherence of Gothic Conventions.' PhD Diss. Yale U, 1975.

Senabre, Ricardo. 'La fuente de una novela de doña María de Zayas.' *Revista de filología española* 46.1/2 (1963): 163–72.

Serrano Poncela, Segundo. 'Casamientos engañosos (Doña María de Zayas, Scarron y un proceso de creación literaria).' *Bulletin Hispanique* 64 (1962): 248–59.

Serrano y Sanz, Manuel. 'María de Zayas.' *Apuntes para una biblioteca de escritoras españolas desde el año 1401 al 1833*. Vol. 2. Madrid: Estado español, 1903. 583–621.

Shakespeare, William. *Hamlet*. Ed. G.R. Hibbard. Oxford: Oxford UP, 1987.

Smith, Paul Julian. *The Body Hispanic: Gender and Sexuality in Spanish and Spanish American Literature*. Oxford: Clarendon P, 1989.

– 'Writing Women in Golden Age Spain: Saint Teresa and María de Zayas.' *MLN* 102 (1987): 220–40.

Stackhouse, Kenneth A. 'Verisimilitude, Magic and the Supernatural in the Novelas of María de Zayas y Sotomayor.' *Hispanófila* 62 (1978): 65–75.

Stallybrass, Peter. 'Patriarchal Territories: The Body Enclosed.' *Rewriting the Renaissance: The Discourses of Sexual Difference in Early Modern Europe*. Ed. Margaret W. Ferguson et al. Chicago: U of Chicago P, 1986. 123–44.

Stevens, John. 'A Letter from Madrid.' *The British Mercury*. 31 Dec. 1712–28 Jan. 1713. np.

Strasser, Ulrike. '"The First Form and Grace": Ignatius of Loyola and the Reformation of Masculinity.' *Masculinity in the Reformation Era*. Ed. Scott H. Hendrix and Susan C. Karant-Nunn. Kirksville, MO: Truman State UP, 2008. 45–70.

Stroud, Matthew D. *Fatal Union: A Pluralistic Approach to the Spanish Wife-Murder Comedias*. Lewisburg, PA: Bucknell UP, 1990.

Suárez de Figueroa, Cristóbal. *El pasajero: Advertencias utilísimas a la vida humana*. Ed. Enrique Suárez Figaredo. Web. 6 Jan. 2010.

Sucquet, Antoni. *Via vitae aeternae. Engravings by Boëtium à Bolswert*. Antwerp: Martinus Nutius, 1620.

Sylvania, Lena E.V. *Doña María de Zayas y Sotomayor: A Contribution to the Study of Her Works*. New York: Columbia UP, 1922.

Tausier, María. 'Taming Madness: Moral Discourse and Allegory in Counter-Reformation Spain.' *History* 94.315 (2009): 279–93.

Taylor, Scott K. *Honor and Violence in Golden Age Spain*. New Haven: Yale UP, 2008.

Teresa de Jesús, Saint. 'Libro de la Vida.' *Obras completas*. Ed. Efren de la Madre de Dios and Otger Steggink. 8th ed. Madrid: Editorial Católica, 1986. 31–232.

Thurston, Herbert. 'Blood Prodigies.' *Studies: An Irish Quarterly* 10.37 (1921): 25–38.

– *The Physical Phenomena of Mysticism.* Ed. J.H. Crehan. Chicago: H. Regnery, 1952.

Tirso de Molina [Gabriel Tellez], attributed author. *El burlador de Sevilla.* Ed. Alfredo Rodríguez López-Vázquez. 7th ed. Madrid: Cátedra, 1995.

Tomás y Valiente, Francisco. *El derecho penal de la monarquía absoluta (Siglos XVI–XVII–XVIII).* Madrid: Editorial Tecnos, 1969.

Truman, Ronald W. *Spanish Treatises on Government, Society, and Religion in the Time of Philip II: The 'De regimine principum' and Associated Traditions.* Leiden: Brill, 1999.

van Praag, J.A. 'Sobre las novelas de María de Zayas.' *Clavileño: Revista de la Associación Internacional de Hispanismo* 15 (1952): 42–3.

Varma, Devendra P. *The Gothic Flame, Being a History of the GOTHIC NOVEL in England: Its Origins, Efflorescence, Disintegration, and Residuary Influences.* New York: Russell & Russell, 1966.

Vasileski, Irma V. *María de Zayas y Sotomayor, su época y su obra.* Madrid: Playor, 1973;

Vega, Alonso de. *Suma llamada Nueva Recopilación y práctica del fuero interior, utilísima para confesores y penitentes, con varias resoluciones de casi innumerables casos de conciencia, tocantes a todas las materias teólogas, canónicas y jurídicas, conforme a la doctrina de los santos y más graves autores antiguos y modernos.* Madrid: Luis Sánchez, 1606.

Vega y Carpio, Lope de. *El castigo sin venganza.* Ed. Antonio Carreño. Madrid: Cátedra, 1990.

Velasco, Sherry M. *Male Delivery: Reproduction, Effeminacy, and Pregnant Men in Early Modern Spain.* Nashville TN: Vanderbilt UP, 2008.

Vigil, Mariló. *La vida de las mujeres en los siglos XVI y XVII.* Madrid: Siglo XXI, 1986.

Vila, Juan Diego. '"En deleites tan torpes y abominables": María de Zayas y la figuración abyecta de la escena homoerótica.' *Escenas de transgresión: María de Zayas en su contexto literario-cultural.* Ed. Irene Albers and Uta Felten. Madrid; Frankfurt: Iberoamericana; Vervuert, 2009. 75–94.

Vilches, Elvira. *New World Gold: Cultural Anxiety and Monetary Disorder in Early Modern Spain.* Chicago: U of Chicago Press, 2010.

Villaseñor Black, Charlene. 'Love and Marriage in the Spanish Empire: Depictions of Holy Matrimony and Gender Discourses in the Seventeenth Century.' *Sixteenth Century Journal* 32.3 (2001): 637–68.

Virtue and Beauty: Leonardo's Ginevra de' Benci and Renaissance Portraits of Women. Ed. David Alan Brown et al. Washington, DC: National Gallery of Art; Princeton: Princeton UP, 2001.

Vives, Juan Luis. *Instrucción de la mujer cristiana.* Trans. Juan Justiniano. Ed. Elizabeth Teresa Howe. Madrid: Fundación Universitaria Española, University Pontificia de Salamanca, 1995.

Vollendorf, Lisa. 'The Future of Early Modern Women's Studies: The Case of Same-Sex Friendship and Desire in Zayas and Carvajal.' *Arizona Journal of Hispanic Cultural Studies* 4 (2000): 265–84.

– 'Reading the Body Imperiled: Violence against Women in María de Zayas.' *Hispania* 78 (1995): 272–82.

– *Reclaiming the Body: María de Zayas's Early Modern Feminism.* Chapel Hill: U of North Carolina P, 2001.

– '"Te causará admiración": El feminismo moderno de María de Zayas.' *Literatura y feminismo en España, s. XV–XXI.* Barcelona: Icaria, 2005. 107–24.

– 'Transatlantic Ties: Women's Writing in Iberia and the Americas.' *Women, Religion, and the Atlantic World (1600–1800).* Ed. Daniella Kostroun and Lisa Vollendorf. Toronto: U of Toronto P, 2009. 79–112.

Voragine, Jacobus de. *Vida de Cristo y leyenda de los santos.* ?Burgos?: ?Juan de Burgos?, ?1497?

Wallensköld, A. *Le conte de la femme chaste convoitée par son beau-frère: Étude de littérature comparée.* Helsingfors: Officina typographica Societatis litterariæ fennicæ, 1907.

Walpole, Horace. *The Castle of Otranto.* Ed. Laura Mandell. New York: Pearson Longman, 2007.

– *The Mysterious Mother: A Tragedy.* London: Strawberry Hill, 1768; J. Foe, 1796.

Walsh, John K. 'The Chivalric Dragon: Hagiographic Parallels in Early Spanish Romances.' *Bulletin of Hispanic Studies* 54.3 (1977): 189–98.

Wardropper, Bruce. 'El horror en los distintos géneros dramáticos del Siglo de Oro.' *Criticón* 23 (1983): 223–40.

– 'El problema de la responsabilidad en la comedia de capa y espada de Calderón.' *Actas del segundo congreso internacional de hispanistas (20–25 agosto 1965).* Ed. Jaime Sánchez Romerado and Norbert Poulussen. Nimega, Holland: Instituto Español de la U de Nimega, 1967. 689–94.

Weber, Alison. 'Spiritual Administration: Gender and Discernment in the Carmelite Reform.' *Sixteenth Century Journal* 31.1 (2000): 123–46.

– *Teresa of Ávila and the Rhetoric of Feminity.* Princeton: Princeton UP, 1990.

Welles, Marcia L. 'María de Zayas y Sotomayor and Her 'novela cortesana': A Re-evaluation.' *Bulletin of Hispanic Studies* 55 (1978): 301–10.

– *Persephone's Girdle: Narratives of Rape in Seventeenth-Century Spanish Literature.* Nashville, TN: Vanderbilt UP, 2000.

Williams, Robert H. 'Review of *Novelas amorosas y ejemplares de doña María de Zayas y Sotomayor.* By Agustín G. de Amézua.' *Hispanic Review* 18.1 (1950): 75–7.

Williamsen, Amy R. 'Challenging the Code: Honor in María de Zayas.' *María de Zayas: The Dynamics of Discourse.* Ed. Judith A. Whitenack and Amy R.

Williamsen. Madison: Farleigh Dickinson UP; London: Associated UP, 1995.
133–51.

– '"Death Becomes Her": Fatal Beauty in María de Zayas's "Mal presagio casar
lejos."' *Romance Languages Annual* 6 (1994): 618–23.

– 'Questions of Entitlement: Imposed Titles and Intrepretation in Sor Juana
and María de Zayas.' *Revista de estudios hispánicos* 31.1 (1997): 103–12.

– 'Re-writing in the Margins: Caro's *Valor, agravio y mujer* as Challenge to
Dominant Discourse.' *Bulletin of the Comediantes* 44.1 (1992): 21–30.

Wilt, Judith. *Ghosts of the Gothic: Austen, Eliot and Lawrence*. Princeton: Princeton UP, 1980.

Yllera, Alicia. Introducción. *Parte segunda del Sarao y entretenimiento honesto
[Desengaños amorosos]*. By María de Zayas y Sotomayor. Ed. Alicia Yllera.
Madrid: Cátedra, 1983. 9–112.

– 'María de Zayas: ¿Una novela de ruptura? Su concepción de la escritura
novelesca.' *La creatividad femenina en el mundo barroco hispánico: María de
Zayas, Isabel Rebeca Correa, Sor Juan Inés de la Cruz*. Ed. Barbara Potthast et al.
Vol. 1. Kassel: Edition Reichenberger, 1999. 221–37.

Zayas y Sotomayor, María de. *Desengaños amorosos, Parte segunda del sarao y
entretenimiento honesto de doña María de Zayas y Sotomayor*. Ed. Agustín G. de
Amezúa y Mayo. Madrid: Real Academia Española, 1950.

– *The Disenchantments of Love: A Translation of the* Desengaños amorosos.
Trans. H. Patsy Boyer. Ed. María Martínez del Portal. Albany: State U of
New York P, 1997.

– *The Enchantments of Love: Amorous and Exemplary Novels*. Trans. H. Patsy
Boyer. Ed. María Martínez del Portal. Albany: State U of New York P, 1990.

– *Exemplary Tales of Love and Tales of Disillusion*. Trans. and ed. Margaret Greer
and Elizabeth Rhodes. Chicago: U of Chicago P, 2008.

– *Novelas amorosas y ejemplares*. Ed. Julián Olivares. Madrid: Cátedra, 2000.

– *Novelas completas*. Ed. María Martínez del Portal. Barcelona: Bruguera, 1973.

– *Obra narrativa completa*. Ed. Estrella Ruiz-Gálvez Priego. Madrid: Fundación
José Antonio de Castro, 2001.

– *Parte segunda del sarao y entretenimiento honesto*. Barcelona: Sebastián de Cor-
mellas, 1649.

– *Parte segunda del sarao y entretenimiento honesto [Desengaños amorosos]*. Ed.
Alicia Yllera. Madrid: Cátedra, 1983.

– *Primera y segunda parte de la novelas amorosas y ejemplares de doña María de
Zayas y Sotomayor, natural de Madrid. Corregidas y emendadas en esta última
impresión*. Madrid: Melchor Sánchez, 1659.

– *Primera y segunda parte de la novelas amorosas y ejemplares de doña María de
Zayas y Sotomayor, natural de Madrid*. Barcelona: Pablo Campins, 1734.

– *A Shameful Revenge and Other Stories*. Trans. John Sturrock. Illustrated. By Eric Fraser. London: The Folio Society, 1963.
– *La Traición en la amistad / Friendship Betrayed*. Ed. Valerie Hegstrom. Trans. Catherine Larson. Lewisburg: Bucknell UP, 1999.
Zeitlin, Froma I. 'Playing the Other: Theater, Theatricality, and the Feminine in Greek Drama.' *Nothing to Do with Dionysius? Athenian Drama in Its Social Context*. Ed. John J. Winkler and Froma I. Zeitlin. Princeton: Princeton UP, 1990. 63–96.
Zuili, Marc. 'César Oudin y la difusión del español en francia en el siglo XVII.' *Actas de primer encuentro hispanofrancés de investigadores / Première rencontre hispano-française de chercheurs, Sevilla 20 Nov.–2 Dec. 2005*. Web. 23 Feb. 2010.

Index